IT Inventory and Resource Management with OCS Inventory NG 1.02

Eliminate inventorying dilemmas by implementing a free & feasible IT Inventory solution

Barzan "Tony" Antal

BIRMINGHAM - MUMBAI

IT Inventory and Resource Management with OCS Inventory NG 1.02

First published: May 2010

Production Reference: 1070510

Published by Packt Publishing Ltd.
32 Lincoln Road
Olton
Birmingham, B27 6PA, UK.

ISBN 978-1-849511-10-0

www.packtpub.com

Cover Image by Parag Kadam (paragvkadam@gmail.com)

Credits

Author
Barzan "Tony" Antal

Reviewer
Jeff Prater

Acquisition Editor
Dilip Venkatesh

Development Editor
Neha Patwari

Technical Editors
Hyacintha D'Souza
Smita Solanki

Copy Editor
Leonard D'Silva

Indexer
Monica Ajmera Mehta

Editorial Team Leader
Aanchal Kumar

Project Team Leader
Priya Mukherji

Project Coordinator
Ashwin Shetty

Proofreader
Lesley Harrison

Graphics
Geetanjali Sawant

Production Coordinator
Melwyn D'sa

Cover Work
Melwyn D'sa

About the Author

Barzan "Tony" Antal is a system administrator and network technician at a significant company that delivers industrial software, system integration, and IT solutions. He is also a professional technical writer with over 150 articles published across a large portfolio of prestigious websites covering topics of computer hardware, IT news, networking, security, software development, SEO/SEM, Web, and other technologies.

The author has acquired a diverse experience in the fields of IT&C by passionately pursuing and attempting to apply everything as many times as possible in the real world. He is a strong believer in practicality, and his down-to-earth approach helps him out as a consultant providing assistance and finding customized feasible solutions. During his writing endeavors, this aching for viability always shines through.

Acknowledgement

First and foremost, I'd like to thank the outrageous support from my parents and close friends. My girlfriend, Dea, for accepting my way of dealing with everything in life. Special thanks to Gabor Bernat, I'm grateful for those well-thought comments regarding the manuscript. My colleague, Ceclan Sandor, for keeping up with support over time. Alina D., Lehel M., and Szilard N. for their encouragements and believing in me.

A huge thank you to my technical reviewer — Jeff Prater, you cannot imagine the impact your input has had on this book. You have definitely gone beyond the call of duty while reviewing and researching. Robert Dunham, for kick-starting me in my writing endeavors many years ago. If it wasn't for you, I wouldn't be a published author now.

Moreover, I'd like to thank the professional and entirely author-centric team from Packt Publishing, especially Ashwin Shetty, Dilip Venkatesh, Duane Moraes, Hyacintha D'Souza, Neha Patwari, Priya Mukherji, Smita Solanki and everyone else. All of your hard work made this book possible. My sincere thanks for putting up with my hectic schedule.

Lastly, I consider this book as a tribute to the developers of OCS Inventory NG, GLPI, and the Open Source community. I also appreciate the readers of this book and truly hope that my work helps a great deal in succeeding to fulfill their IT inventory demands.

And finally, thanks James Payne for understanding my lack of activity from the Shed. Oh, and of course, everyone from the DevHardware Forums — You guys are fantastic!

About the Reviewer

Jeff Prater is the Director of Technology for the Houston County District Attorney's Office in Perry, Georgia. His expertise and knowledge of modern technologies gave him the opportunity to transform an inefficient government department into an efficient, modeled prosecutor's office through the introduction of a document and case management system. In 2007, the Houston County District Attorney's office became the first paperless prosecutor's office in the state of Georgia. Because of his success with government automation and efficiency technologies, he was given the opportunity to speak at the National District Attorneys Association 2007 Annual Conference at the National Advocacy Center, University of South Carolina. To compliment his career in technology, Jeff also writes technical articles for Ziff Davis Enterprise/Developer Shed aimed at individuals with limited technology experience. In his free time, Jeff enjoys spending time with his wife, Beth, and his newborn daughter, Leah.

Table of Contents

Preface

OCS Inventory NG is a cross-platform, open source inventory, and asset management solution. It brings more than plentiful features to the table to satisfy the business needs of small-to-large organizations with up to tens of thousands of computers. However, to put this inventory solution to optimum use requires a lot of skill.

This book will lead you through the steps of implementing OCS-NG until you master working with it. This book aims at reducing efforts involved in resource management. The solution gives a robust foundation on top of which we can implement other third-party applications, plugins, and much more.

This book begins with the basics—it explains what IT inventorying needs are to be met in the real world. Then, it covers a step-by-step approach to everything you need to know to set up and implement OCS-NG as a centralized inventory solution to meet all these requirements. It delves deeper into carrying out inventory tasks with every chapter.

You will learn how to choose the best agent type and deployment method. We discuss the process of gathering inventory data and cover techniques for creating and deploying packages. You will also learn how to acquire added benefits with the use of plugins. We discuss best practices on inventorying and troubleshooting agent-related problems. The book presents real-world inventorying scenarios along with their solutions. You will basically learn how to use OCS-NG to get the most out of it.

As a conclusion, if you want to learn about a free solution that fulfills inventorying necessities of the real world, then this is the book for you.

A practical guide on how to set up, configure, and work with OCS Inventory NG—a cross-platform, open source inventory solution.

What this book covers

Chapter 1, Introduction to IT Inventory and Resource Management presents the importance of IT inventory within any organization or company. It describes some of the must-have features that an automated and centralized solution should provide. OCS Inventory NG comes into the picture saving the day and selecting many of those checkboxes.

Chapter 2, Setting up an OCS Inventory NG Management Server explains the server role requirements of an OCS-NG management server and leads the user through the steps of setting up the requisite software on the chosen platform. Once the system is ready, OCS-NG is installed and configured to collaborate with the agents that will soon be deployed.

Chapter 3, The Zen of Agent Deployment helps you understand the types of agents and the various ways agents can be deployed on client machines. This chapter presents operating system-specific strategies to automate the deployment of agents. Additional components that are required are thoroughly explained.

Chapter 4, Finding your Way through OCS-NG Features exposes the diversified features that OCS-NG sports and gives a rundown on each of them. From this chapter, you will learn how gathering from clients happens, how to sort the results, and accomplish all kinds of administrative tasks with the fresh inventory database.

Chapter 5, Investigating the Process of Gathering Inventory Data goes further beyond the actual mechanism of retrieving information and focuses on how to optimize and tweak this process as well as find leakages. Administrators can determine which devices are inventoried, how frequently they are inventoried, locate hosts that are not inventoried, and resolve synchronization issues.

Chapter 6, Package Deployment through OCS-NG takes a practical look at package deployment and command execution functionalities on inventoried clients. These increase the usefulness of our centralized inventory suite. This chapter opens to view the different ways in which you can do this as well as how to specify on which clients this can be done.

Chapter 7, Integrating OCS-NG with GLPI adds the icing on the cake by introducing integration possibilities with other tools. This chapter gives you the edge by explaining how GLPI empowers our OCS-NG inventory. Opting for GLPI on top of OCS-NG is akin to functionalities on steroids, and you will learn how to make it work.

Chapter 8, Best Practices on Inventorying with OCS-NG deals with all-around repetitive tasks related to IT inventories and management needs and how to get them solved with our setup. This chapter deals with some best practices and other tips of backing up the database. It also deals with everyday situations that can happen and need to be resolved seamlessly.

Chapter 9, Troubleshoot Confidently – Find Solutions and Workarounds continues the string of practical tips and tricks and good-to-know strategies. This chapter covers identifying issues, diagnosing common problems, troubleshooting them, and finding solutions for them.

Appendix, Keeping Pace with Version Updates – Glancing over the changelog of the Latest Release gives a brief overview on how to read changelogs, explains us what they are, and why they are useful to us. Their relevancy is quite high as every open source project has a changelog.

What you need for this book

OCS Inventory NG runs on top of the popular Apache web server, using MySQL's InnoDB engine and the PHP server-side scripting language. In order to install the OCS-NG management server, the system must have these prerequisites installed and configured.

There is an integrated pack that sets up all of the components we must have for a fully functional web server. This package is available for Windows, Linux, Solaris, and Mac OS X operating systems. It's called XAMPP. The developers of OCS-NG thought about making the process seamless on Windows machines. The Win32 installation kit of OCS-NG includes this integrated pack and sets up the prerequisites during the setup process.

The OCS Inventory NG management server consists of the following four server roles:

- **Database server**: It requires MySQL 4.1 or a higher version that uses the InnoDB engine
- **Communication server**: It requires Apache web server 1.3 or higher and some Perl modules (which we are going to present in a minute)
- **Deployment server**: It requires any web server (Apache works here too)
- **Administration console**: It needs Apache Web Server, PHP 4.3 or higher, and some additional ZIP and GD support

Apart from those main server components, the following modules are necessary:

- Apache server needs to be 1.3.X, 2.0.X+ with the following modules:
  - Mod_perl version 1.29+
  - Mod_php version 4.3.2+
- PHP 4.3.2+ with extensions:
  - ZIP library of ZIP file functions and support
  - GD library of image functions

- PERL 5.6+ with the following modules:
  - XML::Simple version 2.12+
  - Compress::Zlib version 1.33+
  - DBI version 1.40+
  - DBD::MySQL version 2.9004+
  - Apache::DBI version 0.93
  - Net::IP version 1.21+
  - SOAP::Lite version 0.66+

- MySQL 4.1+ with following engine:
  - InnoDB

- Any sort of *make* utility to control the generation of executables and similar important files from an application's source code files
  - For example: GNU make.

Who this book is for

The book targets an audience of system administrators and IT professionals who are required to implement, configure, customize, and work with IT inventory and asset management solutions.

The book does not presume any prior knowledge of inventory management. It only requires a solid grasp of the client-server model and familiarity with the chosen operating system along with the necessary web server and database server terminologies. Anyone with an interest in inventorying IT assets and solving real-world resource management dilemmas will enjoy this book.

Conventions

In this book, you will find a number of styles of text that distinguish between different kinds of information. Here are some examples of these styles, and an explanation of their meaning.

Code words in text are shown as follows: "For example, installing a package is done by typing `yum install package-name`."

A block of code is set as follows:

```
memory_limit = 96M
post_max_size = 64M
upload_max_filesize = 64M
```

Any command-line input or output is written as follows:

```
openssl req -new -key server.key -out server.csr
```

New terms and **important words** are shown in bold. Words that you see on the screen, in menus or dialog boxes for example, appear in the text like this: "Clicking the **Next** button moves you to the next screen."

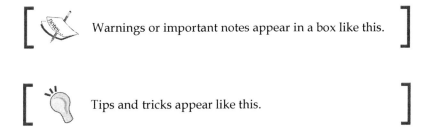

Warnings or important notes appear in a box like this.

Tips and tricks appear like this.

Reader feedback

Feedback from our readers is always welcome. Let us know what you think about this book—what you liked or may have disliked. Reader feedback is important for us to develop titles that you really get the most out of.

To send us general feedback, simply send an e-mail to feedback@packtpub.com, and mention the book title via the subject of your message.

If there is a book that you need and would like to see us publish, please send us a note in the **SUGGEST A TITLE** form on www.packtpub.com or e-mail suggest@packtpub.com.

If there is a topic that you have expertise in and you are interested in either writing or contributing to a book on, see our author guide on www.packtpub.com/authors.

Errata

Although we have taken every care to ensure the accuracy of our content, mistakes do happen. If you find a mistake in one of our books—maybe a mistake in the text or the code—we would be grateful if you would report this to us. By doing so, you can save other readers from frustration and help us improve subsequent versions of this book. If you find any errata, please report them by visiting http://www.packtpub.com/support, selecting your book, clicking on the **let us know** link, and entering the details of your errata. Once your errata are verified, your submission will be accepted and the errata will be uploaded on our website, or added to any list of existing errata, under the Errata section of that title. Any existing errata can be viewed by selecting your title from http://www.packtpub.com/support.

Piracy

Piracy of copyright material on the Internet is an ongoing problem across all media. At Packt, we take the protection of our copyright and licenses very seriously. If you come across any illegal copies of our works, in any form, on the Internet, please provide us with the location address or website name immediately so that we can pursue a remedy.

Please contact us at copyright@packtpub.com with a link to the suspected pirated material.

We appreciate your help in protecting our authors, and our ability to bring you valuable content.

Questions

You can contact us at questions@packtpub.com if you are having a problem with any aspect of the book, and we will do our best to address it.

1
Introduction to IT Inventory and Resource Management

In the past decade or so, we have begun to realize that computers are an indispensable necessity. They're around us everywhere, from the computers in our comfortable households to rovers from other planets. Currently, it is not uncommon at all to have more than a few dozen office computers and other pieces of IT equipment in the infrastructure of a small company that does nothing directly related to that specific area.

It should not surprise anyone that in the case of business environments, there has to be some streamlined inventory, especially when we consider that the network might have a total of several hundred, if not thousands, of workstation computers, servers, portable devices, and other office equipment such as printers, scanners, and other networking components.

Resource management, in its essence, when viewed from an IT perspective, provides a method to gather and store all kinds of information about items in our infrastructure. Later on it supports means to further maintain the said inventory. Moreover, it performs routine tasks based on the collected data such as generating reports, locating relevant information easily (like where is a specific memory module with the model number you're looking for), auditing the type of software installed on workstation computers, and more.

Our plan of action for this chapter is going to be pretty straightforward; we will analyze the IT inventorying needs and some general requisites when it comes to managing those assets. What's more, we'll be presenting the client-server model that is the underlying foundation on which most centralized management solutions are working. This is when **OCS Inventory NG** pops into the picture saving the day. Soon we will see why.

Throughout this book, we will adopting a step-by-step approach to build up our full-fledged OCS-NG, become familiar with its set of features, and excel in fulfilling our inventorying needs on all levels. Once the groundwork is done, we can further discuss more on best practices and learn how to troubleshoot confidently. Moreover, we can present a future possibility to empower what we've already done by building on top of it another asset management system that provides even more functionalities.

We will learn about OCS Inventory NG soon. For now, it's to realize that it's an open source project. No matter how successful a company is, open source solutions are always appreciated by the IT staff and management. Open source projects are preferred as long as they are actively developed, fairly popular, well documented, provides community support, and meets the needs of the company. Among others, open source projects end up modular and flexible.

Inventorying requirements in the real world

One of the general requirements of an IT inventory is to be efficient and practical. The entire process should be seamless to the clients and should require limited (or no) user interaction. Once set up, it just needs to be automated to update the inventory database, based on the latest changes, without requiring manual intervention. Thereafter, the collage of data gathered is ought to be organized and labeled the way we want.

Businesses everywhere have come to realize that process integration is the best method for querying, standardizing, and organizing information about the infrastructure. The age of hi-tech computing made this possible by speeding up routine tasks and saving up employee time, eliminating bureaucracy and unnecessary filing of papers that all lead to frustration and waste of resources. Implementing integrated processes can change the structure and behavior of an organization, but finding the correct integration often becomes a dilemma.

A feasible solution to avoid inevitable havoc

Drifting back to the case of the IT department, the necessity of having an integrated and centralized solution to manage numerous systems and other hardware equipment becomes obvious. The higher the number of systems, the bigger the volume to be managed, the more easily the situation can get out of control, thus leading to a crisis. Everyone runs around in panic like headless zombies trying to figure out who can be held responsible, and what can be done in order to avoid such scenarios.

Taking a rational approach as soon as possible can improve the stability of entire organizations. Chances are you already know this, but usually system administrators tend to dislike working with papers, filling in forms, storing them purely for archiving needs, and then when they least expect it, finding relevant information. A system like that won't make anyone happy.

A *centralized repository* in the form of a database gives almost instant access to results whenever such a query happens. Its actual state of always being up-to-date and reflecting the actual state of the infrastructure can be guaranteed by implementing an updating mechanism.

Later on, once the database is in a healthy state and the process is integrated, tried, and proven, it won't make any significant difference whether you are managing dozens of computers or thousands. A well-designed integrated process is future-proof and scalable. Thus it won't become a setback if and when the company decides to expand.

Streamlining software auditing and license management

As mentioned earlier, it is important to understand that auditing workstation machines cannot be neglected. In certain environments, the users or employees have limited access and work within a sort of enclosed program area, and they can do little to nothing outside of their specialization. There are situations that arise when the employees are supposed to have administrative access and full permissions. It is for the good of both the user and the company to monitor and pay attention to what happens within each and every computer.

Having an up to par *auditing mechanism* can integrate the license management system as well. The persons responsible for this can track the total amount of licenses used and owned by the company, can calculate balance, can notify when this number is about to run out, and so on. It isn't uncommon at all to automate the purchasing of licenses either.

The *license management* process description varies from firm to firm, but usually it's something similar to the following: the user requests for a license, the supervisor agrees, and the request is sent to the relevant IT staff. After this step, the license request gets analyzed. Based on the result, it is either handed out or ordered/acquired if necessary.

If the process is not automated, all this would involve paperwork, and soon you will see frustrated employees running back and forth through departments asking who else needs to sign this paper. The process of automating and printing the end result is elegant and takes no trouble. The responsible department can then store the printed document for archiving purposes, if required. However, the key of the process lies in integration. Inventorying can help here too.

More uses of an integrated IT inventory solution

The count of office consumables can also be tracked and maintained. This is a trickier process because it cannot be done totally unattended, unless by installing some sort of sensor to track the count of printer cartridges inside office furniture or the warehouse. However, you can update this field each time the item in question gets restocked.

A centralized method for tracking consumables means the responsible parties can get notified before running out of stock. Once again, this step eliminates unexpected scenarios and unnecessary tasks.

The beauty of centralized management solutions in the IT world is that if it is done correctly, then it can open doors to numerous other activities as well. For example, in the case of workstation PCs, the integrated process can be expanded into providing remote administration and similar other activities to be carried out remotely on the client machine.

Package deployment and execution of scripts are just few distinctive examples. Think of it as, license is granted, the package is deployed, and the script is run to ensure proper registration of the application, if required. System administrators can usually help fix common issues of employees through remote execution of scripts. Surely, there are other means to administer the machines, but we're focusing on all-in-one integrated solutions.

Another possibility is integrating the *help-desk* and *ticketing system* within the centralized inventory's management control panel as well. In this way, when an employee asks for help or reports a hardware issue, the system administrator can take a look at what's inside that system (hardware specifications, software installed, and so on.).Therefore, the system administrator gets to know the situation beforehand and thus use the right tools to troubleshoot the issue.

Gathering relevant inventory information

We can conclude that in order to have a complete inventory which we can build on and implement other IT-related and administrative tasks, we need, at least, the following:

- Collecting relevant hardware information in case of workstation computers
    ○ Manufacturer, serial number, model number of every component
    ○ When applicable, some of the following: Revision number, size, speed, memory, type, description, designation, connection port, interface, slot number, driver, MAC and IP address, and so on

- Collecting installed software/OS (licensing) information
    ○ Operating system: Name, version, and registration information
    ○ Application name, publisher, version, location
    ○ Customqueries from the Windows registry (if applicable)

- Collecting information about networking equipment and office peripherals
    ○ Manufacturer, serial number, model, type of component, and so on

- MAC and IP address
    ○ When applicable: Revision, firmware, total uptime, and so on

Overall inventory demands to enhance usability

Now let's create a list of criteria that we want our IT inventory solution to meet. In the previous paragraph, we enumerated some of the *must-have* data that cannot be left out from our inventory. Likewise, we have expectancies regarding how the process works.

From the perspective of your users, the process must be transparent and the background software must not become a resource hog. The bandwidth usage that is required to communicate with the centralized management server should be minimal. The inventorying mechanism must be automatic and discover on its own every item within the environment. Once everything is recorded, the copy stored in the database must always be kept up-to-date and backed up.

The inventorying client that sweeps through the entire network should be cross-platform. As always, everyone likes an intuitive and fast user interface. This is especially important when managing inventories and working with large volumes of data. The control panel or management center is the place where we can organize, label, and work with the gathered information. If the interface is too complex or overcrowded, it leads to frustration.

The way information is queried from the database and displayed on screen must be snappy so that we don't have to wait and get bored to tears while some rotating hourglass is animated.

In addition, we want integrated backup functions. It's always possible to manually create database dumps or backup points, but if we can do so directly from the interface, it's much easier and possible for non-IT proficient individuals as well.

Assuming that the web interface can be configured to be accessed by multiple users having different permissions and rights, it can become quite a useful tool for employees working in non-IT departments such as accounting and management. The process of inventorying becomes streamlined, and everyone can work with the inventory information to get their share of tasks done.

In a corporate environment, it might happen quite often that an employee receives a new computer and the older computer is received by another user having different needs. The inventory must be able to automatically detect and diagnose these situations and track the history of a machine.

The ability to custom specify, define, and set labels to the inventoried items is really important. When done professionally, companies might agree upon some naming convention to label inventoried items. An example of this is the following: `pc001` in case of workstation computers, `nt001` for networking equipment, `sv001` for servers, `ph001` for phones, `pr001` for printers, and so on.

This means that we need such functionalities from our IT inventory solution to track these inventory IDs as well. Should you want to take this idea further, you can generate and print barcodes, and stick those on the side of those items. A feature-laden IT inventory can systematize the way tasks are carried out within an organization.

Summing these up, we have looked upon the most common inventorying requirements that each one of us is facing within a corporate environment. These are the necessities, and the solution we require to implement so that our needs are met. In order to understand how it's going to accomplish our demands, we will talk about the client-server model. Once we know that, we are going to overview how OCS-NG ticks those inventory-requisite checkboxes.

Centralization: Introducing the client-server model

Ever since distributed applications appeared, the **client-server model** has become popular. In the simplest terms, the server is a computer (usually, a high performing one) running the service that centralizes some kind of information. It's also able to receive connections from clients, process their requests, and give them the results whenever necessary.

Clients establish a connection with the server in order to request or upload some content. This communication model describes one of the most basic relationship and architecture. Typically, servers can simultaneously accept and process requests. This is done with multithreading programming. Other times, the queries are so fast that sequential execution is enough.

The communication between clients and the server can happen either through the Internet in case of **wide area network (WAN)** or just locally when it's limited to the **local area network (LAN)**. When necessary to enhance scalability, it is possible to incorporate more than one server in the *client-server* model. The servers will be part of a pool and they can share the load between each other. Thus a balanced workload and bandwidth is achieved.

Example of the client-server model—an Internet forum

The service that runs on the servers is a computer application. It usually uses elements of other services. Let's consider the example of a PHP-based web application: forums or bulletin boards. Everyone knows those. The forum application is the service running on the server, and the clients are the members visiting the site, posting, reading posts, and so on.

The forum service cannot run on its own. It needs a set of other vital server components. A web server is necessary to listen, accept, and serve HTTP requests from visitors. In the case of users, the web browser can formulate the HTTP requests, establish the communication with the target web server, and retrieve its HTTP responses. This is how web surfing can be explained from a client-server architecture perspective.

Nevertheless, this is not sufficient for the forum script to function properly. It is heavily dependent on a database service as well. This is the place where the data is stored. If the script is PHP based, then the PHP service is also a prerequisite so that the dynamically generated web pages can be processed. While, other services may also be required, for the sake of keeping things simple and to present the basis of a client-server architecture, these services will suffice.

The client-server model versus the peer-to-peer paradigm

The client-server model has its share of advantages and drawbacks when compared with other similar models such as the peer-to-peer paradigm. First and foremost, the client-server model is based on having only one place where the data is stored, on the server. This provides enhanced security and management. The server can be tightly secured, firewalled, and powered by high-performing components. In addtion, the sever has access to plenty of system resources, is backed up regularly, and must be maintained appropriately.

The data is centralized, and this gives a safer infrastructure to maintain an error-free copy of the actual data on the side of every client. From the client's perspective, the server can be replaced, upgraded, or migrated on another server, without being affected. They know the path and destination of how to reach the server. If the migration or the maintenance is carried out properly, clients will not even be aware of that.

The **peer-to-peer (P2P)** paradigm takes a different approach to the client-server model. The model presumes that every end point can act both as a server and client likewise. Undoubtedly this brings the advantage of greater scalability and flexibility. But it is tougher and time-consuming to maintain an actual up-to-date copy of the database on every end-point client.

The P2P paradigm solves the possibility of network traffic congestion as there's no dedicated server to get overloaded. Ultimately, this is not a magic pill either as all of the clients creating so much cross-talk contributes to increased all-around network traffic.

On the other hand, the client-server model does not provide such a high degree of robustness. If and when the server fails on a hardware level, until it gets replaced, repaired, or fixed, clients won't be able to connect and get any data out of the management server at all. However, there are various workarounds to enhance the uptime of servers and ensure their balanced workflow. Redundancy can also be implemented within the model if it is truly necessary.

IT inventorying based on the client-server model

Each of the paradigms mentioned have their share of best fit scenarios where using one in favor of the other is a better decision. In case of IT inventorying and resource management solutions, the first model-which is the client-server model, centralization is a better approach. The chance of overloading the server is lower because the volume of data that is exchanged is really low, a few kilobytes at most. The bandwidth usage is light.

Most importantly, the server-client model yields immediate access to the actual information stored (that is secured) in the database. Centralization is an advantage here.

How does OCS Inventory NG meet our needs?

OCS Inventory NG stands for **Open Computer and Software Inventory Next Generation**, and it is the name of an open source project that was started back in late 2005. The project matured into the first final release in the beginning of the year 2007. It's an undertaking that is still actively maintained, fully documented, and has support forums. It has all of the requirements that an open source application should have in order to be competitive.

There is a tricky part when it comes to open source solutions. Proposing them and getting them accepted by the management requires quite a bit of research. One side of the coin is that it is always favorable as everyone appreciates cutting down licensing costs. The problem with such a solution is that you cannot always take for granted their future support.

In order to make an educated guess as to whether an open source solution could be beneficial for the company, we need to look at the following criteria: how frequently is the project updated, check the download count, what is the feedback of the community, how thorough is the documentation, and how active is the support community?.

OCS-NG occupies a dominant position when it comes to open source projects in the area of inventorying computers and software.

Brief overview on OCS Inventory NG's architecture

The architecture of OCS-NG is based on the client-server model. The client program is called a **network agent**. These agents need to be deployed on the client computers that we want to include in our inventory.

The **management server** is composed of four individual server roles: the database server, communication server, deployment server, and the administration console server. More often than not, these can be run from the same machine.

OCS Inventory NG is cross-platform and supports most Unices, BSD derivates (including Mac OS X), and all kinds of Windows-based operating systems. The server can also be run on either platform. As it is an open source project, it's based on the popular LAMP or WAMP solution stack. This means that the main server-side prerequisites are Apache web server, MySQL database server, and PHP server. These are also the viable components of a fully functional web server.

The network agents communicate with the management server under standardized HTTP protocols. The data that is exchanged is then formatted under XML conventions. The following screenshot gives a general overview of the way clients communicate with the management server's sub-server components:

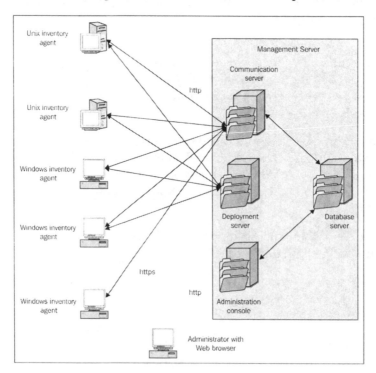

Rough performance evaluation of OCS-NG

The data that is collected in the case of a fully-inventoried computer adds up to something around 5KB. That is a small amount, and it will neither overload the server nor create network congestion. It is often said that around one million systems can be inventoried daily on a 3GHz bi-Xeon processor based server with 4 GB of RAM without any issues.

Any modest old-generation server should suffice for the inventory of few thousand systems. When scalability is necessary such as over 10,000-20,000 inventoried systems, it is recommended to split those 4 server-role components on two individual servers.

Should this be the case, the database server needs to be installed on the same machine with the communication server and on another system with the administration server and the deployment server with a database replica. Any other combination is also possible.

Although distributing the server components is possible, very rarely do we really need to do that. In this day and age, we can seamlessly virtualize up to four or more servers on any dual or quad-core new generation computer. OCS-NG's management server can be one of those virtual machines. If necessary, distributing server components in the future is possible.

Meeting our inventory demands

First and foremost, OCS Inventory NG network agents are able to collect all of the *must-have* attributes of a client computer and many more. Let's do a quick checkup on these:

- **BIOS**:
  - System serial number, manufacturer, and model
  - Bios manufacturer, version, and date

- **Processors**:
  - Type, count (how many of them), manufacturer, speed, and cache

- **Memory**:
  - Physical memory type, manufacturer, capacity, and slot number
  - Total physical memory
  - Total swap/paging memory

- **Video**:
  - ◦ Video adapter: Chipset/model, manufacturer, memory size, speed, and screen resolution
  - ◦ Display monitor: Manufacturer, description, refresh rate, type, serial number, and caption

- **Storage/removable devices**:
  - ◦ Manufacturer, model, size, type, speed—all when applicable
  - ◦ Drive letter, filesystem type, partition/volume size, free space

- **Network adapters/telephony**:
  - ◦ Manufacturer, model, type, speed, and description
  - ◦ MAC and IP address, mask and IP gateway, DHCP server used

- **Miscellaneous hardware**:
  - ◦ Input devices: Keyboard, mouse, and pointing device
  - ◦ Sound devices: Manufacturer name, type, and description
  - ◦ System slots: Name, type, and designation
  - ◦ System ports: Type, name, caption, and description

- **Software information**:
  - ◦ Operating system: Name, version, comments, and registration info
  - ◦ Installed software: Name, publisher, version (from **Add/ Remove software** or **Programs and Features** menu)
  - ◦ Custom-specified registry queries (applicable to Windows OS)

Not only computers, but also networking components can be used for inventorying. OCS Inventory NG detects and collects network-specific information about these (such as MAC address and IP address, subnet mask, and so on.). Later on, we can set labels and organize them appropriately.

The place where OCS-NG comes as a surprise is its unique capability to make an inventory of hosts that are not on the network. The network agent can be run manually on these offline hosts and are then imported into the centralized management server.

One of its features includes intelligent auto-discovering functionalities and its ability to detect hosts that have not been inventoried. It is based on popular network diagnosing and auditing tools such as *nmap*. The algorithm can decide whether it's an actual workstation computer or rather just a printer. If it's the former, then the agent needs to be deployed. The network scanning is not done by the management server. It is delegated to network agents.

In this way, the network is never overcrowded or congested. If the management server itself scans for populated networks spanning throughout different subnets, the process would be disastrous. In this way, the process is seamless and simply practical. Another interesting part is the election mechanism based on which the server is able to decide the most suited client to carry out the discovery. A rough sketch of this *in action* can be seen in the next figure:

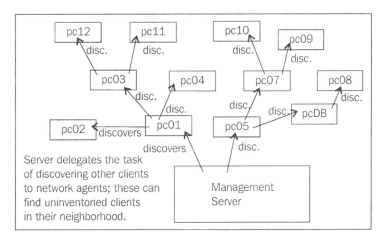

Set of functions and what it brings to the table

At this moment, we're fully aware that the kind information that the network agents are getting into the database are relevant and more than enough for our inventorying needs. Nevertheless, we won't stop here. It's time to analyze and present its web interface. We will also shed a bit of light on the set of features it supports out of the box without any plugins or other mods yet. There will be a time for those too.

Taking a glance at the OCS-NG web interface

The web interface of OCS Inventory NG is slightly old-fashioned. One direct advantage of this is that the interface is really snappy. Queries are displayed quickly, and the UI won't lag.

The other side of the coin is that intuitiveness is not the interface's strongest point. Getting used to it might take a while. At least it does not make you feel that the interface is overcrowded. However, the location and naming of buttons leaves plenty of room for improvement. Some people might prefer to see captions below the shortcuts as the meaning of the icons is not always obvious. After the first few minutes, we will easily get used to them.

A picture is worth thousands of words, so let's exemplify our claims.

The buttons that appear in the previous screenshot from left to right are the following:

- All computers
- Tag/Number of PC repartition
- Groups
- All softwares
- Search with various criteria

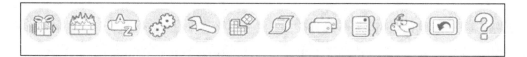

In the same fashion, in this case, the buttons in the previous screenshot stand for the following features:

- Deployment
- Security
- Dictionary
- Agent
- Configuration (this one is intuitive!)
- Registry (self-explanatory)

- Admin Info
- Duplicates
- Label File configuration
- Users
- Local Import
- Help

When you click on the name of the specific icon, the drop-down menu appears right below on the cursor.

All in all, the web interface is not that bad after all. We must accept that the strongest point lies in its snappiness, and the wealth of information that is presented in a fraction of a second rather than its design or intuitiveness.

We appreciate its overall simplicity and its quick response time. We are often struggling with new generation Java-based and AJAX-based overcrowded interfaces of network equipment that seem slow as hell. So, we'll choose OCS Inventory NG's UI over those anytime!

An incentive on functionalities

Now that we are familiar with the look of the web admin panel of OCS Inventory NG, let's find out the kinds of functionalities that are hiding beyond those icons.

Firstly, we have the *All computers* option to enumerate the entire inventory. We can customize the type of columns we want to track. One of the most common configurations is the following setup: Tag, Last Inventory, Computer, User, RAM, and CPU. This seems intuitive and could suffice for most usages. Whenever necessary, we can fine-tune this by adding or removing columns from the following possibilities:

- Bios Manufacturer, Bios Version, Bios Date
- CPU number (stands for core number), CPU Type
- Company
- Description
- Domain
- Fidelity
- IP address
- Last come
- Manufacturer, Model
- OS Version

- Owner
- Quality
- Serial number
- Service pack
- Swap
- User Agent, User Domain
- Win Product ID, Win Product Key

This gives us a global view of the inventory. Should we want to find more about a specific computer, we click on its name. Then, we are redirected to a dedicated page for that item.

The following two images give us a sense of what to expect.

```
Name:
Domain:
Userdomain:
Last inventory:      10/26/2009 16:06:18
IP address:
User:
Memory:              4096
Swap:                4677
Network name 1:
Network name 2:      0.0.0.0
```

```
OS Name:             Microsoft Windows XP Professional
OS Version:          5.1.2600
Service pack:        Service Pack 2
Comments:
Windows user:        System Administrator
Windows licence:
Windows key:
User agent:          OCS-NG_windows_client_v4054
```

What's more, we can also find details about the hardware components inside the computer, details about the software applications installed, and even investigate the behavior of **IpDiscover**. This is how the automatic network diagnosis feature is called. We're going to get in depth of this concept in a later chapter as we progress and build our inventory.

There are situations when we need to repartition and categorize computers into several groups based on some attributes. This is when the TAG-based repartitioning feature comes out as a winner. We can configure network clients to submit the inventory data accompanied with *TAG* information. This option is practical when departments or different sites are inventoried in the same database. A simple tag makes all the difference.

The searching functionalities are impressive. We're able to forge any kind of query using parameters such as processor speed, manufacturer, IP address, OS version, and the ones mentioned earlier. The modifiers are **EXACTLY**, **DIFFERENTLY**, or **LIKE**. In this way, we can build complex search queries in a rather simple fashion.

Check out the following example. Let's find Windows-based **Test** machines in that IP range.

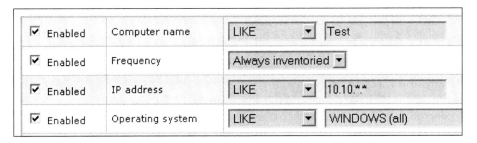

From the OCS-NG web interface, we can set up users with different levels of access. This is one of our inventory requirements as well. Lots of other functionalities are worth mentioning, such as categorizing software applications, and setting up ignored ones, which do not matter from our point of view (for example, freeware and open source applications do not require licensing).

The package deployment and remote execution functionalities might be appreciated by some. They won't make or break the deal of choosing OCS-NG anyway. The real benefit comes from its lightweight structure and the intelligent auto-discover routines. On top of these, the modular build of the inventory makes it possible for further extensions.

Until now, we have seen that OCS-NG seems to meet all of the inventorying demands we specified earlier. This means that we're beginning a journey to build an entire fully-fledged inventorying solution from ground up.

We can guarantee a practical ride!

Summary

In this introductory chapter, we have kick started our venture to understand and solve IT inventory requirements that exist in almost every firm in the real world. We presented the practical uses of having a mature inventory coupled with a healthy database ready to serve requests. No doubt we have realized that implementing such an integrated process is a necessary method before the situation gets out of control.

Together we created a list of criteria and expectations that we demand from our integrated inventory solution. By having all of these in place, the way work is done inside an organization becomes streamlined. Moreover, we can eliminate unnecessary paperwork. The responsible parties that will be managing their own departments will be able to get their tasks done even more efficiently.

We have realized that centralization is the best solution for an inventory and asset management system. After analyzing and comparing two of the most popular networking and distributed computing paradigms with each other, we backed up our suppositions. We have learned the mechanism of the client-server model as well as the peer-to-peer paradigm architecture.

We have set the scene for the book by presenting an incentive on OCS Inventory NG and overviewing the set of features it brings to the table. Moreover, we can tackle this situation further and build from ground up our OCS-NG inventory on a step-by-step basis.

So let's go ahead and begin setting up our OCS-NG central management server.

2
Setting up an OCS Inventory NG Management Server

There's one fantastic analogy to building servers, even though it might seem hilarious. The process is like architecture, for example, building a house. Shocking, isn't it? Yes! Nevertheless, it makes sense. First, we need a rock solid foundation. Depending on your point of view, this can either be the hardware platform or the server software backend platform.

The foundation requires the necessary materials. These are akin to software prerequisites in case of software application, for example, Perl modules. When the foundation is laid, and when it seems to be solid (meaning the material is conglomerated), which means every module and component gets along well with the other items, we can say we are ready to begin building the house. The house itself can stand for the application we're going to install.

Right now, the house we're going to install is the OCS Inventory NG management server. The foundation is a well-rounded AMP stack web server with the necessary modules. After the house is built, and assuming it does not fall apart right away (meaning no errors), the final step before moving in is its interior design.

Naturally, the interior design of fresh homes represents the initial configuration of server variables. Getting the fences up consists of setting passwords and eliminating security flaws. Now, depending on how large our family gets, we might find out that the way we designed our home is not appropriate. The groundsill might be weak, and the home can prove to be small and uncomfortable. Jokes aside, it's self-explanatory how this analogy continues.

In this chapter, let's get the following tasks done:

- Get to know the platform on which OCS-NG management server runs
- Set up the software prerequisites on Linux distributions

- Install the OCS Inventory NG management server on Linux distributions
- Learn the installation on Windows with the help of an integrated installation kit
- Carry out some initial configuration and get the server ready for agents.

Getting ready for the OCS-NG installation

The *OCS-NG* management server encloses all of the four server roles that our inventory solution entails. It is the centralized heart of the inventory. In this chapter, we're going to look through the necessary steps to prepare our system in order to fulfill the general requirements of running OCS-NG management server. As it is a cross-platform project, we will cover the installation on specific Linux flavors and on a Windows server operating system.

The actual installation process is console based on Linux environments. It is verbosely logged, and the steps can be easily followed. It is straightforward. On Microsoft Windows operating systems, there is a de facto standard Win32 setup-like installation wizard.

OCS Inventory NG runs on top of the popular Apache web server, using MySQL's InnoDB engine and the PHP server-side scripting language. In order to install the OCS-NG management server, the system must have these prerequisites installed and configured.

On Linux distributions, we'll look into a brief overview of the steps involved for installation. This checkup helps us to refresh our memory. Under most circumstances, should you desire to install OCS-NG on a Linux server, this suggests that you are familiar with working in Linux/Unix environments. Therefore, setting up basic server roles should not cause you any problems.

There is an integrated pack that sets up all of the components we must have for a fully functional web server. This package is available for Windows, Linux, Solaris, and Mac OS X operating systems. It's called XAMPP. The developers of OCS-NG thought about making the process seamless on Windows machines. The Win32 installation kit of OCS-NG includes this integrated pack and sets up the prerequisites during the setup process.

Regardless of which platform we choose to install the OCS-NG management server on, the next step is the initial configuration. After fiddling with a few security pointers, we can finally declare that our server is pretty much ready for further action. Thus, our objective is met.

This is our action plan for this chapter!

Setting up prerequisite software on Linux flavors

The OCS Inventory NG management server consists of the following four server roles:

- **Database server**: It requires MySQL 4.1 or a higher version that uses the InnoDB engine
- **Communication server**: It requires Apache web server 1.3 or higher and some Perl modules (which we are going to present in a minute)
- **Deployment server**: It requires any web server (Apache works here too)
- **Administration console**: It needs Apache Web Server, PHP 4.3 or higher, and some additional ZIP and GD support

 From now on, in the case of software versions, the "+" suffix at the end of version numbers is akin with the "or higher" expression. For example, MySQL 4.1+ means MySQL with at least version number 4.1 or higher.

Apart from those main server components, the following modules are necessary:

- Apache server needs to be 1.3.X, 2.0.X+ with the following modules:
    - Mod_perl version 1.29+
    - Mod_php version 4.3.2+
- PHP 4.3.2+ with extensions:
    - ZIP library of ZIP file functions and support
    - GD library of image functions
- PERL 5.6+ with the following modules:
    - XML::Simple version 2.12+
    - Compress::Zlib version 1.33+
    - DBI version 1.40+
    - DBD::MySQL version 2.9004+
    - Apache::DBI version 0.93
    - Net::IP version 1.21+
    - SOAP::Lite version 0.66+

- MySQL 4.1+ with following engine:
  - ° InnoDB

- Any sort of *make* utility to control the generation of executables and similar important files from an application's source code files
  - ° For example: GNU make.

The list might look overwhelming at first. However, in the real world, setting up these components isn't any hassle at all. Almost every Linux distribution comes with these (and many more) server roles that can be enabled easily during setup or after. The addition of these modules and certain extensions can be done in less than five minutes.

The process of installing new applications inside a Linux environment is usually assisted by package management software. These are distribution-specific utilities that download software packages from maintained repositories and automate the installation process. If all goes well, "dependency hell" is avoided seamlessly. From the user's point of view, these package managers handle everything. As a result, they are confused with installers.

Demystifying package management

The overall list of tasks that a package manager is responsible for performing is quite long. Firstly, these tools track and organize libraries and other applications present on the operating system. They know each and every program that is installed, their version, where they are installed, the packages they are dependent upon, and more.

Ever since the evolution of Linux operating system, newcomers to this world were terrified of the "dependency hell." As we all know, Linux brings lots of options when it comes to the kind of software we can choose from. There are hundreds of applications for every simple task. Usually these applications rely on already created libraries, but a problem arises when there are numerous versions of a certain library. It is hard to keep track of them manually.

The everlasting dilemma of solving dependency hell

Years ago, users were required to resolve this "dependency hell" themselves. This meant figuring out the list of dependencies in case of a software. Somehow, one had to find those necessary packages and libraries (that is, download them from the Web), and set them up. Once these were done, one had to try to install the application again. New dependency problems might have appeared again. Rinse and repeat. It was a long-winded process.

Package management software was designed to automate all of the preceding installations. Each distribution has an official repository of *certified software,* which is pretty much guaranteed to work on the said operating system. The dependencies is resolved really fast. The required libraries are downloaded from the repository as well.

This solution works fantastically in the case of popular applications as these are all officially supported. From a pragmatic point of view, this method is not a magic pill. It is not possible to officially support and certify all of the software that exists. In rare cases, the user still needs to struggle and fight with dependencies like our forefathers did.

Nevertheless, the management server of OCS-NG requires tried and proven open source server components. LAMP is the acronym for Linux, Apache, MySQL, and PHP/Perl. This software stack is one of the most widely recognized bundles with regards to setting up a general-purpose web server. This means that no matter what distribution you've chosen, these server components are going to be available via their official repos.

Before we actually begin to set up Apache, MySQL, and PHP/Perl on our Linux distro, we are going to look into some of the most common package managers. Once we know how to work with each, installing those server daemons and packages is child's play.

Getting familiar with your distribution's package manager

Nowadays, most Linux distributions come with at least one full-fledged package manager. By default, these connect and grab those binary packages from officially supported software repositories. Most package management software achieves the same functionality under a different layout, shape, form, or by using a different approach.

As a memory refresher, we cannot forget that installing packages and/or updating our Linux distributions requires root access. Despite the controversy it created, some distros allow the installation of signed packages from their official repository even without a root password, but in most cases we need root access to do administrative tasks on an operating system. Therefore, working under our favorite package manager also requires root access.

Yum on RPM-based Linux distributions

One of the most widely implemented package managers these days is **yum**. Yum comes from **Yellowdog Updater**. It is RPM-compatible and, thus, it is equipped in most distributions that support RPM packages. By its nature, yum is console based, but there are many **graphical user interface (GUI)** frontends available.

The advantage of using package management software such as yum comes mainly from making the update procedure really trivial. Every time a new package is installed via yum, it is stored in your software/package database. When a new version is released and added to the repository, you can find out whether you're lagging behind and update it if required. Nevertheless, not every repository is always up-to-date. This is to be kept in mind.

Opting for software that is distributed via package management comes with a certain guarantee. In case of really popular software packages, like the server components we are going to install soon (Apache Web Server, MySQL, and PHP/PERL), this is critical. Their installation becomes seamless, and they are guaranteed to work on your specific distributions. If you're running an old Linux distro, then you'll get an old version of those too.

The following Linux distributions are equipped with yum right from scratch:

- Red Hat Enterprise Linux
- Fedora/Fedora Core
- Mandrake/Mandriva
- CentOS
- SuSE Linux/openSUSE
- Yellow Dog Linux
- And others

Working with yum is quite easy. For example, installing a package is done by typing `yum install package-name`. To check whether an update is available for a package, we type `yum update package-name`. Without specifying a package-name, type `yum update`, it checks and updates each of them if updates are ready. In order to find out if a package is installed or not, we can simply type `yum list installed package-name`.

Then there are situations when we aren't sure of a package's full name. In such cases, we type `yum list perl*` and this way it enumerates every package that begins with `perl`. We can use wildcards. Removing packages can be done with `yum remove package-name`.

For more information and other useful tips on how to fully use yum, type `man yum`.

APT and Aptitude/Synaptic on Debian and its derivates

Advanced Packaging Tool (APT), was designed as a package manager user interface for Debian-based Linux distributions. Initially, it was just a frontend for dpkg, which is the core package manager on Debian derivates; it works with .deb packages.

For a moment, let's think of a pyramid. On the lowest layer, there is dpkg. It is the core of Debian package management. It is the tool that provides the functionality to install, remove, and extract information out of .deb packages. On top of dpkg sits APT. It is a friendlier interface. It is well designed, and it provides robust means to find out the best possible order for packages necessary to be installed or removed for great performance.

Some enthusiasts swear by APT, and they claim it's one of the main reasons why they stick with Debian variants. Over the years, APT was extended, and it now supports RPMs too.

Drifting back to our pyramid, on the top layer we can find *Aptitude or Synaptic*. These are graphical user interfaces to the previously mentioned APT. They provide a comfortable frontend and powerful searching features. Aptitude also has a **command-line interface (CLI).** Should you want to find more information about these applications, type man followed by command name. Right now, let's learn about the most frequently used APT commands.

The most basic APT command deals with installing packages, we can do this with apt-get install packagename. We can remove the said package with apt-get remove packagename. Upgrading packages can be achieved with apt-get -u upgrade, where the -u argument tells the system to print out the packages that are going to be updated.

As mentioned earlier, APT was ported to RPM and the tool that deals with RPM packages is called APT-RPM. The rest of the commands and arguments are similar. The configuration of APT can be quite complex, depending on your needs. Be sure to check the manual.

The following list contains a few Linux distributions that support APT:

- Debian GNU/Linux
- Ubuntu
- Conectiva (APT-RPM, they did the port to RPM)
- Mandrake
- SuSE

- Sun Solaris
- Red Hat
- PLD
- Vine Linux
- ALT Linux
- Yellow Dog Linux
- And others

Emerge and Portage, the heart of Gentoo Linux

Gentoo Linux takes a different approach when considering a package management system. Originally developed on the idea of FreeBSD ports, Gentoo's powerful package manager is called **Portage**. Portage works with *ebuilds*, which are bash scripts that deal with the installation of applications. In essence, the process encapsulates the tasks of downloading the sources, configuring, making, compiling, and finally installing them appropriately.

Emerge is the utility that works with Portage. Using emerge is a double-edged sword. While it comes with lots of advantages, it can become quite complex at the same time. What we need to know is how to use emerge to install some of the necessary prerequisite packages in order to have our platform ready for OCS-NG management server. Should you really want to get your feet wet with Portage, there's plenty of documentation.

There are more than 25,000 ebuilds available through Gentoo official mirror servers. We can synchronize our local repository with these mirror servers by executing the `emerge --sync` command. This updates the repository with the latest version packages. We can grab a package by typing `emerge packagename`. This downloads the respective ebuild(s) and starts the installation process. Usually, the compiling steps are (or can be) lengthy.

Despite the original approach of not supporting binary packages, Portage does contain **Pre Compiled Binary Packages** (**PCBP**) for really popular applications that are time consuming to compile. No user fancies waiting for hours just to get a complex application suite like `OpenOffice.org` up and running. We can add the `--bin` argument to search for an available binary package. If there's one, then emerge utility will get that instead of the ebuild.

Installing Apache, MySQL, and PHP/Perl on Linux systems

We want to install Apache, MySQL, and PHP/PERL (also known as AMP solution stack) on our Linux system as our OCS-NG inventory is going to run on top of these. Apache is the web server daemon, and it's going to provide a web-based user interface for us too. MySQL will serve database requests, and it's the heart of the inventory after all. In order to provide dynamic content, we also need PHP and Perl interpreters.

After having learnt how to use package managers of various Linux distributions, let's put our knowledge to some practical use. We will focus on yum, then APT, and finally emerge.

Installing the AMP stack with yum

First things first, we can install all packages with one simple command line as follows:

```
# yum -y install httpd php mysql mysql-server php-mysql
```

Now that we have these basic packages installed, we can check whether there are updates available for them by using the yum check-update httpd command In order to find out which version we installed, we can type the following command:

```
rpm -qa | grep -i httpd
```

```
[root@fedorabox /]# rpm -qa | grep -i httpd
httpd-2.2.11-2.fc10.i386
httpd-tools-2.2.11-2.fc10.i386
```

Then, if an update is available, we can simply type yum update httpd to update the package. This command can be applied to every package. Here httpd was used for exemplification.

When we're trying to get all of the necessary packages with that one-liner yum command, what happens if our Linux distribution already comes with some of these packages installed? Well, the yum utility is fairly smart and can decide if there's a higher version for some of them. It also checks and resolves the dependencies.

We can update each package manually with the yum update packagename, but it is a bit pointless to do it that way. Instead, we just command the installation of those packages, and the installer figures out if they are already on the machine and what to do in that situation.

Check out the next screenshot. Some packages are updates while others are already up-to-date.

```
[root@fedorabox /]# yum -y install httpd php mysql mysql-server php-mysql
Loaded plugins: refresh-packagekit
Setting up Install Process
Package php-5.2.9-2.fc10.i386 already installed and latest version
Package php-mysql-5.2.9-2.fc10.i386 already installed and latest version
Resolving Dependencies
--> Running transaction check
---> Package httpd.i386 0:2.2.14-1.fc10 set to be updated
--> Processing Dependency: httpd-tools = 2.2.14-1.fc10 for package: httpd-2.2.14-1.fc10.i386
---> Package mysql.i386 0:5.0.88-1.fc10 set to be updated
--> Processing Dependency: mysql-libs = 5.0.88-1.fc10 for package: mysql-5.0.88-1.fc10.i386
---> Package mysql-server.i386 0:5.0.88-1.fc10 set to be updated
--> Running transaction check
---> Package httpd-tools.i386 0:2.2.14-1.fc10 set to be updated
---> Package mysql-libs.i386 0:5.0.88-1.fc10 set to be updated
--> Finished Dependency Resolution
```

The previous screenshot shows only one-third of the process. The entire downloading, updating, and cleanup processes are skipped. What matters is that it handles updates seamlessly. Each action is verbosely logged. It should not require user interaction.

You can check the version of MySQL installed by using the following command:

```
# mysql -V
mysql  Ver 14.14 Distrib 5.1.42, for redhat-linux-gnu (i386) using
readline 5.1
```

```
mysql  Ver 14.14 Distrib 5.1.42, for redhat-linux-gnu (i386) using readline 5.1
```

We need to add them as services so that they start automatically with the operating system:

```
# chkconfig httpd on
```

```
# chkconfig mysqld on
```

Let's manually start the services now, as we don't want to reboot.

```
# service httpd start
Starting httpd:          [  OK  ]
# service mysqld start
Starting MySQL:          [  OK  ]
```

Now, we need to specify the MySQL root password. Here's how to do this:

```
# mysqladmin -u root password 'password-goes-here'
```

Do not ignore the simple quotes, as the password goes inside those apostrophe marks.

As a rule of thumb, it is recommended to execute the `mysql_secure_installation` shell script. This bash script is shipped with MySQL packages, and it performs the following initial security configurations:

- Changes root password, if applicable. We did that earlier.
- Removes the anonymous user access.
- Disables root login from remote access (only allowed from 'localhost').
- Removes the default sample database.

Installing AMP stack with apt

First, we will install the Apache2 web server daemon using the following command:

```
# apt-get install apache2
```

Next, we will install the rest of PHP 5 packages using the following command:

```
# apt-get php5 libapache2-mod-php5 php5-cli php5-common php5-cgi php5-gd
```

MySQL related packages are then installed using the following command:

```
# apt-get install mysql-client mysql-common mysql-server php5-mysql
```

> In case, we do not specify the version number, such as PHP 5, the latest version is picked by the package management software. Therefore, as an example, `php` also suffices.

Once they are installed, we recommend running the `mysql_secure_installation` shell script here too. If you decide not to run it, then at least don't forget to set the root password.

Installing AMP stack with emerge on Gentoo

Here's how we install Amp stack under Gentoo with Emerge:

First we add *Apache2* and *MySQL* to the **USE** flag in `/etc/make.conf`:

```
# emacs -nw /etc/make.conf
```

Now we execute the emerge utility:

```
# emerge -av apache
# emerge -av mysql
# emerge -av php
# emerge -av mod_perl
```

Let's add them as services to start on each restart:

```
# rc-update add apache2 default
# rc-update add mysql default
```

We need to enable PHP 5 in our Apache2 config file:

```
# nano -w /etc/conf.d/apache2
at the end of "APACHE2_OPTS=" line add "-D PHP5"
```

> It should be noted that the -av argument stands for *ask* and *verbose* functionalities.

Working with Gentoo Linux sometimes requires patience. Generally, if one runs a distro like Gentoo, some sort of experience with that environment is assumed. Thus, should you struggle getting an AMP stack set up together, don't hesitate to research for information. There are step-by-step guides available that are dedicated to that topic.

Installing the AMP stack with an XAMPP precompiled package

XAMPP is an open source project that contains an Apache distribution containing other critical web server elements such as MySQL server, PHP, and Perl. It also installs some good-to-have applications such as PhpMyAdmin, ProFTPd (FTP server). The installation requires downloading, extracting, and installing. The script is automated.

For more information, please visit the project's official web page at:

```
http://www.apachefriends.org/en/xampp-linux.html
```

You can download XAMPP from the previously mentioned site as well. It comes with installation instructions.

Setting up the necessary modules on Linux systems

Besides having a functional AMP stack, our web server needs a few additional modules. These are Perl modules, some of which deal with compression, while others provide extension means (SOAP). Getting these installed requires just a minute's work.

Here's how we can do this using the following commands in yum:

```
# yum install perl-XML-Simple
# yum install perl-Compress-Zlib
# yum install perl-DBI
# yum install perl-DBD-MySQL
# yum install perl-Apache-DBI
# yum install perl-Net-IP
# yum install perl-SOAP-Lite
```

We can do the same with APT as well by using the following commands:

```
# apt-get install libxml-simple-perl
# apt-get install libcompress-zlib-perl
# apt-get install libdbi-perl
# apt-get install libdbd-mysql-perl
# apt-get install libapache-dbi-perl
# apt-get install libnet-ip-perl
# apt-get install libsoap-lite-perl
# cpan -i XML::Entities
```

And in the case of Portage, we run the following `emerge` commands:

```
# emerge dev-perl/XML-Simple
# emerge perl-core/IO-Compress
# emerge dev-perl/Apache-DBI
# emerge dev-perl/Net-IP
# emerge dev-perl/SOAP-Lite
# emerge app-portage/g-cpan
# g-cpan -i XML::Entities
```

As a final note, it does not matter if some of the modules are already installed. Running the commands just mentioned on either package management system won't do any harm. They will be checked, and if they are found to be present, a warning will be printed on the screen.

The SOAP-related modules are optional. They can be installed when needed later on, too.

Setting up the OCS-NG management server on Linux operating systems

Before we begin, let's initiate a terminal session at the Linux server. This is going to be the server on which we will install the OCS-NG server. It is recommended to start an encrypted shell such as SSH. You may even work locally on the server, if possible.

We are going to look into two individual ways of installing the OCS-NG management server. You may pick either. The first installation modality will be via RPMs. Ever since OCS-NG has become popular and recognized in the open source community, several Linux distributions have started to include it into their package repository. The advantage of this is that they are officially supported, fully maintained, and kind of guaranteed to work.

While installing software, when there's an RPM, it takes barely one line of command, and the process is fully automated. The second modality that we will cover is slightly longer, as the user is required to download and extract the latest OCS-NG server archive. The user can then follow the instructions throughout the verbosely logged and interactive setup.

We agree that whenever possible, using RPMs to install and remove packages is generally recommended. In this way, you are keeping things consistent, and the software database is updated and reflects the overall state of all your applications. One thing is clear, we won't get into the source code versus RPM debate here. It's pretty long winded.

What really matters is that we know the real installation modality, if and when you fail to find an RPM package based on the version of OCS-NG you want to install.

Although these software repositories seem to be quite up-to-date, keep in mind that they are always lagging behind their official releases. Moreover, as you find yourself getting familiar with the entire OCS-NG architecture, you will want to try and play around with beta and release candidate versions.

Then again, we might also use a Linux distribution that is not RPM based. Summing these issues up, it is important to know both installation modalities. If you're using one of the popular distributions that support RPMs such as Red Hat, Fedora, SUSE, Mandriva, and others, opting for this keeps things integral. But perhaps in the official repo, there's an older version of OCS-NG. We consider it's worth taking those few minutes to install OCS-NG without precompiled packages. This is entirely your choice. We can make an inventory on either.

Another key point needs to be mentioned: OCS-NG is based on web technologies. It does not need to be compiled. A lot of people are terrified of having to compile source code in order to install an application. The OCS-NG installation package needs to be extracted and copied where you want. Once this step is done, you just launch the shell script.

Now that we know what to expect, let's get down to the real deal.

Installing OCS-NG server via an RPM package

Every time we look forward to installing an application via precompiled packages, we have to first ask our package management software repository what to do with the package (search, install, check the version, and so on). In case of OCS-NG, when it comes to these packages, most repositories are called **ocsinventory.**

Therefore, provided that we're dealing with Yum, we run the following query:

```
#yum search ocsinventory

Loaded plugins: refresh-packagekit

======================Matched: ocsinventory=====================

ocsinventory.noarch : Open Computer and Software Inventory Next
Generation

ocsinventory-agent.noarch : Open Computer and Software Inventory NG
client

ocsinventory-ipdiscover.i386 : Open Computer and Software Inventory NG
client

ocsinventory-reports.noarch : OCS Inventory NG - Communication server

ocsinventory-server.noarch : OCS Inventory NG - Communication server
```

```
Loaded plugins: presto, refresh-packagekit
============================== Matched: ocsinventory ==============================
ocsinventory.noarch : Open Computer and Software Inventory Next Generation
ocsinventory-agent.noarch : Open Computer and Software Inventory Next Generation client
ocsinventory-ipdiscover.i686 : Open Computer and Software Inventory Next Generation client
ocsinventory-reports.noarch : OCS Inventory NG - Communication server
ocsinventory-server.noarch : OCS Inventory NG - Communication server
```

Based on the previous output, we have found out that there is some kind of
`ocsinventory` package inside the yum repository of our distribution. In order
to find out more details regarding the version, release, size, and so on, we are
going to run the `yum info ocsinventory` command. The output can be seen
in the following screenshot. **Version 1.02.1** is available.

```
[root@fedorabox /]# yum info ocsinventory
Loaded plugins: refresh-packagekit
Available Packages
Name        : ocsinventory
Arch        : noarch
Version     : 1.02.1
Release     : 3.fc10
Size        : 4.7 k
Repo        : updates
Summary     : Open Computer and Software Inventory Next Generation
URL         : http://www.ocsinventory-ng.org/
License      : GPLv2
```

Now, we're quite lucky because the version found inside the repository matches the
latest stable version released. This means that we can get the OCS-NG management
server up and running just like installing any other application by running the
following query:

`yum install ocsinventory`.

As always, this command resolves the dependencies and proceeds to install
the software. We're going to be asked to confirm the transaction summary
(six packages are needed for this).

There is another modality when we want to get an RPM package that matches
the version number of our Linux distribution. We can give a try to RPM packet
search engines. RPM PBone is just an example. You can find Pbone at
`http://rpm.pbone.net/`. There are others like Rpmfind, which you can
find at `http://www.rpmfind.net/`.

Luckily, for those who love to deal with RPMs, there's an enthusiast and developer
called Remi who maintains an RPM repository dedicated to OCS Inventory-NG
and GLPI. We will cover the latter in a future chapter when we get to extensions
and how to integrate OCS-NG with other tools. Remi has a blog at `http://blog.`
`famillecollet.com/pages/OCS-GLPI-en` where he has also posted instructions.

On this link, we can find instructions on how to install OCS-NG via RPMs provided
by Remi as well. We can either configure our package management system to look

into his repository, or we can just download the RPM packages ourselves and get them installed.

Check out his entire RPM collection. Keep in mind, these are not officially maintained. The community is thankful to Remi for his work and dedication.

```
http://rpms.famillecollet.com/
```

Here's a quick example on how to download and install Remi's release for Fedora 11:

```
#wget http://rpms.famillecollet.com/remi-release-11.rpm

#rpm -Uvh remi-release-11.rpm
```

Should we choose to install one of Remi's releases without a package management system like yum or APT, there's a preliminary step. The RPM validity check requires the GNU Privacy Guard (GnuPG or GPG) of Remi to be imported. For instructions on how to do this, you can refer to the following link:

```
http://blog.famillecollet.com/pages/Config-en
```

The command is `rpm --import RPM-GPG-KEY-remi` after we downloaded the key.

These modalities should suffice, if you really opt for getting OCS-NG up and running via precompiled RPM packages. However, if we end up struggling to find the right version from repositories, then we don't need to worry. The script-based installation is the way to go.

Installing OCS-NG server via installation script

The installation script automates the setup procedure. The user is required to be present as the setup is interactive. Depending on the configuration we are trying to work with, we can install all of the server roles of OCS-NG on the same server.

In most cases, you don't really need a distributed setup where two or more servers are dedicated just for inventorying needs. A few million computers can be inventoried with today's modern servers. Any modest computer (not even a *real* dedicated server) can deal with thousands of inventories by itself.

These rather shy performance requirements also mean that the OCS-NG management server can be made virtual. Nowadays, most companies have server needs that are virtual and centralized. Should this be one of your concerns, it does work well with OCS-NG too.

As with every other software, it is strongly recommended to use the latest *final* and stable release for production use. In case of test environments, beta versions and release candidates are alright. In scenarios where unknown behavior cannot be allowed: for example, production use, always choose fully tested stable versions.

The real benefit of opting for the script-based installation comes mainly from the fact that we are getting the latest versions right from the OCS-NG developers. We have the liberty to choose whichever version to install on whatever Linux distribution (or Windows), and as the installation of OCS-NG does not require compiling of sources, it goes smoothly.

Downloading and extracting the OCS-NG server package

The first step of the installation process is grabbing the latest version of the OCS-NG. Point your favorite browser to the **Downloads** section of the official OCS-NG website:

```
http://www.ocsinventory-ng.org/index.php?page=downloads
```

On the left side of the web page, you can see the versions enumerated from newest to the oldest. At the time of writing this book, the latest version is **1.02.1**. Don't be led into doubt, as this does not mean that the product is in its early development stages. This is one of the project's traits, slowly increasing in version numbers. As of November 6, 2009, a new beta 2.1.3 version was released and is going through initial testing. For now, we'll work with 1.02.1.

Download the OCS Inventory NG server in a `.tar.gz` archived format. You should find the file in the following format:

```
OCSNG_UNIX_SERVER-1.02.1.tar.gz.
```

 # wget http://downloads.sourceforge.net/project/ocsinventory/OCS%20 Inventory%20NG/1.02/OCSNG_UNIX_SERVER-1.02.1.tar.gz

```
Resolving downloads.sourceforget.net... 216.240.187.150
Connecting to downloads.sourceforget.net|216.240.187.150|:80... connected.
HTTP request sent, awaiting response... 200 OK
Length: 1282 (1.3K) [text/html]
Saving to: `OCSNG_UNIX_SERVER-1.02.1.tar.gz.1'

100%[================================================================>] 1,282

2010-03-03 02:07:49 (49.9 MB/s) - `OCSNG_UNIX_SERVER-1.02.1.tar.gz.1' saved [1282/1282]
```

```
# ls -l
-rw-r--r-- 1 root root 1488981 2009-05-30 11:21 OCSNG_UNIX_SERVER-
1.02.1.tar.gz
```

The next step is extraction. The archive contains a folder so we don't need to create it.

```
# tar -xvzf OCSNG_UNIX_SERVER-1.02.1.tar.gz
```

As you can see, we have used the tar command with -xvzf options to extract the archive. Tar is one of the most basic GNU archiving tool in Linux. The specified parameters stand for the following: -x for *to extract*, -v for *verbose logging*, -z for *gzip* to process the archiving through gzip and ungzip, and finally -f is followed by the target filename.

The following directory is created: OCSNG_UNIX_SERVER-1.02.1 (version dependent)

```
#ls -l
drwxr-xr-x 5 root root    4096 2009-05-30 10:53 OCSNG_UNIX_SERVER-1.02.1
```

Alright, the chances are we have not encountered any problems. It is time take a peek into the extracted folder.

```
#cd OCSNG_UNIX_SERVER-1.02.1
#ls -l
total 132
drwxr-xr-x 5 root root  4096 2009-05-30 10:53 Apache
-rw-r--r-- 1 root root 36923 2009-05-30 10:52 ChangeLog
drwxr-xr-x 3 root root  4096 2009-05-30 10:53 dtd
-rw-r--r-- 1 root root 17987 2009-05-30 10:52 LICENSE.txt
drwxr-xr-x 9 root root  4096 2009-05-30 10:53 ocsreports
-rw-r--r-- 1 root root  3946 2009-05-30 10:52 README
-rwxr-xr-x 1 root root 54851 2009-05-30 10:52 setup.sh
```

```
total 132
drwxr-xr-x. 5 tony tony  4096 2009-05-30 10:53 Apache
-rw-r--r--. 1 tony tony 36923 2009-05-30 10:52 ChangeLog
drwxr-xr-x. 3 tony tony  4096 2009-05-30 10:53 dtd
-rw-r--r--. 1 tony tony 17987 2009-05-30 10:52 LICENSE.txt
drwxr-xr-x. 9 tony tony  4096 2009-05-30 10:53 ocsreports
-rw-r--r--. 1 tony tony  3946 2009-05-30 10:52 README
-rwxr-xr-x. 1 tony tony 54851 2009-05-30 10:52 setup.sh
```

The LICENSE.txt is the **GNU Public License (GPL) v2** of **End User License Agreement (EULA)**. As always, we should not proceed further without reading the license thoroughly. Fortunately for many of us, we're quite familiar with the GNU Public License (GPL) v2 already.

The README file is a short description of the OCS Inventory NG setup procedure. A More detailed documentation is available on the online wiki from the OCS Inventory NG's website:

http://wiki.ocsinventory-ng.org/

It is available in the following languages: English, French, Spanish, Deutsch, and Italian.

The setup.sh is a console-based installation shell script that requires user interaction.

We are going to execute this script with either ./setup.sh or sh setup.sh.

Warning:
Do not attempt to take a coffee break now — your participation will be required!

Running the installation script and checking prerequisites

When we hit *Enter* to the launching command, we are greeted by the OCS Inventory NG welcome screen in the terminal window.

A caution related to upgrading is pointed out, as shown in the following figure:

```
+-------------------------------------------------------------+
|                                                             |
|  Welcome to OCS Inventory NG Management server setup !       |
|                                                             |
+-------------------------------------------------------------+

CAUTION: If upgrading Communication server from OCS Inventory NG 1.0 RC2 and
previous, please remove any Apache configuration for Communication Server!

Do you wish to continue ([y]/n)?█
```

Any earlier Apache configuration needs to be wiped out when upgrading the communication server from 1.0 RC2. Assuming this is our first installation, we ignore it.

The installation script checks the existence of MySQL on the server and then queries its version number. You should pass this step as we did with the prerequisites earlier.

```
Your MySQL client seems to be part of MySQL version 5.1.

Your computer seems to be running MySQL 4.1 or higher, good ;-)
```

Now, we are asked to specify our MySQL database network information. Where it is located? If it's on the same server, then we hit **Enter** for **localhost**.

```
Which host is running database server [localhost] ?

OK, database server is running on host localhost ;-)
```

On which port does it run? If it's set to the default port 3306, then we hit **Enter** here too.

```
On which port is running database server [3306] ?

OK, database server is running on port 3306 ;-)
```

```
+------------------------------------------------------------+
| Checking for database server properties...                 |
+------------------------------------------------------------+

Your MySQL client seems to be part of MySQL version 5.1.
Your computer seems to be running MySQL 4.1 or higher, good ;-)

Which host is running database server [localhost] ?
OK, database server is running on host localhost ;-)

On which port is running database server [3306] ?
OK, database server is running on port 3306 ;-)
```

Once the database configuration is gathered, it asks for the Apache web daemon. Assuming the daemon is binary on the default path: /usr/sbin/httpd, we hit *Enter*.

```
Where is Apache daemon binary [/usr/sbin/httpd] ?

OK, using Apache daemon /usr/sbin/httpd ;-)
```

Now comes the main configuration file of Apache. Unless modified, it's on the default path.

```
Where is Apache main configuration file [/etc/httpd/conf/httpd.conf] ?

OK, using Apache main configuration file /etc/httpd/conf/httpd.conf ;-)
```

The right permissions also need to be set. In order to do this, the script asks for the Apache user account and user group. By default, these are both `apache`.

```
Which user account is running Apache web server [apache] ?

OK, Apache is running under user account apache ;-)

Which user group is running Apache web server [apache] ?

OK, Apache is running under users group apache ;-)
```

```
+-----------------------------------------------------------+
| Checking for Apache web server daemon...                  |
+-----------------------------------------------------------+

Where is Apache daemon binary [/usr/sbin/httpd] ?
OK, using Apache daemon /usr/sbin/httpd ;-)
+-----------------------------------------------------------+
| Checking for Apache main configuration file...            |
+-----------------------------------------------------------+

Where is Apache main configuration file [/etc/httpd/conf/httpd.conf] ?
OK, using Apache main configuration file /etc/httpd/conf/httpd.conf ;-)
+-----------------------------------------------------------+
| Checking for Apache user account...                       |
+-----------------------------------------------------------+

Which user account is running Apache web server [apache] ?
OK, Apache is running under user account apache ;-)

+-----------------------------------------------------------+
| Checking for Apache group...                              |
+-----------------------------------------------------------+

Which user group is running Apache web server [apache] ?
OK, Apache is running under users group apache ;-)
```

Moving on, the script automatically detects the `Apache Include configuration` directory. This is the place where the OCS Inventory NG configuration file is also placed. The user is asked for confirmation of the `Apache Include configuration` folder. If there are multiple installations of Apache and the installer gets confused, then just hit *Enter* on default.

```
Setup found Apache Include configuration directory in /etc/httpd/conf.d/.
Setup will put OCS Inventory NG Apache configuration in this directory.
Where is Apache Include configuration directory [/etc/httpd/conf.d/] ?
OK, Apache Include configuration directory /etc/httpd/conf.d/ found ;-)
```

After these two main components of the LAMP solution stack are configured, we're finally getting to the last letter of the acronym. The script asks for the path of the PERL interpreter. It should be automatically detected. Just hit *Enter*, unless you know it's at another place.

```
Found PERL Intrepreter at </usr/bin/perl> ;-)
Where is PERL Intrepreter binary [/usr/bin/perl] ?
OK, using PERL Intrepreter /usr/bin/perl ;-)
```

```
+--------------------------------------------------------------+
| Checking for Apache Include configuration directory...       |
+--------------------------------------------------------------+

Setup found Apache Include configuration directory in
/etc/httpd/conf.d/.
Setup will put OCS Inventory NG Apache configuration in this directory.
Where is Apache Include configuration directory [/etc/httpd/conf.d/] ?
OK, Apache Include configuration directory /etc/httpd/conf.d/ found ;-)

+--------------------------------------------------------------+
| Checking for PERL Interpreter...                             |
+--------------------------------------------------------------+

Found PERL Intrepreter at </usr/bin/perl> ;-)
Where is PERL Intrepreter binary [/usr/bin/perl] ?
OK, using PERL Intrepreter /usr/bin/perl ;-)
```

We know that there are different ways to set up the roles of OCS-NG management server such as distributed setups where the communication server is on another server. This is when you're asked whether you want to install the communication server on the same machine as well. If so, then hit **y** for yes.

```
Do you wish to setup Communication server on this computer ([y]/n)?y
```

Right away, the setup automatically detects the make utility. Now it won't ask for confirmation.

```
OK, Make utility found at </usr/bin/make> ;-)
```

Mod_perl is an amazing Perl interpreter for your Apache web server. This mod is required for OCS Inventory NG's communication server to function properly. The installation script will try to detect the presence of mod_perl along with its version.

```
Checking for Apache mod_perl version 1.99_22 or higher
Checking for Apache mod_perl version 1.99_21 or previous
```

If all goes well, the setup recognizes its version. Chances are it's going to be 1.99_22+.

```
Checking for Apache mod_perl version 1.99_22 or higher
Found that mod_perl version 1.99_22 or higher is available.
OK, Apache is using mod_perl version 1.99_22 or higher ;-)
```

However, don't worry if it cannot auto-detect the correct version. The following output may be presented on your terminal screen:

```
Setup is unable to determine your Apache mod_perl version.
Apache must have module mod_perl enabled. As configuration differs from
mod_perl 1.99_21 or previous AND mod_perl 1.99_22 or higher, Setup must
know which release Apache is using.
You can find which release you are using by running the following command
   - On RPM enabled OS, rpm -q mod_perl
   - On DPKG enabled OS, dpkg -l libapache*-mod-perl*
Enter 1 for mod_perl 1.99_21 or previous.
Enter 2 for mod_perl 1.99_22 and higher.
Which version of Apache mod_perl the computer is running ([1]/2) ?2
```

```
+----------------------------------------------------------+
| Checking for Make utility...                             |
+----------------------------------------------------------+

OK, Make utility found at </usr/bin/make> ;-)


+----------------------------------------------------------+
| Checking for Apache mod_perl version...                  |
+----------------------------------------------------------+

Checking for Apache mod_perl version 1.99_22 or higher
Checking for Apache mod_perl version 1.99_21 or previous
Setup is unable to determine your Apache mod_perl version.
Apache must have module mod_perl enabled. As configuration differs from
mod_perl 1.99_21 or previous AND mod_perl 1.99_22 or higher, Setup must
know which release Apache is using.
You can find which release you are using by running the following command
  - On RPM enabled OS, rpm -q mod_perl
  - On DPKG enabled OS, dpkg -l libapache*-mod-perl*
Enter 1 for mod_perl 1.99_21 or previous.
Enter 2 for mod_perl 1.99_22 and higher.
Which version of Apache mod_perl the computer is running ([1]/2) ?2
OK, Apache is using mod_perl version 1.99_22 or higher ;-)


+----------------------------------------------------------+
| Checking for Communication server log directory...       |
+----------------------------------------------------------+

Communication server can create detailled logs. This logs can be enabled
by setting interger value of LOGLEVEL to 1 in Administration console
menu Configuration.
Where to put Communication server log directory [/var/log/ocsinventory-server] ?
OK, Communication server will put logs into directory /var/log/ocsinventory-server ;-)
```

You can find out your correct version of `mod_perl` by following the instruction which is as follows:

```
[root@fedorabox tony]# rpm -q mod_perl
mod_perl-2.0.4-7.i386
```

We have chosen the second option as our version is higher than 1.99.2. If you don't have `mod_perl` installed, then it's not too late to fix this problem. Fire up another terminal/console shell on your Linux server, and using your package management software, grab it.

There are a few more steps in the installation. Now, we are asked where the server should place the communication server's logs. It defaults to a rather self-explanatory path.

```
Where to put Communication server log directory [/var/log/ocsinventory-
server] ?

OK, Communication server will put logs into directory /var/log/
ocsinventory-server ;-)
```

The installation is going to check those prerequisite Perl modules we talked about earlier.

```
Checking for DBI PERL module...
Found that PERL module DBI is available.
Checking for Apache::DBI PERL module...
Found that PERL module Apache::DBI is available.
Checking for DBD::mysql PERL module...
Found that PERL module DBD::mysql is available.
Checking for Compress::Zlib PERL module...
Found that PERL module Compress::Zlib is available.
Checking for XML::Simple PERL module...
Found that PERL module XML::Simple is available.
Checking for Net::IP PERL module...
Found that PERL module Net::IP is available.
```

```
+-------------------------------------------------------------+
| Checking for required Perl Modules...                       |
+-------------------------------------------------------------+

Checking for DBI PERL module...
Found that PERL module DBI is available.
Checking for Apache::DBI PERL module...
Found that PERL module Apache::DBI is available.
Checking for DBD::mysql PERL module...
Found that PERL module DBD::mysql is available.
Checking for Compress::Zlib PERL module...
Found that PERL module Compress::Zlib is available.
Checking for XML::Simple PERL module...
Found that PERL module XML::Simple is available.
Checking for Net::IP PERL module...
Found that PERL module Net::IP is available.
```

It also checks for optional ones. These are not necessary unless the **Simple Object Access Protocol (SOAP)** web service functionality is required. In a nutshell, SOAP is an XML-based protocol that simplifies information exchange over HTTP. SOAP opens up numerous doors for further extensions and easy data access through third-party applications. We will learn more about this in *Chapter 7, Integrating OCS-NG with GLPI* when we discuss extensions and plugins.

```
Checking for SOAP::Lite PERL module...
Found that PERL module SOAP::Lite is available.
Checking for XML::Entities PERL module...
Found that PERL module XML::Entities is available.
```

The real work behind the scenes of the script

Once this step is over, the installation script begins the real work, which is as follows:

- Configures Communication server Perl modules
- Checks if the kit is complete
- Writes the Makefile for Apache::Ocsinventory
- Prepares Communication server Perl modules
- Installs Communication server Perl modules
- Creates Communication server log directory
- Fixes file permissions on the log directory, configures log rotation
- Configures Apache web server

```
+----------------------------------------------------------------+
| OK, looks good ;-)                                             |
|                                                               |
| Configuring Communication server Perl modules...             |
+----------------------------------------------------------------+
Checking if your kit is complete...
Looks good
Writing Makefile for Apache::Ocsinventory
+----------------------------------------------------------------+
| OK, looks good ;-)                                             |
|                                                               |
| Preparing Communication server Perl modules...               |
+----------------------------------------------------------------+
+----------------------------------------------------------------+
| OK, prepare finshed ;-)                                        |
|                                                               |
| Installing Communication server Perl modules...              |
+----------------------------------------------------------------+
+----------------------------------------------------------------+
| OK, Communication server Perl modules install finished;-)|
|                                                               |
| Creating Communication server log directory...               |
+----------------------------------------------------------------+
Creating Communication server log directory /var/log/ocsinventory-server.

Fixing Communication server log directory files permissions.
Configuring logrotate for Communication server.
Removing old communication server logrotate file /etc/logrotate.d/ocsinventory-NG
Writing communication server logrotate to file /etc/logrotate.d/ocsinventory-server
```

The setup can ensure that mod_perl is loaded up before the OCS-NG Communication server is launched. This requires some renaming, and the user is asked for confirmation. Hit **y** for yes.

```
To ensure Apache loads mod_perl before OCS Inventory NG Communication
Server, Setup can name Communication Server Apache configuration file
'z-ocsinventory-server.conf' instead of 'ocsinventory-server.conf'.

Do you allow Setup renaming Communication Server Apache configuration
file

to 'z-ocsinventory-server.conf' ([y]/n) ?y
```

Finally, the script arrives to the last component of the OCS-NG management server suite. It asks you whether you desire to set up the **Administration Server (Web Administration Console)** on the same machine. Unless you're looking for a distributed setup, say **y** forYes.

Do you wish to setup Administration Server (Web Administration Console) on this computer ([y]/n)?y

```
+----------------------------------------------------------+
| OK, Communication server log directory created ;-)       |
|                                                          |
| Now configuring Apache web server...                     |
+----------------------------------------------------------+

To ensure Apache loads mod_perl before OCS Inventory NG Communication Server,
Setup can name Communication Server Apache configuration file
'z-ocsinventory-server.conf' instead of 'ocsinventory-server.conf'.
Do you allow Setup renaming Communication Server Apache configuration file
to 'z-ocsinventory-server.conf' ([y]/n) ?y
OK, using 'z-ocsinventory-server.conf' as Communication Server Apache configuration file
Removing old communication server configuration to file /etc/httpd/conf.d//ocsinventory.conf
Writing communication server configuration to file /etc/httpd/conf.d//z-ocsinventory-server.conf

+----------------------------------------------------------+
| OK, Communication server setup sucessfully finished ;-)  |
|                                                          |
| Please, review /etc/httpd/conf.d//z-ocsinventory-server.conf
| to ensure all is good. Then restart Apache daemon.       |
+----------------------------------------------------------+


Do you wish to setup Administration Server (Web Administration Console)
on this computer ([y]/n)?y
```

Another caution is thrown on the terminal screen. Ignore it if you are installing it for the first time as we're doing now. Either way, the script verbosely explains the situation and asks you what to do. If you are upgrading, you will know the tasks to carry out.

After we get past that caution, we are asked where to copy the Administration Server static files.

```
Where to copy Administration Server static files for PHP Web Console
[/usr/share/ocsinventory-reports] ?
OK, using directory /usr/share/ocsinventory-reports to install static
files ;-)
Where to create writable/cache directories for deployement packages and
IPDiscover [/var/lib/ocsinventory-reports] ?
OK, writable/cache directory is /var/lib/ocsinventory-reports ;-)
```

```
+----------------------------------------------------------+
| Checking for Administration Server directories...        |
+----------------------------------------------------------+

CAUTION: Setup now install files in accordance with Filesystem Hierarchy
Standard. So, no file is installed under Apache root document directory
(Refer to Apache configuration files to locate it).
If you're upgrading from OCS Inventory NG Server 1.01 and previous, YOU
MUST REMOVE (or move) directories 'ocsreports' and 'download' from Apache
root document directory.
If you choose to move directory, YOU MUST MOVE 'download' directory to
Administration Server writable/cache directory (by default
/var/lib/ocsinventory-reports), especialy if you use deployement feature.

Do you wish to continue ([y]/n)?y
Assuming directories 'ocsreports' and 'download' removed from
Apache root document directory.

Where to copy Administration Server static files for PHP Web Console
[/usr/share/ocsinventory-reports] ?
OK, using directory /usr/share/ocsinventory-reports to install static files ;-)
Where to create writable/cache directories for deployement packages and
IPDiscover [/var/lib/ocsinventory-reports] ?
OK, writable/cache directory is /var/lib/ocsinventory-reports ;-)
```

The script checks those necessary Perl modules again. We're skipping that part now.

Once they are alright, as a final step, it copies and fixes the permissions for the new files.

`Creating PHP directory /usr/share/ocsinventory-reports/ocsreports.`

`Copying PHP files to /usr/share/ocsinventory-reports/ocsreports.`

`Fixing permissions on directory /usr/share/ocsinventory-reports/ocsreports.`

`Creating database configuration file /usr/share/ocsinventory-reports/ocsreports/dbconfig.inc.php.`

`Creating IPDiscover directory /var/lib/ocsinventory-reports/ipd.`

`Fixing permissions on directory /var/lib/ocsinventory-reports/ipd.`

`Creating packages directory /var/lib/ocsinventory-reports/download.`

`Fixing permissions on directory /var/lib/ocsinventory-reports/download.`

`Configuring IPDISCOVER-UTIL Perl script.`

`Installing IPDISCOVER-UTIL Perl script.`

`Fixing permissions on IPDISCOVER-UTIL Perl script.`

`Writing Administration server configuration to file /etc/httpd/conf.d//ocsinventory-reports.conf`

```
+-----------------------------------------------------+
| Installing files for Administration server...       |
+-----------------------------------------------------+
Creating PHP directory /usr/share/ocsinventory-reports/ocsreports.
Copying PHP files to /usr/share/ocsinventory-reports/ocsreports.
Fixing permissions on directory /usr/share/ocsinventory-reports/ocsreports.
Creating database configuration file /usr/share/ocsinventory-reports/ocsreports/dbconfig.inc.php.
Creating IPDiscover directory /var/lib/ocsinventory-reports/ipd.
Fixing permissions on directory /var/lib/ocsinventory-reports/ipd.
Creating packages directory /var/lib/ocsinventory-reports/download.
Fixing permissions on directory /var/lib/ocsinventory-reports/download.
Configuring IPDISCOVER-UTIL Perl script.
Installing IPDISCOVER-UTIL Perl script.
Fixing permissions on IPDISCOVER-UTIL Perl script.
Writing Administration server configuration to file /etc/httpd/conf.d//ocsinventory-reports.conf
+-----------------------------------------------------+
| OK, Administration server installation finished ;-) |
|                                                     |
| Please, review /etc/httpd/conf.d//ocsinventory-reports.conf
| to ensure all is good and restart Apache daemon.    |
|                                                     |
| Then, point your browser to http://server//ocsreports
| to configure database server and create/update schema. |
+-----------------------------------------------------+

Setup has created a log file /home/      /OCSNG_UNIX_SERVER-1.02.1/ocs_server_setup.log. Please, save this file.
If you encounter error while running OCS Inventory NG Management server,
we can ask you to show us his content !

DON'T FORGET TO RESTART APACHE DAEMON ! <---------------------

Enjoy OCS Inventory NG ;-)
```

The installation script quits specifying where the log file was saved and stresses on the fact that one should not forget to restart the Apache web server daemon. Before doing that, you are advised to revise the `config` file as follows:

`/etc/httpd/conf.d/ocsinventory-reports.conf`

Setting up the OCS-NG management server on Windows operating systems

Over the years, people from all walks of life got familiar with the Microsoft Windows OS. The reason for that is simple; their focus lay on the standard definition of user friendliness. No matter what the task to be carried out using Windows was, it needed to be automated, wizard based, and intuitive with a beautiful user interface.

The same goes for software installations. We expect wizards and we expect to be able to go through the stages of an application's setup just by clicking **Next**, accepting the license agreement, filling out some text fields, browsing for the target location, and eventually ticking some checkboxes identifying what we really need. However, this last step is hidden under the name of *advanced* or *expert* mode. For the average user, the typical configuration should suffice.

Regardless of the application type and what purpose it's going to serve, most people would expect such an installation using Windows. Those expectations were instilled into consumers. As such, developers are conforming to those desires. Right now, we want to install OCS Inventory NG management server. As we know, it requires the AMP stack (Apache web server, MySQL relational database system, and PHP/Perl interpreters).

XAMPP for Windows, the warm-up stage

It should not surprise anyone that developers thought about finding integrated solutions to provide seamless modalities to set up such an AMP suite. That is how the XAMPP suite was born. It is an automated setup that sets up an AMP solution stack and some other useful tools. It supports Windows 2000, Server 2003, XP (SP2 and SP3), Server 2008, as well as Vista and Windows 7. Besides, it's also available for Linux, Solaris, and OS X.

The latest version of XAMPP for Windows at the time of writing is **1.7.2**. It was tested and it indeed is fully functional on Windows 7. Should you encounter problems while installing one of the XAMPP versions, then please head over to the support forums. The project is fairly well documented, and there's a little dedicated English section within the forums.

XAMPP 1.7.2 is a collection of the following software products:

- Apache 2.2.12 (IPv6 enabled) + OpenSSL 0.9.8k
- MySQL 5.1.37 + PBXT engine
- PHP 5.3.0
- phpMyAdmin 3.2.0.1
- Webalizer 2.21-02 + GeoIP lite
- FileZilla FTP Server 0.9.32
- msmtp 1.4.17

From these components, we need the first three. Unless we don't ever plan to run an FTP server from this machine, installing Filezilla FTP Server is optional. The rest of the tools may turn out useful.

We know what you're thinking about right now; in the beginning of this chapter, we were mumbling about an *integrated installation* package that sets up everything seamlessly. While that is true, it may not be the best decision after all. Let's demystify the situation.

OCS-NG developers integrated the XAMPP package into their installation kit. This gesture is to be appreciated as it helps most people to get the inventory server up and running under Windows OS. The only drawback of the situation is that XAMPP is more often updated than OCS-NG. Since that integrated setup suite was developed, more than a few XAMPP versions were released. This does not mean that the older version isn't enough to set up OCS-NG.

In the case of web servers and relational database systems, it is important to always be on the bleeding edge by having up-to-date releases. We don't want to risk having some uninvited guests from the dark side of *wild-wild-web*. The latest OCS-NG 1.02.1 setup incorporates the XAMPP 1.6.6a. It is a few releases behind the current stable 1.7.2 one.

Please visit the OCS-NG download section at the official web page:

```
http://www.ocsinventory-ng.org/index.php?page=downloads
```

On downloading, if we go ahead and execute the setup, the following warning pops up:

From the previous screenshot, we realize that indeed the setup comes with XAMPP 1.6.6a. In situations where the OCS-NG management server is not going to be located in a **DMZ (demilitarized zone)**, meaning *out there* on the Internet available to everyone, this may not result in problems. The truth be told, this should never happen. An inventorying system and asset management suite should only be available on the intranet.

However, in the case of really large companies where the intranet gets wide enough and different people have access to specific areas, the situation can get tricky again. Most security flaws are thoroughly discussed, exposed (to the public), but fixed right away. This means that if you stick with an older but vulnerable version, anyone can exploit the said security hole; but if you update to the latest and patched release, the problem is solved.

All in all, the decision is ours. We can go through the integrated setup and choose to install XAMPP 1.6.6a along with the OCS-NG server, or we can download and install the latest XAMPP version beforehand. Once XAMPP is up and running, we can set up OCS Inventory NG server, and the installation wizard detects its presence and won't pop up that warning message.

You can download the latest version of XAMPP for Windows from the following link:

```
http://www.apachefriends.org/en/xampp-windows.html
```

We recommend downloading the self-extract archive (`.exe` format), but either one is alright. Once it's downloaded, we are asked where to unpack it. Let's give a common path like:

```
%WINDIR%\%PROGRAMFILES%\xampp
```

After the archive is unpacked, an automated script is executed. Our interaction might be required, but the instructions are straightforward and the actions are verbosely logged.

We can control the status of those services via the XAMPP control panel. That is also the place from where we can administer those roles as well. Either way, if we can see that Apache and MySQL are started and their status is **OK** ,we can install the OCS Inventory NG server.

Warning: XAMPP 1.6.8-1.7.1—a known issue and solution

There's one final warning regarding XAMPP 1.6.8 or higher version. There was a rather unfinished migration from mod_perl 5.8 and 5.10 and they have forgotten to rebuild the MySQL support for 5.10. This is further detailed in a forum post by *dliroulet* who is an OCS-NG team member and developer. Check out the following post:

```
http://forums.ocsinventory-ng.org/viewtopic.php?id=4598
```

Should you experience problems with the XAMPP 1.7.2 version or higher, there is a known solution. Some necessary Perl 5.10 modules need to be recompiled. Fortunately, EBH (who is also a forum member) posted for us the recompiled package in an archive. We just download and extract into the XAMPP folder!

We can download the updated modules from the following link:

```
http://oslinux.free.fr/xampp_1.7.1_perl510_update_modules_for_OCS_
inventoryNG1.02.1.zip
```

They are also mirrored at the following address:

```
http://www.primeranks.net/storage/ocsng/xampp_1.7.1_perl510_update_
modules_for_OCS_inventoryNG1.02.1.zip
```

You should not experience problems with XAMPP 1.7.2 and OCS-NG 1.02.1. However, no matter what, you now know what can be done if such a situation occurs.

Launching the OCS-NG integrated installation

Launching the setup wizard automatically detects the presence of Apache web server along with the required Perl module. This way, it goes further, and the warning message box will not pop up anymore. We click **Next** and then accept the license agreement once we have gone through the text. After this, the window where we need to choose our install type is displayed. The choices are double: either with or without XAMPP Web Server.

Assuming we have installed XAMPP earlier, then the **XAMPP Web Server** component will be *unticked* by default, and only the **OCS Inventory NG Server** will be chosen to be installed. This kind of install is around 3.5 MB.

On the other hand, if you decided to remain with the integrated XAMPP 1.6.6a, then the setup automatically *checks* that component as well. This latter situation can be seen in the following screenshot:

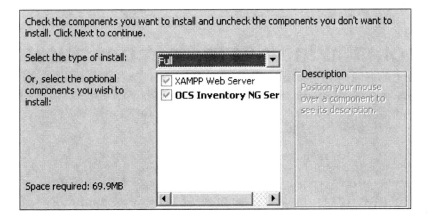

Keep in the mind that you cannot even start the setup without XAMPP! So that means that one way or another, you must install XAMPP earlier than the OCS-NG server.

An integrated installation (XAMPP and OCS-NG server) takes up to 70 MB of disk space. The setup is fast, regardless of whether we choose to install XAMPP or not this time. Once this is done, the following link is opened in a new browser window:

```
http://localhost/ocsreports/install.php
```

This link is valid in situations where all four server components of OCS-NG were installed on the same system. This means the installation has finished and there are just a few steps left from having the full-fledged OCS-NG management server ready.

The XAMPP status can be tracked from the **Security** section as well. This is the web page through which we can administer the installed services.

```
http://localhost/xampp/index.php
```

Component	Status	Hint
MySQL database	ACTIVATED	
PHP	ACTIVATED	
HTTPS (SSL)	ACTIVATED	
Common Gateway Interface (CGI)	ACTIVATED	
Server Side Includes (SSI)	ACTIVATED	
Perl with mod_perl	ACTIVATED	
SMTP Service	DEACTIVATED	
FTP Service	DEACTIVATED	

As a final step, it is important to set the root password for MySQL.

```
http://localhost/security/xamppsecurity.php
```

A pragmatic look at initial configuration

Arriving at this stage means that we have installed the OCS-NG management server. If we had chosen to install the server on Linux, then we would need to fire up our favorite browser and visit the following link. On Windows installations, a new browser is redirected to the following URL:

```
http://localhost/ocsreports/install.php
```

This is when we need to specify the MySQL database log in information for our inventory solution. This is important as it must be able to communicate with the database. The user must have the eligible rights to create databases and tables. Under normal circumstances, this user is `root`. The password is the one we specified earlier. Hostname is `localhost`, if the MySQL server runs on the same machine as the OCS-NG server (like we did).

OCS Inventory Installation

MySql login :	
MySql password :	
MySql HostName :	

Send

This step creates a new database called `ocsweb`, and a new MySQL user `ocs` with password *ocs*. The database schema is created according to the specifications OCS-NG is able to work with. It is he user `ocs` through which our Communication server and Administration server components can exchange information with each other.

Don't worry about security right now, we will discuss it in a later chapter. We can find all of these located in the `dbconfig.inc.php` file. When we decide to use another user or a password (most importantly) for that user, we will know which file we need to fiddle with.

During this process, everything is verbosely logged as well. Pay attention to the output presented on the web page. The necessary tasks should be carried out without hassles. We are asked to fill in a TAG (if you choose to use that feature), but let's ignore that for now.

As such, we're going to leave that field empty. It is quite annoying as a pop up will appear on the very first run of every client agent later on. TAG can be used *silently* as well. When we will discuss the TAG field, we will cover methods which can be used to do this elegantly.

Once everything is done, we can log into the administration console by clicking on the blue hyperlink that redirects our browser to `http://localhost/ocsreports`, the initial username is **admin** with the password **admin**. We should change these as soon as possible.

Enjoy the administration console. It's a place where you will spend a great deal of time.

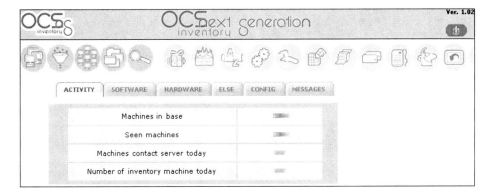

Congratulations! This means that your OCS-NG server has been successfully installed.

Summary

In this chapter, we learnt how to set up the OCS-NG management server. At first, we examined the architectural requirements of the server. We understood how the central management server is composed out of four components: communication server, database server, deployment server, and administration console.

The management server can be installed on Linux distributions and Microsoft Windows operating systems. We were required to get into package management systems and learn how to deal with packages and dependencies. This is usually tricky, and unfortunately, some people have had their share of bad experience equivalent to dependency hell.

Once we got to know some of the most popular package management systems, we could then set up the required AMP stack solution rather easily. This web server served as the foundation of the OCS-NG server.

Enthusiastically, as we were fulfilling the prerequisite checks, we moved on to install the OCS-NG management server. We have looked into two possible modalities on how to do this on Linux and one integrated solution to do this on Windows. We made sure that regardless of our chosen platform, the server got up and running with flying colors.

Now that we have finally put together our OCS-NG management server, it's time to get familiar with agent deployment. Agents will fill our inventory with useful data. After all, that is what inventorying is about — retrieving and storing data. By now, we have a centralized place to store data. Let's move on to learn how to deploy clients to gather data.

3
The Zen of Agent Deployment

So far, we have set up the OCS Inventory NG central management server, but its database is lacking in content. The database without information is just as worthless as a deserted factory without employees and work to do. Agents will be serving the purpose of gathering inventory data, and then providing them to the OCS-NG management server.

In this chapter, our sole focus will be on agents. Thanks to the rather diversified operating system compatibility range, we have numerous scenarios to look into. There are also more than a few techniques to get these agents on the client machines. It is important to realize the key differences in order to make the right decision that best fits the situation.

Throughout this chapter, we will learn how to accomplish the following tasks:

- Rationalize what happens behind the scenes of agents
- Understand the differences between agent types
- Find out about the deployment modalities on various operating systems
- Decide the right agent type and deployment modality for your configuration
- Acquire step-by-step information on carrying out those deployment methods
- Comprehend the *know-how* of getting agents up and running not only on Windows, Linux, and Mac OS X client machines, but also on mobile devices

Behind the scenes: How agents earn their living

The inventory software that runs on client machines is not called an agent just by pure coincidence. If we look up the definition of the noun 'agent', we end up with something like this: a representative who acts on behalf of other persons or organizations.

No doubt, the inventory agent fulfils that status quo. The organization for which the agent works is the central management server. Their work is clearly defined; they gather information, and send them back to the central server. They can also act as spies on identifying other hosts that are not inventoried. Network discovery is covered in *Chapter 5, Investigating the Process of Gathering Inventory Data.*

Besides these tasks, the agent also serves as a key position with regards to package deployment. When this situation occurs, the agent can ask for the file information from the deployment server, request the package, and prepare it for deployment execution.

We have enumerated the tasks of agents in terms of **priority**. The first and foremost task is sending in the inventory data, if it is required to do so. The task of identifying hosts that are not scanned from the network is the second most useful. It enhances network detection and reduces the bandwidth usage by adding distributed scanning into the mix. The server would otherwise be overwhelmed to scan the entire network, all by itself.

Package deployment is an optional feature of the OCS-NG inventory. In those configurations, where this functionality is not required, agents are not required to execute this task.

In situations that are networked, there is some kind of connectivity between the agents and the central management server; the agents always initiate the contact first. We can imagine this as the agent initiating the communication. This way, we do not need to open a port on the firewall and neither set up port forwarding. If browsing works, then this works too.

Communications happens through the HTTP and HTTPS protocols. On client machines, when the executables are monitored for outgoing traffic (by some kind of firewall), we might need to allow traffic to go back and forth from the OCS inventory agent file.

After the agent contacts the central management server, it replies with the task(s) to do, just like the big boss of an organization for which the agent is secretly working for. There are situations when there's nothing to do for the agent, and in these cases, the central server does not assign any of the tasks. This means that there is no mission available.

The agent always maintains an up-to-date inventory stored in an XML format. This is stored locally. After each communication query is initiated by the agent, the management server checks whether the inventory stored of that client is out of date or not. This is specified with the frequency value and a server-side variable on the OCS-NG server.

The value is specified in days, and it is used to determine how old the inventory is. We will learn about it in the next chapter. The deal is that once the last inventory date gets older than this value, the task of sending in the new inventory data is assigned to the client agent. Once received, the mission is carried out right away and the new inventory is sent in. The other tasks (network discovery and package deployment) are assigned in the same fashion.

There are exceptions to every situation. Inventorying is also possible on those machines that are not connected to the network where the OCS-NG server lies. For example, the client machines might be offline or might initiate a connection on user request. These require offline inventory mechanisms. The agent works in the same way. It gathers and stores the data locally. On hosts, that are not networked, it just won't be able to send them into the server.

In these situations, we need to manually transfer the inventory file (.ocs extension) to the central management server, and then manually import the file via the administration console.

Choosing the best agent type

In most production environments and organizations in the past decade, there were numerous Microsoft Windows-based operating systems. In order to satisfy the multitude of requirements, there are two possible agent types when it comes to Windows agents. The most recommended agent is the **service** type. This stands for installing the agent as a standard Windows service. As such, it is executed on each startup like the other services.

Another possibility is opting for the **standalone agent** type. This solution is best fit for those scenarios where the client machine is not networked, and it is not supposed to contact and provide the central management server with the gathered inventory. It may rarely happen that due to some side company regulations, we are not allowed to install more services. The same situation applies to laptops that are in the field the majority of the time. In these cases, opting for this kind of agent is our only solution.

The standalone agent gathers and saves the inventory locally. The exported results can then be imported. Should we require an update to the database, we need to execute again the standalone agent on the said computer so that it refreshes the inventory, and then we'll head over to import again. This can also be scheduled and automated. We're going to discuss this in detail in a later chapter when we get into inventorying client hosts that are not networked.

In short, unless the host is not able to network or strict company policies are restricting the installation of new Windows service, we should always choose the first route.

Setting up the agent as a service has many benefits:

- Hosts are inventoried even when users are not logged in. Should the employee be on vacation, the machine is still inventoried on a predefined basis.

- Package deployment functionality is possible. It happens in the background, and it will not require user interaction. The employee can work seamlessly.

By default, the service is installed to be launched under the **LocalSystem** account.

Demystifying the LocalSystem account of Windows OS

Years ago, most system level services were run under the LocalSystem account. It was the only account that provided such privileges. It was the most powerful as well. Later on, Microsoft implemented two derivates of the almighty *System* account: *LocalService* and *NetworkService*. Depending on their needs, services are now run under either of these. The OCS-NG client agent has remained under the almighty LocalSystem account.

These accounts are all predefined local accounts. LocalSystem is the only account that can access the security database located at HKLM\Security inside the Windows registry. Other than these, it has unrestricted access to local resources. It has enough privileges to bring down a system to its knees (or worse), if the server is a harmful one.

LocalService and NetworkService are limited privileges accounts. The latter provides more security by protecting local resources, but it won't protect remote ones. Services logged in under the NetworkService account are authenticated using the computer's account within the domain. In this way, if they try to access remote shares, the policy that determines this eligibility is determined on the system that initiates the connection.

In case of LocalService accounts, the services are authenticated as *no one* — technically, it is a kind of anonymous connection. Should the same service running under LocalService want to access remote shares, the requests are only allowed if the shares are available to everyone. As you can see, the LocalService makes it tougher to take over remote clients.

> For more information regarding how to tighten down these security permissions, please refer to the following Microsoft documentation. It is a comprehensive guide on how services are working, how to strip their privileges from the token, and so on. Refer to the document titled *Services and Service Accounts Security Planning Guide* at:
>
> http://technet.microsoft.com/en-us/library/cc170953.aspx

As mentioned earlier, the OCS-NG agent is set under the powerful SYSTEM account. One side of the coin is that it won't struggle to gather the necessary inventory data and it gets its job done. However, if we are security conscious and we want to tighten down these permissions, we need to follow the previously mentioned Microsoft's planning guide.

In a robust environment, which is otherwise firewalled, protected, and monitored against miscellaneous behavior, the chances are really slim (close to none) that the OCS-NG agent will be exploited in order to access some unrestricted network resource. Thus, we do not consider this as a priority at all. It is just food for thought. It does not mean that leaving the service under that account will open a dangerous security hole.

The real deal is to know how to deal with SYSTEM accounts, like in the case of unknown services, things can get messy fast. That was the reason why we demystified them. In our case now, the OCS-NG agent is popular, and under no means has malicious attempts.

Another option is to create a special log on account for service, if used within a domain environment. Neither of these is the best option that universally applies to every kind of situation. Ultimately, it depends on the environment, and these are all options. We need to make the best use of each of these options, read that Microsoft guide on security planning regarding services and design the best approach. In the end, it's always up to us to tighten our security.

Choosing the best deployment method

As always, we are given different methods to deploy the agents. We know that in the case of large environments, we long for remote and unattended solutions. No one can expect us to run through offices, and press the same buttons on every machine in order to install a certain application. That would be funny, imagine the system administrators skating through halls and departments on rollerblades. All jokes aside, point taken!

Then there are those situations where there are just a few computers to be managed, and asking for outstanding remote deployment solutions is just silly. The entire process of understanding, setting up, and getting around such a deployment method would be more time consuming than just doing it through a brute-force search.

Therefore, we are given more than a few options in this case too. We can install the OCS-NG agent manually. We can do the manual install on either the service version or the standalone type as well. This requires user interaction. On Windows machines, this means going through the steps of the installation wizard using the de facto standard: **Next**, **Agree**, **Next**, **Next**, **Install**, **Finish** style.

Then, we have the more interesting remote deployment methods. One of the ways is to use the **Active Directory Group Policy Objects** (GPOs), and set up a new policy or edit an existing one. What we want to accomplish is to find the appropriate policy's *Script* section. Soon, we will find out how to include the script here. Depending on the type of policy, the script is going to be executed either on the start of a computer or when the user logs in.

The other modality is pushing the deployment via **login scripts.** Yes, this is a slight variation to the technique just mentioned, which works best if the computer startup policy is used (this way it does not require a user to log in). You can set up login scripts via Active Directory GPOs too, but right now we're discussing session login scripts. These require the user to log in. We set these up on the domain controller. We'll see how we do this later on.

A final solution, considering remote deployment is to opt for third-party tools. The first thought that comes to mind for most system administrators is **PsExec** of **PsTools**. On the right section, we will see how to use this third-party tool to execute remote commands.

There are also a few best practices when using these methods. How can we know whether the agent would be set up or not? We create some sort of feedback files, or we push the scripts via PsExec during business hours on all computers that are currently online. We monitor the output and will know all the computers that are offline. Then, we can use either of the previously mentioned methods (computer startup scripts or login scripts) to set up the agent.

There is no best solution to how to set up the agent. It depends on our particular setup. If we have just a handful of computers, we might opt for the manual installation. The wizard has just a few steps, it's light weight and really fast. In the case of *populated* environments, we can opt for remote solutions. Otherwise, the process is time consuming.

It is a matter of preference which method we opt for. If you have a domain, you can use domain login scripts or computer startup scripts. It's also quite handy to use a combination of all of the methods.

We will now look into each of the solutions in greater detail.

Deploying agents on Windows operating systems

The first step, when we want to install an application is to download the latest version. We head over to the official OCS Inventory NG website and locate the latest Win32 agent binaries in the archived format in the **Download** section. At the time of writing, the latest final version of the agent is 1.02, also known as internal version 4.0.5.4.

The archive is named in the following way: `OCSNG_WINDOWS_AGENT_1.02.zip`, where the last digits stand for the version number. Its size is around 2.5MB. Once it is downloaded and extracted, we find the following files:

- `ocsagent.exe`: Installs the standalone agent
- `OcsAgentSetup.exe`: Launches the installation wizard (service type)
- `OcsLogon.exe`: Downloads the binaries from the communication server, or if it's already installed, the agent is launched again (it can install both types)
- `Changelog`: Contains the change log of the latest modifications
- `LICENSE.txt`: The GPL v2 License

There are various command-line arguments that are supported, which are discussed in the next section.

Getting familiar with command-line arguments

At first, we have the `OcsAgentSetup.exe`. It's the installation wizard. Under normal circumstances, we just follow the installation steps, and the agent is set up seamlessly. However, we can use one or more of the following wizard-specific argument switches:

- `/S`: This option is used to execute *silent mode* as this disables user interaction.

- `/UPGRADE`: This option upgrades the service agent (if an upgrade is needed).

- `/NOSPLASH`: This option disables the splash screen.

- `/NoOcs_ContactLnk`: This option eliminates the **Ocs-Contact** link from the **Start** menu.

- `/D=path`: This option is used to specify a custom install folder, quotes are not supported

    ○ Warning: This must be the last parameter (if using more than one).

 At this point, do not worry if some of the command-line switches seem confusing. We're listing all of them for future reference. As progress is made, each one of them will be debunked and discussed in detail.

Besides the aforementioned switches, all of the command-line switches of the agent are also supported, which are listed as follows:

- `/server:name_of_ocs_server`: Specifies the name of the OCS management server.

- `/np`: *No proxy*, disables the proxies defined in the Internet Explorer settings.

- `/pnum:XX`: Here XX is the port number via which HTTP communication is possible and the web server can be contacted. In the case of caching proxies (that is Squid) that could be 3128 or other proxies on 8080.

    ○ By default, port 80 is used (use this option to specify other ports).

- `/local`: This option executes the agent in the local inventory mode. It gathers and saves the inventory data in a `[hostname].ocs` format in the agent folder.

    ○ The results are stored in a compressed XML format.

- ◦ The agent does not try to contact the OCS-NG communication server.

- /file: This saves everything just like using the /local tag, but it contacts the communication server. This one is useful when we need the file for future use.

- /xml: Just like the previous one, it creates a file but in a non-compressed XML format.

  - ◦ If used in conjunction with /local, the agent won't contact the server.

  - ◦ If used without the /local tag, the agent contacts the communication server.

- /nosoftware: When this option is used, the agent will not report the installed software.

- /notag: When this option is used, the agent will not require the TAG value.

- /tag:my_tag: Here my_tag stands for the custom-specified TAG value.

- /hkcu: The agent looks into the HKCU registry hive for installed software.

- /debug: A useful command which enables logging. A file called [hostname].log will be created.

- /force: When this option is used, the agent will be forced to send in the inventory data.

  - ◦ This is required when the database needs to be updated right away, and we cannot allow waiting for the frequency countdown again.

- /uid: When this option is used, the agent generates a new user ID.

- /dmi: When a computer serial number cannot be retrieved through WMI, the agent will opt for using DMI tables via the BiosInfo.exe tool.

- /biosfunc: Just like the previous switch, but it forces the agent to use BIOS functions

- /conf:configfile: Here configfile specifies the configuration file.

  - ◦ By default, the Ocsinventory.dat is taken as the configuration file.

- /test: This argument tests the HTTP connection.

  - ◦ It is meant to be used in correlation with /debug, /np, or /pnum.

  - ◦ If all goes well, an ok.ok file is created in the agent's directory.

- /fastip: In this way, the agent checks only five IPs if elected by the server as the IPDISCOVER host. This tag should never be used for production use.

- /ipdisc:X: This mode forces the agent to run the IpDiscover feature on the network number X, but only if the server asks for an inventory.

  - To ensure that it is going to be executed, it needs to be used with the /force tag. In this way, the agent will contact the server and perform the aforementioned steps.

In addition to the already extensive list of command-line switches, we need to add a few more command-line switches, which can be used with the OcsLogon.exe launcher:

- /DEPLOY:XXXX: This switch specifies the agent version number
- /INSTALL: This one picks the service agent type instead of the standalone
- /PATH:path: This option specifies the installation path

Manual installation strategies

Both agent types can be installed manually. The setup wizard installs the service type.

In the beginning of this chapter, we were given a hint of what to expect. The manual installation sports a standard Windows installation wizard. Of course, you can opt for command-line switches in order to enable its silent mode, but let's not get ahead of ourselves. Assuming we have downloaded and unpacked the latest stable version of the OCS-NG agent for Win32 operating systems, we then execute the OcsAgentSetup.exe file.

The following screenshot shows the first screen of the setup wizard.

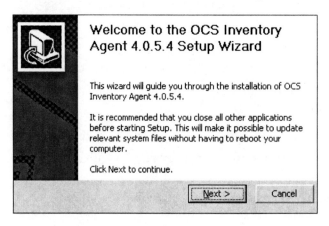

The next screen should not surprise anyone. The license agreement will be displayed inside that textbox. In our case, the license is the GPL v2.

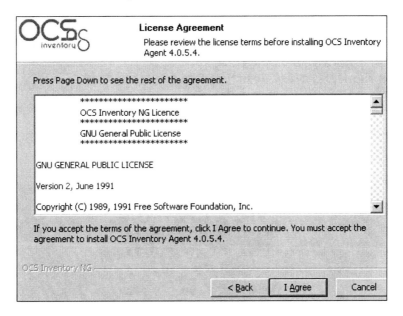

After accepting the license, the next screen finally shows some options.

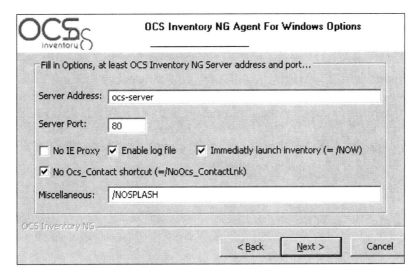

The first field to fill in is the **Server Address** of the OCS-NG management server. The second field, that is, **Server Port**, requires the HTTP port through which it can be accessed. The checkboxes stand for those command-line switch arguments we enlisted earlier. Then, there's an entire field left for **Miscellaneous** arguments.

In the example mentioned, we have selected the **Enable log file, Immediately launch inventory**, the **No OCS_Contact shortcut** link, and added the **/NOSPLASH** tag. The **OCS_Contact shortcut** is a shortcut that appears in the Windows start menu. It points to %PATH%\Ocs_contact.exe /S and has the following shortcut icon. It is a harmless shortcut, but some people might not like it due to the presence of a new application on their machine. On an enterprise level, silence is required. The **OCS_contact** shortcut can be seen in the following screenshot:

Now that we have configured the agent according to our needs, we can click **Next**. The wizard proceeds to ask us for the destination path. Here we either browse to specify a custom path or just hit *Enter* by moving forward—leaving the default %ProgramFiles%\OCS Inventory Agent folder. The size of the fully-installed agent is 3.40 MB.

Once the wizard has finished the installation, you can check whether the service was installed. Here's one way we can check this. Go to **Start | Run | services.msc**, browse through the list of services, and find **OCS INVENTORY SERVICE**. Its **Description** is **OCS Inventory NG Service: Automatic inventory and software deployment system**. If all went well, it should already be **Started** (at the **Service status**). Its **Startup type** is set to **Automatic**.

Should we examine the **Properties** of the service, we will see a screen similar to the following screenshot:

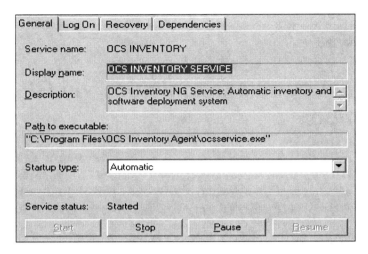

We have selected the **Immediately launch inventory** checkbox during the setup, so this means that, by now, our system should be inventoried and the management server has provided us with the gathered data. We can check the `[hostname].` `logfile` located inside the agent's directory. All of the tasks carried out are verbosely logged and are self-explanatory.

Should we want to execute an unattended installation of the wizard, we will use the silent command-line argument (`/s`). Everything will go smoothly as long as we specify all of the other necessary parameters (like server name, port number, no proxies if need be, and so on).

```
OcsAgentSetup.exe /s /server:name_of_OCS_server /pnum:80 /np /now /
debug
```

Nevertheless, if we want to install the standalone agent, then we are going to use the other manual deployment solution. We will execute the `OcsAgent.exe` executable along with the `/local` argument. The setup will try to install the agent to the `C:\ocs-ng` directory. If it does not have sufficient privileges, then it tries to install the agent in the temporary folder of the user, under which it is executed. Thus, it is advised to launch it with administrative rights.

The setup of the standalone agent will ask where to store the exported inventory results. When we are launching for the first time, the wizard will ask us to specify the TAG. Unless we want to use TAG-based categorization, we can leave this field empty. *Chapter 4, Finding your Way through OCS-NG Features* will look into TAG repartition. Now, let's leave it blank just for testing.

The standalone agent can be rerun later on using the `Ocsinventory.exe /local` execution. This means that we can set up a schedule or make an unattended script for those machines that are not networked, and on which the standalone agent is the only solution. Then, we will refresh the inventory after a certain period of time, and manually import the result files.

Using OcsLogon.exe to deploy via GPO or login scripts

In order to understand how this remote agent deployment solution works, we first need to explain what `OcsLogon.exe` is about. It is a launcher tool. It is basically designed to work inside login scripts and **Active Directory Group Policy Objects (GPOs)**. Once executed on a client machine, it checks whether the agent is installed or not. If not, it then proceeds to install the agent. Otherwise, the agent is just launched.

The launcher downloads the latest binaries from the communication server if it finds out that the agent is not installed on the client machine. The launcher can set up both agent types. The only way to differentiate between these is by using the `/install` command-line switch. By doing so, we are opting for the service type agent. On the contrary, the standalone agent is set up.

The way it contacts the communication server is described here. At first, it is assumed that we should have the `ocsinventory-ng` DNS name defined in our DNS server. That hostname should point to our OCS-NG central management server (also the communication server, or tune it appropriately in case of distributed configurations).

There is another solution to provide the path to the communication server if we do not plan to add that DNS name within our scopes. The `OcsLogon.exe` executable can be renamed so that its filename (excluding the `.exe` extension) points to the OCS server. It can either be called as the server's correct hostname if it appears inside DNS and can be resolved appropriately or by simply using the IP address. Here are a few examples:

- `ocs-server.mydomain.co.uk.exe`
    - The `ocs-server.mydomain.co.uk` points to your OCS server
- `10.10.10.05.exe`
    - In this case, the `10.10.10.05` is the IP address of the OCS server

As you can see, the launcher will strip off the `.exe` executable part and consider the rest as the path to the server. Therefore, let's not forget to name this file accordingly, if we cannot set up the DNS `ocsinventory-ng` to point to our OCS server, and, of course, if we plan to use the launcher to remotely deploy the agent on client machines.

Memory refresher: The `OcsLogon.exe` launcher supports all of the command-line switches we mentioned earlier. Please go back a few pages, when in doubt.

Now that we know how the `OcsLogon.exe` launcher works, let's find out how the dedicated agent packager works. Right after that, we need to discuss the preliminary steps of getting the agent uploaded on the communication server. This can be done via the administration console. Either kind of service type can be installed as command-line switches are supported. It all depends on the agent package you prepare for deployment.

Using the packager to create the deployable agent

The development team behind OCS-NG created a so-called **OCS Inventory NG Packager** utility. This tool works together with the Windows service internals and is able to register anything as a service, even without administrator privileges. The admin account is specified prior to creating the package. The installer will run under that account. It was designed to package the `OcsLogin.exe` launcher according to your agent preference.

Once the package is installed, it's called `OcsPackage.exe`, and it means that we can hook it up on the OCS-NG communication server. The final step is deploying the package.

Let's not get ahead of ourselves now. We can download the packager from the same OCS NG repository on SourceForge. Check the following URL:

`http://sourceforge.net/projects/ocsinventory/files/OCS%20Inventory%20NG`

The latest packager at the time of writing is the 1.02. Download and extract it.

Inside we will find only one executable. Its interface is straightforward.

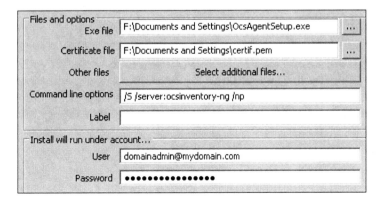

The **Exe file** is going to be the `OcsAgentSetup.exe`. We discussed its command-line switches, and we know that it is much more than just a GUI installation wizard. It can be scripted, run in silent mode, with specific commands, and thus, it's exactly what we need.

We can use SSL certificates to check the server prior deployment. This means that clients are given certificates which can act as fingerprints to authenticate the deployment server. This is critical as package deployment and remote command execution is practically an open door for exploits and malicious undertakings. In this way, we can always be sure that the source server of packages is not compromised. Clients can test this themselves.

Finally, the last step, which is the most important one, is that we need to specify the account through which the installer runs. In the case of a domain, this account must have administrative privileges on the local machine to install new services and copy files. As such, it's recommended to create a special account dedicated to this task that has the necessary privileges.

Using the domain admin account is dangerous, but it works (please refer to the Microsoft service security planning guide linked earlier in this chapter). It depends on how the overall security is tightened and monitored. It can be any other account with local administrative rights. The same applies in the case of workstations.

The next window asks for the destination where the packaged end result is placed.

Getting the agent package on the OCS-NG server

The `OcsPackage.exe` needs to be uploaded on the OCS-NG server. We're going to do this by logging into the administration console. Keep in mind that this time, we won't get into each and every functionality that lies there because that is what the next chapter will cover. Right now we are taking an action-oriented approach.

We point our browser to the OCS-NG administration console interface's URL:

```
http://ocsinventory-ng/ocsreports
```

In the previous path, `ocsinventory-ng` stands for the OCS-NG server name. If we haven't changed our admin user and password yet, then we log in with *admin* and *admin*. On the **Users** toolbar, we can find the predefined users, edit them, and set up new ones. Once we are in, we will navigate to the agent toolbar, it's the fourth icon on the right (the longest) toolbar. It looks like two gears working.

Alright, now we're already seeing the path to the source of the package we just created. On uploading the `OcsPackage.exe`, the agent is practically ready to be deployed.This means that the OCS-NG communication server can serve the requests of agents. Deployment happens in the following fashion:

- `OcsLauncher.exe` is executed on the client computer
  - It's the launcher we mentioned earlier
- It requests the `OcsPackage.exe` (the agent) from the communication server
- Once downloaded, the `OcsPackage.exe` is executed
  - It logs into the specified account and runs the agent installer

As you can see, the OCS-NG Packager can be used to install and set up other files as well. The `OcsLauncher.exe` just checks whether an agent exists on the client machine. If it finds it installed, it executes it. If no agent can be found, it proceeds to request one from the OCS-NG server, and depending on the specified flags it sets up either of the agent types.

It downloads the entire `OcsPackage.exe` just as it was uploaded on the OCS-NG server. Therefore, if we want to build in more files, then we can use the Packager's **Select Additional Files** option to add them. In this way, once it logs into the specified account, along with the `OcsAgentSetup.exe`, the other files are downloaded to the client machine.

We can also remotely execute Visual Basic script files (`.vbs`). We add the `Cscript.exe` path to the `Exe` file. Add our `.vbs` script via the **Select Additional Files** option, and finally write `script.vbs /B` in the command-line options.

Deployment via Active Directory GPOs

It is beyond the scope of this book to explain what Active Directory is about or what group policies are about. As such, we will assume the following; if we want to use these deployment methodologies, we can deduce that we have some kind of familiarity with these Microsoft administration technologies.

If you are managing such a tiny environment that these concepts are unknown to you, but still want to get your feet wet with remote agent deployment, then we wholeheartedly recommend the PsExec solution that's going to be covered in the following pages.

Here we're going to create a **login script** and enforce it via **group policies**.

Now that we're past the general assumptions, let's launch the *Active Directory Users and Computers* MMC snap-in. **Start | Run | dsa.msc**. Find your Active Directory domain or organizational unit that you are managing. For the sake of keeping things simple and uniform, let's call our domain mydomain.com. Once you selected your domain, right-click and select **Properties**.

Out of those tabs, let's navigate to the **Group Policy** tab. There we can find our policies (if there are any). We can either edit an existing one or create a new one. Whichever option we pick, there are two main categories, namely, computer policies and user policies. The former is computer specific, and in our case, they are executed when the computer starts up. The latter is user specific, and requires some user to log in.

Nowadays, there is a new MMC snap-in called gpmc.msc — Group Policy Management. This tool is installed by default on Windows Server 2008 operating systems but not on Windows 2003 or earlier. This snap-in gives us a slightly more advanced interface. It lists the forest, inside which we can pick our domain mydomain.com.

Here we are going to find our organization units and **Group Policy Objects**. When we expand the GPO field by clicking on the '-' (minus), all of our policies will be displayed (if there are any). We can also monitor which ones are enforced, which are linked, and so on. This is also the place of security filtering, such as deciding whether the policy applies to specific users, groups, or computers. Under most circumstances, this is **Authenticated Users**.

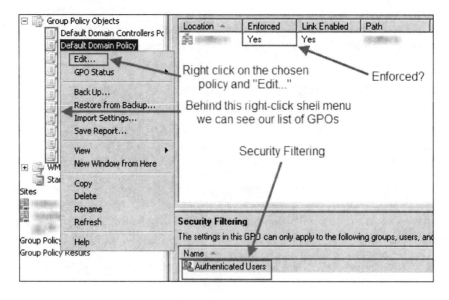

Without trying to sound like an Active Directory tutorial, let's focus on how to edit such a policy with this new **GPMC** snap-in. Right-click on one of the existing policies or create a new one. The Group Policy Management Editor will pop up as a new window. From this point onwards, everything remains the same. We have computer and user policies too.

Scripts that are inside computer policies are called **Startup** and **Shutdown** scripts. These are executed on computer startup and shutdown. What matters to us right now is the startup category. That's where we should place the inventory agent.

The scripts that are inside user policies are called **Logon** and **Logoff** scripts. The reason for that is self-explanatory, these are executed when a user either logs in or logs off. The agent can be deployed this way too, though in most situations it's not an ideal option.

The following screenshot gives us a sense of where to find these scripts inside the GPO:

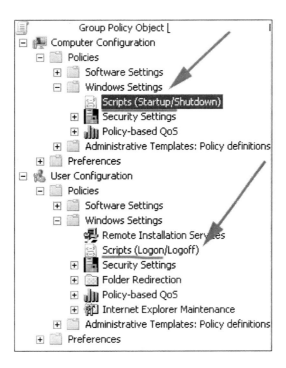

Now, let's right-click on the **Scripts** (**Startup/Shutdown**) right inside the **Windows Settings** tree. We pick **Startup** and select **Properties**. A new window will be displayed, and we can see our already existing startup scripts (if there are any). Before we head over to add a new script, click on the **Show Files** button. It will bring up an Explorer window showing the destination where these scripts are located.

This is where we are going to copy our `OcsLogon.exe` launcher. Let's not forget that there are situations when this file gets renamed. If that's the case, then copy the renamed launcher. Once the file is stored there, you can click on **Add** on the **Startup Scripts** window. This will bring up a new window where you can specify the path of the new script. As we just copied there, you can easily specify this.

The command-line arguments can be added to the special parameters field. These are additionally added at the end of the launcher, just like if it were done manually. This means that if we want to install the service type agent, now is the time to specify the `/install` command-line switch. Also add the `/S`, `/DEBUG`, and other parameters.

The following screenshot shows a simplified version of the tasks that were mentioned:

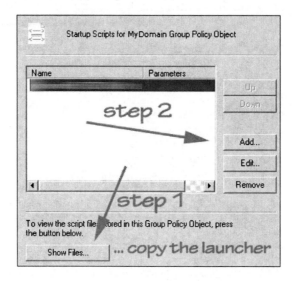

Should we opt for the login scripts instead of startup scripts, it can be done in a similar fashion. Instead of messing with computer policies, we fiddle with user policies.

Keep in mind that deploying scripts via Active Directory GPOs is not the only solution.

Initiating deployment with OcsLogon.exe via login script

At first glance, these two solutions are similar. The previous modality was based on policies. This meant we could enforce different policies on **Organizational Units(OUs)** based on whatever criteria we wanted. This has given us flexibility, which is necessary in specific cases, but there are those situations when we don't want to use group policies. For example, if we have just one domain, and we're looking for a solution to deploy the agents based on users.

This time, we want to set up a **session login script** across our domain.

The first step is to copy the `OcsLogon.exe` launcher to a place on the network that is going to be readable by everyone from the domain. It's advised to set up that location as shared to *Authenticated Users*. The script that we're going to create will download the launcher from this path. That's why it is critical to be available (readable).

The script can be either a traditional batch file or vbscript. What we want to do is quite trivial. We want to execute the launcher from that path using a few command-line switches.

Here's an example where the renamed launcher is on `file-serv` at the `ocsagent-kit` folder:

```
\\file-serv\ocsagent-kit\10.10.10.05.exe /debug /np /install /s
```

This line can be thrown into a batch script, with an `@echo off` in the first line in order to prevent echoing on the display. In this way, no output will be presented, just a flashing command/terminal box at most. The extension must be `.bat` as expected.

Once the script is done, the next step is to copy into our primary domain controller's scripts folder. This is along the lines of the `c:\windows\sysvol\sysvol\<mydomain.com>\scripts` path.

Now, fire up the *Active Directory Users and Computers* MMC snap-in (`dsa.msc`). Find your users within the domain tree, and then link the scripts to each of them. We can do this by clicking **Properties**, and then we have the following alternatives. We either set it up as a **User Profile | Logon Script**: [specify the path] using **Browse,** or at the **Environment** tab, we check the box **Start the following program at logon** and add our script.

As you can see, this modality is much more recommended when there are just a handful of users. We pick those users, set the agent up as a login script, and we are done with it. We can add the creation of response files, such as create `ok.txt` on some predetermined folder. The script checks whether this `ok.txt` exists, and if yes, then the agent is already installed, and it is not executed anymore. You can also check this manually.

Command execution, via scripts, opens up lots of doors. In corporate environments, usually there are login and logoff scripts, and users are categorized into different organizational units. We might also have dozens of groups, but it's not that hard to decide which options are better. The best practice is to use a combination of the previously mentioned solutions. Furthermore, we can mix in a little bit of PsExec. This is what we're going to cover right now.

Unattended installation via the PsExec.exe tool

Chances are that we cannot find a system administrator that has managed a predominantly Windows-based environment and hasn't heard about the PsTools suite. This collection of command-line tools is useful to get most of the administrative tasks done. It was originally developed by a *Sysinternals,* but then it was taken over by Microsoft. Check out the suite's page at:

```
http://technet.microsoft.com/en-us/sysinternals/bb896649.aspx
```

PsExec is one component of the PsTools package. It's a telnet-like replacement that was specifically designed for remote execution of processes on client computers. It allows full interaction with applications. We can literally launch any command on a remote system, while having the output displayed on our screen. That is, if we have sufficient privileges.

We can download the entire PsTools suite directly from the following URL:

```
http://download.sysinternals.com/Files/PsTools.zip
```

It does not require an installation on client machines. We simply download, extract, and fire up a command prompt under administrative privileges, and find the path where we unpacked PsTools. Launch PsExec, and a descriptive help is printed out. Examine its command-line switches. Then decide the kind of deployment you're looking for.

A few examples of how to perform specific deployments are given as follows:

- Sweep through the domain and deploy the agent on *already logged on* hosts:

  ```
  PsExec.exe \\* -s \\file-serv\ocsagent-kit\OcsLauncher.exe /debug
  /np /install /s
  ```

- Install the agent on a specific computer:

  ```
  PsExec.exe \\Sarah-PC -s \\file-serv\ocsagent-kit\OcsLauncher.exe
  /install /s
  ```

- Deploy the agent on a list of computers by using a text file to specify them:

  ```
  PsExec.exe @hosts.txt -s -u mydomain\domainadmin \\file-serv\
  ocsagent-kit\OcsLauncher.exe /debug /np /install /s
  ```

The previous command will ask for the domain admin password. Nothing will appear, and you will need to type in the password and hit *Enter.* The hosts.txt should be on the same folder from where you are executing the PsExec. This file is an ordinary text file where each computer name appears on a separate new line.

We can think of various other scenarios. We can log the output into a text file, should we somehow not be able to monitor the output. We can do this by adding the `> log.txt` at the end of the `PsExec` command. This copies all the output into the text file. Keep in mind that by doing so, we will prohibit the printing of any output on the display as well.

In the previous section, *Unattended installation via PsExec.exe tool*, we mentioned a little about the best practices in deployment. Let's say we launch the remote execution of the agent installation during business hours on all of the already logged in users. We will create a response file, monitor the output, and find out the hosts that were offline.

We can also opt to create a text file that contains all of the hosts within our domain (list all hosts into a text file), and then run the command on the file. The results can be printed into a logfile using the `>` operator. In this way, we will know which computers were skipped. These were, presumably, unavailable. Alright, so what's next?

We set up a logon script via AD GPOs or session login script for those users sitting beside those hosts. The said script should create a feedback that we can monitor later on in order to decide what happened.

Finally, we can also opt to use PsExec's targeted deployment on those specific hosts that were skipped until this point. There are lots of other alternatives as well.

Deploying agents on Linux operating systems

Installing the agent on Linux operating systems can be done locally. Should we have an already implemented remote execution solution on those machines, we can use them. Either way, if we are performing the installation locally, we also have two possibilities. We have an interactive setup and an automated and unattended setup without user interaction.

The chances are that we can find **ocsinventory-agent** in our distribution's software repository. If we prefer that the installation be lead by the software package manager, then we can first verify whether the agent exists, and if so, what kind of version it is.

By now, we should be familiar with our distribution's package manager:

- Installing OCS Inventory NG agent with YUM:

  ```
  yum install ocsinventory-agent
  ```
- Installing OCS Inventory NG Agent with APT-GET:

  ```
  apt-get install ocsinventory-agent
  ```

If we cannot find the ocsinventory-agent package, we can try `ocsinventory-client`.

There is no real advantage of this modality other than keeping our software repo consistent. The manual installation shell is script-based such that it automatically checks the prerequisite modules. If some are not found, it is able to set them up.

The only drawback is that if the modules are found in an older version than the minimum requirement. In this scenario, the setup cannot upgrade, but this situation is unlikely to happen in this day and age. These bare minimum dependencies are quite old.

We are going to cover those two installation possibilities, namely, interactive and scripted install. The first one requires user interaction, while the latter is unattended. Either setup solution creates a verbosely logged setup log. We can use this for troubleshooting, if it is required.

The first step is downloading the latest agent archive from the official website's download section. Of course, we are redirected to the SourceForge repository. We are going to make sure that we select the Linux agent. In our case, the exact URL used is:

`http://sourceforge.net/projects/ocsinventory/files/OCS%20Inventory%20`
`NG/1.02/OCSNG_WINDOWS_AGENT_1.02.zip/download`

The file is named in the following fashion: `OCSNG_LINUX_AGENT_1.02.tar.gz`, where `1.02` is the version number. We can download with `wget` or via your favorite browser and then open up a shell to extract the archive.

`$tar -xvzf OCSNG_LINUX_AGENT_1.02.tar.gz`

From this step, we are going to discuss the distinctive installations. The setups are similar for both scenarios: when the computer is networked (meaning it can reach the OCS-NG central server via HTTP) and hosts that are not networked (the inventory is stored locally).

Installing agents on Linux with user interaction

Open up a new shell terminal window and get into the folder where the agent was unpacked.

We can execute the setup shell script with the following command:

`#sh setup.sh`

Right away, the setup begins. The first question is, which method we will use to generate and store the inventory, meaning, whether the computer is networked or not. The first option applies for networked hosts (http), while the second stores the inventory locally. We use the latter for hosts that are not networked when we upload the inventory file manually.

If we opt for the first, we are asked information about the OCS-NG communication server such as where it is located (for example, server address: `http://ocsinventory-ng`) and what is the server port (default HTTP port: 80). We can then specify a TAG value if we want to take advantage of the TAG-based repartition (separately inventories computers based on TAGs, ideally to differentiate offices from various locations, and so on).

Once these are answered, the server begins to check for the dependencies. It verifies the existence of the PERL interpreter, C/C++ compiler, and some kind of `make` utility (such as the GNU make). The following module dependencies are checked:

- Compress::Zlib PERL module
- XML::Simple PERL module
- Net::IP PERL module
- LWP::UserAgent PERL module
- Digest::MD5 PERL module
- Net::SSLeay PERL module
- dmidecode binary

 dmidecode is a Linux tool to decode the computer's DMI (SMBIOS) table into a human-readable format. The SMBIOS table contains hardware-specific information (serial number, manufacturer, model, and so on).

If these are verified (or chosen to be installed), the setup moves to the following steps:

- Compiles the IpDiscover binary
- Configures, builds, and installs the OCS-NG agent Perl module
- Creates the `/usr/sbin/ocsinv` symbolic link
- Creates the logging directory, sets up the daily log rotation
  - Default log folder: `/var/log/ocsinventory-NG`
  - Default log rotation file: `/etc/logrotate.d/ocsinventory-client`

- Creates the OCS-NG agent configuration file
  - ° By default on `/etc/ocsinventory-client/ocsinv.conf`
- On the same path as the configuration file, it sets up the administrative info file
  - ° `ocsinv.admfile`: It stores TAG and other values
- Sets up the cron task for daily execution of the agent
- Launches the OCS Inventory NG agent for the first time

The entire process is verbosely logged, and each step is detailed and printed on screen as well. If there are problems, its cause is almost always clearly explained. On another note, let's also present an example of the `ocsinv.conf` configuration file:

```
<CONF>
  <DEVICEID>OCS_AGENT_DEVICE_ID-2009-11-20-23-51-24</DEVICEID>
  <DMIVERSION>2.9</DMIVERSION>
  <IPDISCOVER_VERSION>3</IPDISCOVER_VERSION>
  <OCSFSERVER>10.11.22.33:80</OCSFSERVER>
</CONF>
```

Installing agents on Linux without user interaction

The same installation bash shell script can be run in silent mode. This silent mode does not require user interaction. As such, we need to supply the answers to those questions as arguments when calling the setup shell. Here's an example with the arguments:

```
sh setup.sh <SETUP DEPENDENCIES> <SRV ADDRESS> [<SRV PORT> <TAG VALUE>]
```

Here is an example of how this should look:

```
sh setup.sh 1 10.11.22.33 80 mytag_name
```

The `<SETUP DEPENDENCIES>` value must be either `1` or `0` (without < >'s). This binary value is specified if we want the automated installation of all required dependencies. If we are unsure of their existence, we need to pick `1`. The `<SRV ADDRESS>` is self-explanatory. We can type the DNS name of the server if it can be resolved or the IP address. In the case of computers that are not networked, we type `local` there (without quotations marks).

The rest of the arguments are optional. The HTTP port through which the communication server can be reached can be specified. By default, this is 80. TAG is obviously optional.

The entire setup procedure is similar; each step is totally the same as the one discussed earlier such as the interactive setup. Therefore, once it is finished, the *ocsinv* symbolic link is created. Thus, we can manually execute the agent using that link. The configuration and log files can be found on the same path as well.

We need to mention the support for the following agent switches under Linux:

- `-local`: It specifies the local inventory, and it won't send in the inventory results.

- `-xml`: Using this switch, the output can be obtained in an uncompressed XML format. Here, we are asked for the path.

- `-tag=chosen_tag`: This switch is used to specify a tag.

- `-nosoft`: This switch is used so that it won't check for any installed software.

- `-force`: This switch forces the agent to send in the results to the OCS-NG server.

- `-info`: This switch prints details about the agent execution on the screen.

- `-debug`: This switch enables the debug mode, logging becomes more verbose.

Installing the OCS agent with the shell script is trivial. We also have the option to use the Unified Unix agent (it comes with a detailed readme) that supports Linux, Solaris, and AIX.

Deploying agents on Mac OS X operating systems

The OCS inventory agent installation on Mac OS X operating systems requires minimal effort. We can download a ready-to-run PKG precompiled package. The installation using PKGs takes just a single command execution. It is similar to installing RPMs or DEBs on Linux and Debian-based distributions.

Once the installation is finished, we need to edit the configuration file. Who else will provide the OCS-NG central server's address if not us? But before we get there, let's see where we can download that PKG. The first option is to navigate to the official OCS-NG inventory download section. Here we can download the prepackaged Unix Unified agent for Mac OS X 10.3.9 (Panther) or higher from the following link:

```
http://www.ocsinventory-ng.org/index.php?page=1-02-1
```

In the download section, we can also find a so-called Mac OS X installation builder. As its name suggests, it is a tool that creates installations. We can supply in advance the required information such as OCS management server address and even certificates, if required. The installer PKG is created. Then we can install it in the same fashion as we're used to.

 When asked for a certificate, we can supply a blank file, for example, named `cacert.pem`. The inventory will work, although the SSL certificate will not be verified as the one given is empty. This is a drawback when package deployment is needed.

The configuration file can be found as `ocsinv.conf`, and we can edit it later on too.

```
sudo vi ocsinv.conf
```

The installation path of OCS agent on Mac OS X is on `/etc/ocsinventory-client`.

As always, the agent can be executed manually. In this way, we are forcing an immediate inventory. The following command under Mac OS X is used to do this:

```
sudo php /usr/local/sbin/ocs_mac_agent.php
```

Please check the kind of tasks you have in the `cron tab`. By default, the installation package of Mac OS X agents installs the agent in the `/Applications` and sets it up as a daemon. The worst thing you can do is to set up another daily cron, even though the agent is run on every system startup. This is not that bad, especially in the case of workstation computers that are not rebooted. Nevertheless, this is just a pointer, so we're closely watching our actions.

In case of troubleshooting, we can find the logfile at `/var/log/httpd/error.log`. Please do find the problem (such as server gives a 500 error, perhaps a problem with the database, and so on). After a successful execution, the client will respond with an HTTP 200 message. The **200 OK** means **Request is OK**. Error messages often sport **500** as that stands for **Internal Server Error**. For a full overview of HTTP error messages, refer to the following URL:

```
http://www.w3schools.com/TAGS/ref_httpmessages.asp
```

As soon as we get a successful inventory run, we realize that it's time to automate the process, especially if the computer is networked. We need to add a new task into the cron tab. Inventorying is usually advised to be run daily or 2-3 times a week. It is possible to run the task more often, but this is rarely required. Under most circumstances, once a day suffices.

Here's an example of a daily cron scheduled on 21:15. The agent is launched. We can edit the `cron tab` file using the `crontab -e` command. We need a new line like this:

```
15 21 * * * /usr/local/sbin/ocs_mac_agent.php
```

Deploying agents on mobile devices

It is a rather neglected process to make an inventory of mobile devices as well. This should not be the case with OCS-NG as we have this option too. We can set up the agents on mobile devices running Windows mobile platforms (version 5, 6+) and Java platforms.

On the devices running Java, we need to have a working **Java virtual machine (JVM)** supporting JDK version 1.4 or higher. Here we can mention IBM's **J9 JDK** or **phoneME**, the open source project that aims to bring support for Java technologies on cell phones.

Let's not get ahead of ourselves now, should you need more information, check out the following link.

```
https://phoneme.dev.java.net/
```

For handsets based on Windows Mobile, **ActiveSync** is required on the computer. The successor of ActiveSync is **Windows Mobile Device Center**. One of these utilities is required for data synchronization between a computer host and a mobile device.

Getting these requirements installed and enabled are the preliminary steps. There is a lot of documentation available, and if we plan on doing something like this, the chances are that we already have these resolved. These should not give us headaches.

The name of the project that resulted in the porting of the inventory agent to mobile phones is called OCS Inventory Mobile. It was possible thanks to the **OpenMobileIS**, an open source Java framework for mobile applications. For more information, please check out the following link:

```
http://www.openmobileis.org/
```

Alright, now that we know how the ported agent came to life, let's see from where we can download, and how to install on either Java-based handsets or WM platforms.

```
http://ocsinventory.svn.sourceforge.net/viewvc/ocsinventory/trunk/
mobile_devices/
```

In order to install the mobile agent on Java platforms, we need to generate a JAR file. We can either download a version that is hosted by someone, or we can make our own JAR exportation. To do this, we will need to download a Java IDE, such as Eclipse, checkout the official OCS Inventory SVN, and then we can export the project as JAR. Other Java editors work too.

The JAR file can be launched through the virtual machine on your system. Usually this command is something along the lines of Java `jar path/ocsmobile.jar doSynchro`. Please refer to the user guide of your JVM. We can also check the following mobile installation guide:

`http://www.ubikis.com/OCSInventory/HowToOCSmobile.pdf`

There is a file called `NetDevice.dll`, and it should be placed on the same directory where the JAR file is. The location of the configuration file is `server.properties` in the `conf` folder right inside the OCS folder. That's where we set the IP address of the OCS-NG central server. Thereafter, each mobile agent execution can be done using the JAR file.

The installation on Windows mobile-based smartphones is even more trivial. The setup has an installation wizard totally similar to the one we presented earlier for Windows agent. The wizard asks us for the OCS-NG communication server's address.

Once we supply the required information, we can configure the location of the installation files on the computer machine that will serve as the synchronization host. We are given an option to select the components to be installed. The typical setup should suffice for most configurations. Summing this up, once the setup is finished, we can hook up the mobile device to the host computer, and initiate the inventorying process. Everything is seamless.

Summary

Throughout this chapter, we elaborated agent deployment. First, we analyzed what happens behind the scenes when agents are inventorying, and how they do their work in order to serve the central server. As every situation can be different, we have two agent types as well as numerous modalities to hook up our machines with one of those agents.

We can install agents on all kinds of platforms, starting from Microsoft Windows up to Linux distributions, Solaris, Mac OS X, and even mobile devices. We can either opt for *interactive setups* or simply *automated installations* with the help of scripts and remote deployment tools. In a corporate environment, it's important to deploy in the background.

The agent is a piece of software that supports command-line switches as parameters. We have enlisted and explained each of these arguments. There are certain scenarios when we want to use a combination of these to achieve a specific purpose. During the installation process, we might experience hassles and we need to know where to start. Once we found out how to log verbosely, from troubleshooting to finding answers is just a step.

No doubt it is a fantastic benefit that the agent can be set up on virtually any kind of operating system, but we must agree that in most cases, the Windows-based agent will be most commonly used. It shouldn't surprise anyone that Microsoft Windows is the predominant operating system on workstation machines. Due to this, we have covered more deployment possibilities for Windows hosts (especially remote ones).

In order to back up the above assumptions, let's rely on the official *download counts* of the latest agent version. We should take them with a grain of salt as agents can be downloaded from other places (though, unlikely in large numbers), and in the case of multi-computer environments, each agent type is grabbed only once.

The Windows agent was downloaded over 48,300 times, while the Linux agent slightly over 16,000 times. The Mac OS X download count is around 3,500. The numbers speak for themselves. We can always glance over and see these numbers for ourselves

OCSNG_Mac_OS_X_Agent-1.02.tar.gz	3,476
OCSNG_WINDOWS_AGENT_1.02.zip	48,319
OCSNG_UNIX_AGENT-1.02.tar.gz	16,129

By now, we have a fully functional OCS-NG central management server, and we have just deployed our agents across our environment. Our database has grown from nothing into an organized inventory. We are going to move on, and look into the functionalities of the OCS-NG inventory platform. There are important features to debunk. The next chapter covers the ways to accomplish all-around administrative tasks with our inventory.

4
Finding your Way through OCS-NG Features

Our inventory platform is already set up by now. The central OCS-NG inventory server is up and running, and agents have been deployed throughout our network. No doubt, this means that we have plenty of entries in our database. Now, we need to learn to work with the inventory, how to perform administrative tasks, and how to get the most out of each function.

This chapter, deals with the user interface of the web-based OCS-NG admin and user console. Each toolbar item will be explained, and by the end of this chapter, we will know where to find the most common functionalities. At first, we log in using the default admin user, then we change its password (if we haven't done that already), and finally we set up more users. Once this is done, we can get into best practices and administrative tasks.

In this chapter, we will get to learn about the following:

- Achieve familiarity with the user interface of the web administration console
- Get around to do some preliminary configuration best practices
- Understand TAG-based repartitioning and its implementation to our needs
- Find out how to maintain a clean inventory, and solve common pitfalls
- Generate reports, and search for software and other inventory-related data
- Implement and get the most out of registry query function
- Upload the inventory data of computers that are not networked

In a nutshell, our area of action is going to be the web-based user interface of OCS-NG. We need to understand how to carry out those tasks inside a web browser. As a matter of fact, this is the chapter that gets into the real deal. So far, we have laid out the preliminary steps in order to build the inventory platform from ground up. Right now, we will see how to use its features, and see the advantages of having such an inventory at our hands.

With all of this said, let's kick-start our journey, and learn to use the OCS-NG web interface.

Getting familiar with the OCS-NG web interface

Fire up your favorite web browser and point it to the following URL of the OCS-NG server:

```
http://<ocs-servername>/ocsreports
```

If we are accessing the OCS-NG web interface from the same machine from where the server daemon is run, we can access the administration console using the *localhost* instead of using the `ocs-servername` in the hyperlink syntax previously mentioned. Otherwise, the hostname gets resolved. We can also opt for the IP address of the server instead of hostnames.

Logging in

The login screen will pop up. It will ask for the **User** and **Password**. By default, there is only one predefined user who has administrative privileges. The username is **admin** and the password is also **admin**. Type these into the empty text fields and log in.

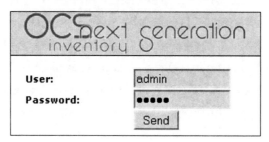

The password of the predefined **admin** user can be changed, but that is not what we're going to do. Soon, we will deal with some preliminary configurations, and learn how to set up new users. Next, we can set up new users with appropriate access rights, and delete the predefined **admin** account. Everyone knows that OCS-NG is among many web-based applications that comes (by default) with the **admin** for **User** and **admin** for **Password** credentials.

In the upper-right corner of the login screen, we can find the language bar right below the place where the version number is displayed. Multilingual support is appreciated. Over the course of this book, we are obviously going to work with the English user interface.

Make sure you pick your language because the tiny icons in the toolbar will be applied. Also, if you find spelling mistakes, don't forget to send in suggestions for improvements.

Looking around and examining the view

Now that we have successfully logged in, let's look around, and examine the administrative interface. As a side note, chances are we are using a decent modern browser with JavaScript support, and of course, we have also enabled this support.

The main interface can be split into the following main components:

1. **Logout/Change password toolbar**: It is placed on the upper-right corner.
2. **Query toolbar**: This is the blue background toolbar with five options.
3. **Administration toolbar**: This is the orange-yellowish toolbar with 12 options.
4. A middle section that sports six sub-tabs, and by default it shows some general statistics about the inventory. The **Activity** tab is displayed as the first tab in the middle section.

Each of the toolbars can be easily identified and are also marked accordingly in the following screenshot:

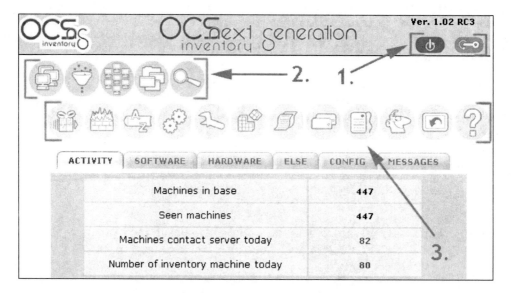

Although the shortcuts might not seem intuitive, once you get familiar with them and get into the pace of working inside the web console, you will get used to them. For starters, it helps that a comment tooltip appears if you move your mouse pointer over one of those shortcuts inside a toolbar. We will examine each of them in a while.

Elaborating the overview section of statistics

The overview section in the middle of those six tabs provides a general reach for most reports regarding inventory numbers. We can also fine-tune some configuration variables, and alter the behavior of these displayed statistics so that they are organized. Furthermore, we can set up new messages, and display them on a specific group of hosts, if not on each of them.

The **SOFTWARE** tab displays the number of different operating systems that were inventoried as well as agent types. The following screenshot shows the **SOFTWARE** tab:

ACTIVITY	SOFTWARE	HARDWARE	ELSE	CONFIG	MESSAGES
Number of different OS				7	
Different agent				2	

Useful tip:

Every time there is some text or a number displayed in blue color, it means that it is a hyperlink, and this applies to the OCS web console too. At the click of a mouse it enlists details regarding that number. In the screenshot previously shown, for example, if we click on **2** it will enumerate both of those agent types!

The next tab we will present now is the **ELSE** tab. Don't worry, we won't skip the **HARDWARE** tab.

This tab displays generic information about everything else that does not meet the criteria of earlier tabs such as **ACTIVITY**, **SOFTWARE**, and **HARDWARE**. Here, we can find out how many workgroups were found, the number of TAGs we implemented into repartitioning, as well as the count of different IP subnets within our infrastructure. Should we have package-related errors or pending deployments, they will be reported as well.

The next screenshot gives a sense of what to expect from the **ELSE** tab:

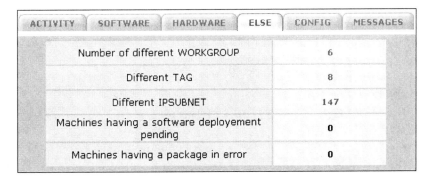

The **HARDWARE** tab prints detailed statistics about hardware specifications. For example, we can find how many different processors and resolutions can be found within our entire inventory. We also have some general numbers such as those below or above specific values for memories, hard disk size, and processor sizes.

Of course, we won't be using these statistics every day, but in case a rare situation pops up, we can pull these numbers out with a big grin on our faces. The following screenshot shows the **HARDWARE** tab:

ACTIVITY	SOFTWARE	HARDWARE	ELSE	CONFIG	MESSAGES		
Different processors						62	
Different resolutions						21	
Machines with a processor >= 3000 MHz						43	
Machines with a processor =< 1000 MHz						**0**	
Machines with a processor between 1000 MHz and 3000 MHz						385	
Machines with RAM >= 512 MB						446	
Machines with RAM =< 128 MB						1	
Machines with RAM between 128 MB and 512 MB						3	
hard disk number with remaining size > 4000 Mo						1078	
hard disk number with remaining size < 500 Mo						6	
hard disk number with remaining size between 500 Mo and 4000 Mo						70	

The next tab of this middle section is the **CONFIG** tab as we covered **ELSE** earlier. Here, we will find the advanced configuration regarding this middle section. We can add and/or remove fields from general statistics that are laid out inside **ACTIVITY**, **SOFTWARE**, **HARDWARE**, and **ELSE** tabs. We can configure this in the statistics middle section.

Should we add more fields into this section, then the opportunity to configure and set values that are specific to those fields will also appear exactly in the same fashion as **PROC_MINI**, **PROC_MAX**, and other options. The next screenshot presents these options:

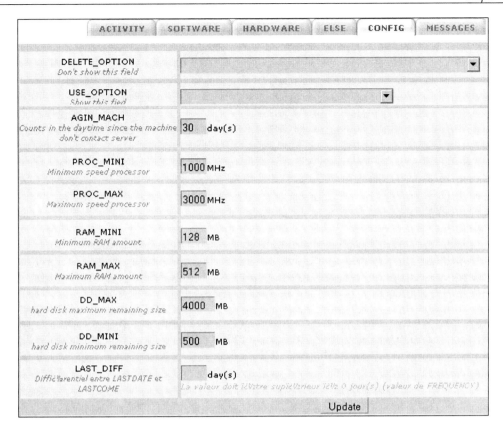

The **MESSAGES** panel is used for creating messages that we can send to specific groups.

The **MESSAGES** panel is shown in the next screenshot:

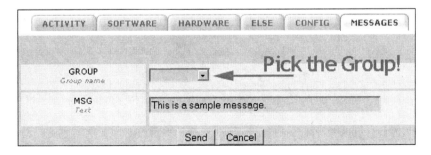

Finally, let's also cover the first tab: **ACTIVITY**. This tab is displayed by default every time we log into the OCS-NG web interface. It gives a general overview of our inventory database. The **ACTIVITY** tab is shown in the following screenshot:

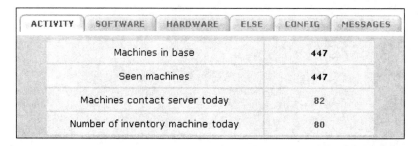

Machines in base	447
Seen machines	447
Machines contact server today	82
Number of inventory machine today	80

We will see over time that there is no toolbar or menu item that brings up this middle section. If we further navigate the interface, for example, if we click on the **CONFIG** tab, we cannot go back to the main interface that brings up the middle section anymore. Do we need to log in again in order to see it? No way!

At any time, we can bring up the middle section by clicking on the **OCS-NG Inventory** top logo on the upper-left corner of the page or by clicking on the **OCS next generation Inventory** at the title of the page in the center. Both are hyperlinks to the following URL:

```
http://<ocs-servername>/ocsreports/index.php?first
```

Getting to know the blue query toolbar

This **query toolbar** is situated on the left side, and its background is in blue. The shortcuts are self-explanatory, but we will do our best to give you a run down on each functionality.

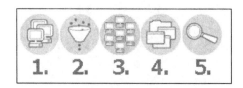

Understanding the first two queries

The first icon represents **All computers,** and it basically lists all of the inventory contents. We can customize how many rows are displayed (by default it is 20). We can also set the order and type of columns that we want to display. For example, in the following screenshot we've opted for: **Tag**, **Last inventory**, **Computer**, **User**, **RAM (MB)**, and **CPU (MHz)**. We can set any field there out of dozen of attributes.

Tag ✕	△ Last inventory ✕	Computer ✕	User ✕	RAM(MB) ✕	CPU(MHz) ✕	
	12/01/2009 19:38:38			2048	2193	✕
	12/01/2009 18:39:02			1024	3010	✕
	12/01/2009 18:18:45			1024	2998	✕
	12/01/2009 18:01:07			3572	2401	✕
	12/01/2009 17:41:37			2048	1995	✕
	12/01/2009 17:34:53			2048	2161	✕
	12/01/2009 16:35:57			2048	2999	✕
	12/01/2009 16:21:12			1519	2992	✕
	12/01/2009 16:02:57			2048	1662	✕
	12/01/2009 15:20:04			1977	2394	✕
	12/01/2009 15:16:58			2030	2333	✕
	12/01/2009 14:48:55			3317	1864	✕
	12/01/2009 14:39:22			3070	2671	✕
	12/01/2009 14:01:26			1007	2793	✕

We can remove one of the columns by clicking on the red **X** icon to the right of the column name. On the other hand, every time we add a new column, it gets attached to the right side. If we want to swap the order between **RAM** column and **CPU** column, we must first remove the **RAM** column, and then the **CPU** column. As **CPU** column gets into its left place of its previous neighbor, we again add the **RAM** column such that it gets attached onto the right, so it becomes **CPU's** column right side neighbor.

Useful tip:

When we configure these columns and rows based settings according to our requirements, we don't need to worry as they are saved between user sessions. Logging in again will maintain your customized view.

Demystifying TAG-based repartitioning

The second icon in the toolbar represents **TAG/Number of PC Repartition**.

Now, we are going to take a quick break and explain what TAG-based PC repartition is all about. Right away, we will continue our coverage of each menu function.

In a nutshell, this feature adds the possibility of site-based categorization. In the case of a company that has eight locations/sites or perhaps four locations each with two floors, we can repartition the hosts based on some TAGs. For example, **LOC1_FL1**, **LOC1_FL2, LOC2_FL1**, and so on. There are many other uses for TAGs as well, of which location repartitioning is just one.

The **TAG / Number of PC Repartition** query is shown in the next screenshot:

Tag / Number of PC repartition	
Tag	**△ Computer count**
LOC1_FL1	42
LOC1_FL2	33
LOC1_FL3	67
LOC2_FL1	79
LOC2_FL2	15
LOC3_FL1	137
LOC3_FL2	28
LOC3_FL3	46

In our example, we have these eight TAGs. From the previous screenshot, we can see the computers are enumerated based on their TAGs, such as **LOC1_FL1** has **42** hosts, the second tag has **33** hosts, the third has **67**, the fourth has **79**, and so on. Should we click on one of those numbers, we are redirected to the **SEARCH** function, which basically searches for and prints out the results in the following syntax; all of the hosts having exactly that tag.

Understanding the other three queries

The third shortcut from the toolbar represents **Groups**. This is the place where we can deal with **Groups**. The **DYNAMICS GROUPS** and **SERVERS GROUP** are displayed. We can also set up new **STATICS GROUPS**. Just like the other toolbar items, this one also does a query. The next screenshot shows the **Groups** query:

DYNAMICS GROUPS	STATICS GROUPS	SERVERS GROUP			
Show: 20 ▼					
Number of recording 1					
name	**description**	**creat**	**nbr**	**del**	**Visible**
Static Group Example	This is a static group.	2010-03-05 21:58:24	0	✕	☐

The fourth icon in the toolbar represents **All softwares**. This one is a fancy tool that helps searching within software. We can search for software applications using their beginning letter or using their exact names (such as finding **Notepad++**), or add another factor into the search queries, when their count is lower, equal, or higher than a value.

name	nbre
NVIDIA Drivers	72
Notepad++	47
Nokia PC Suite	28
Nokia Connectivity Cable Driver	20
Nero 7 Essentials	12

The previous screenshot was a sample of clicking the letter **N** meaning listing all software that are found starting with the letter N. Of course, we have shown only the top five of the results.

The last query item from the toolbar stands for **Search with various criteria**. This is the interface pane where we can build up custom search queries based on literally any of those inventoried attributes. The list is really exhaustive, but the real benefit of this is that no matter how complex our search query might become, we know it can be dealt with.

Using the drop-down box we can add parameters to search for. The common altering operators are the following: **EXACTLY, DIFFERENT, LIKE, BEFORE, AFTER, SMALLER, BIGGER, BETWEEN**, and other SQL query-like operators. Thankfully, due to user friendly interface and mechanism, we don't need any SQL knowledge to use the search function.

The **Search with various criteria** query is shown in the following screenshot:

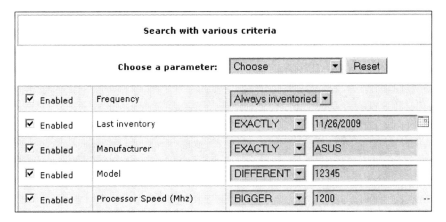

In the previous screenshot, we put together a sample query. We searched for hosts that were **Always inventoried**, where their **Last inventory** is EXACTLY **11/26/2009**, **Manufacturer** is EXACTLY **ASUS**, and the **Model** is DIFFERENT to **12345**, and the **Processor Speed** is BIGGER than **1200**. It is as simple as that, but please pay attention to those **Enabled** checkboxes.

We have covered the query toolbar. Next is the orange-yellowish administrative toolbar.

Getting to know the administrative toolbar

This toolbar is situated on the right side of the web interface. We will enumerate the tiny toolbar icons as we're going to give a run down on each of them.

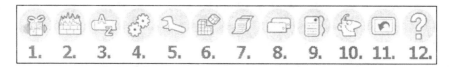

The toolbar is composed of 12 items. Two of them sport a drop-down menu with even more functionalities. The others are click-to-go shortcuts. If we move our mouse pointer on top of one, here again a tooltip appears explaining what it's going to do. The various items that compose the administrative toolbar are described as follows:

1. **Deployment**: This option deals with **Deployment**. It has a drop-down menu and this is the place where we can **Build**, **Activate**, and customize the **Rules of affectation** of the packages we are planning to deploy.

The following screenshot shows the three options of the drop-down menu:

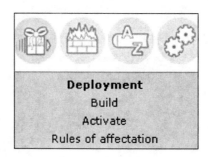

The next screenshot gives a brief overview on **New package building** mechanism:

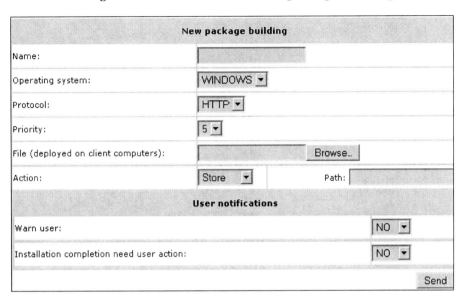

2. **Security**: Under this item, we can find **Network information** and **Config**. We can find which hosts are inventoried, where IpDiscover lies, the ranges, and subnets that are inventoried or not, and so on. We can edit the fields, set up new subnets, and so on.

The following screenshot shows the **Security Menu**:

3. **Dictionary:** Here we find a software related **Dictionary**, meaning we can search for software, and specify which are to be ignored or left unchanged. The others are pulled under the **NEW** tab. This is important in case of licensed applications.

If we want to custom track the count of some licenses, we may prefer to leave those software **UNCHANGED**. As such, we need to add them into that category. On the other hand, we should ignore service packs, common trial/demo software, .NET Framework, codec packs, flash/video players, and stuff that we don't care about.

The next screenshot shows the options of the **Dictionary** menu:

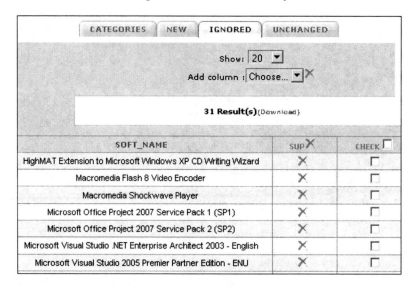

We can also track MS Office suites regardless of their version number. This option is really useful when we integrate GLPI as asset management software on top of our OCS-NG inventory platform. This is discussed thoroughly in *Chapter 7, Integrating OCS-NG with GLPI.*

4. **Agent:** Here we upload new agent packages. We covered this in the previous chapter that was dedicated to agent deployment.

The following screenshot shows the interface where we can submit new agents.

5. **Configuration:** Here we find another drop-down menu.

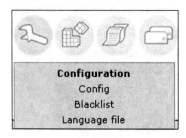

The first option is **Config**. This one leads to server-based configurations, and from this place we can tune the behavior of agents as well. Many of the options we can work with here are related to the following: **Inventory, server, IpDiscover, Deployment, Groups, Registry, Redistribution Servers, Inventory files, Filters, Webservice, Interface**.

Let's view the following screenshot of the **Config** pane:

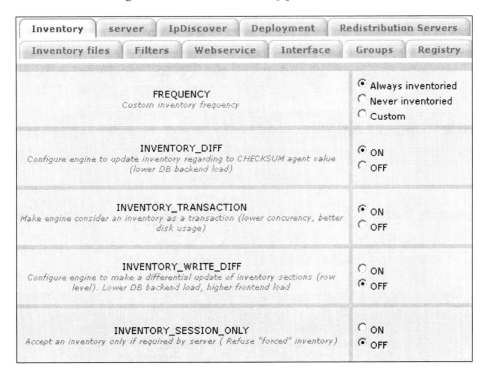

The previous screenshot shows only one-eleventh (1/11) of the **Config** pane as only the **Inventory** tab is displayed. Here we can see the inventory-specific variables.

In a later section, we will cover these configuration options too. Right now, we can surf through them in order to achieve familiarity. So, if and when such a situation occurs we will know where to look.

The **Blacklist** option is the second from the drop-down menu. Here we can blacklist MAC addresses and serial numbers. MAC addresses such as 00:00:00:00:00:00, FF:FF:FF:FF:FF:FF, 44:45:53:54:00:00, 44:45:53:54:61:6F, and so on should be blacklisted. There are many other addresses that are not valid Ethernet addresses or we recognize them as VMware, VirtualBox, or other virtualization software's virtual network adapters.

The **Language file** is the third option from the drop-down menu, and this is where we can edit the translated definition files of each message box and line. You can give it a go.

6. **Registry**: This option pulls up the **Registry** query function. We will cover this later.

The following screenshot displays the **Registry** query function:

Registry requests	
Name (you choose) :	Blizzard Games
Registry hive :	HKEY_CURRENT_USER ▼
Path of the key (Ex: SOFTWAREMozilla) :	SOFTWARE\Blizzard Entertainment
Name of the key that will be read (* for all) :	*

Send   Cancel

7. **Admininfo**: We can add/remove **Administrative data** to/from the **administrative info** table.

The next screenshot shows the **AdminInfo** query function:

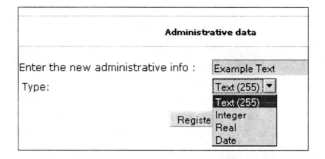

8. **Duplicates**: This is where we can deal with *redundancies*, check their summary, see which hosts are duplicates, and ultimately merge them according to our preferences.

This function is thoroughly explained in the *Maintaining a clean inventory: Solving common pitfalls, eliminating redundancies* section later in this chapter.

9. **Label file configuration**: We can specify new **label files** here.

The next screenshot shows the **Label file configuration** function:

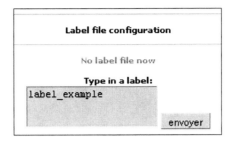

10. **User**: This is where we can add and/or remove users. Here we can specify user privileges. Removing users is done by clicking on the red **X** at the end of each row from the table.

The following screenshot shows the **User** function:

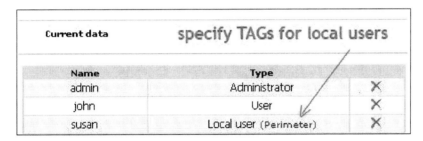

11. **Local import**: This is where we can upload inventory files of hosts that are not networked.

The following screenshot shows the **Local import** function:

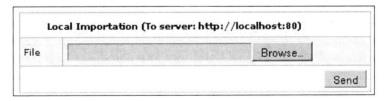

12. **Help**: This option basically opens up a new tab inside your browser, and loads up the Wiki URL of OCS-NG at:

```
http://wiki.ocsinventory-ng.org/
```

Summing these up, we have covered in short both toolbars. There's just one tiny two-option toolbar left on the upper-right corner. The **power down** button shortcut with the red background can be used to logout and the button next to it is used to change the password of the currently authenticated user. The latter is represented by a key that is turning in a lock.

Now let's move forward and look at some preliminary configuration tips.

Preliminary configuration tips and best practices

The first and foremost best configuration practice is to get rid of the default admin account. This is something that is generally applicable everywhere. The problem is that everyone knows the default account password, so if we don't change it, let alone delete the account altogether, some malicious users could get access to our database. The following screenshot shows the **Add a new user** function:

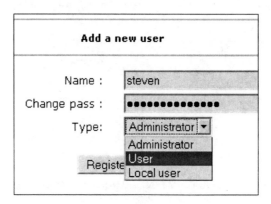

We navigate to the **Users** icon on the administrative toolbar. Then we add a new **User**. At first we should add an **Administrator**. Once this is done, we can specify many other users with either **User** or **Local user** privileges. The difference between **User** and **Local user** is that the latter is limited to viewing only particular TAG-based hosts (if this feature is activated, of course). Moreover, the **User** has *global* viewing rights to the database.

If we use TAGs to delimit separate locations of the company, then this function makes sense.

Explaining configuration parameters

In this chapter's *Getting to know the administrative toolbar* section we briefly presented the **Configuration** menu option and its **Config** sub-pane. We mentioned that there are many variables that we can configure.

The time has come for us to glance over the definition of these **config** parameters. We are going to consider tweaking these according to our needs only if we understand their use. Over the course of this book, we will hand out performance tips here and there when the situation seems right for those occasions.

Now, we want to have a complete list for reference usage.

 The original meaning of each variable was posted on the Wiki documentation of OCS-NG at `http://wiki.ocsinventory-ng.org/index.php/Documentation:Administration`

Variable	Description
AUTO_DUPLICATE_LVL	Duplicate computer detection. Select which values to use in duplicate detection. If multiple values are selected, they all must match for two machine records to be considered duplicate.
DEPLOY	Activates or disables the automatic deployment of new agents.
DOWNLOAD	Activates or disables the package deployment feature. Turning off DOWNLOAD stops this functionality on the server and on the agents. With DOWNLOAD off, once agents will have contacted OCS server, they will stop the current download without cleaning packages.
DOWNLOAD_CYCLE_LATENCY	Time in seconds to wait between each download cycle.
DOWNLOAD_FRAG_LATENCY	Time in seconds to wait between each fragment download.
DOWNLOAD_PERIOD_LATENCY	Time in seconds to wait between each download period.
DOWNLOAD_PERIOD_LENGTH	Number of cycles per period.
DOWNLOAD_TIMEOUT	Validity in days of a package on an agent. If the time used to download a package is over the DOWNLOAD_TIMEOUT days, the package will be cleaned and ERR_TIMEOUT will be sent to the ocs server.

Variable	Description
FREQUENCY	Specify the frequency in days of inventories.
INVENTORY_DIFF	Enable or disable differential inventory to speed up the server. With differential inventory, only changes are stored by the server, not the full inventory
INVENTORY_TRANSACTION	Enable or disable database transactions on the server. With transaction, an inventory is stored only if all the data has been processed correctly.
IPDISCOVER	Specify the number of agents that will run the IP discovery feature for each gateway (subnet). If you leave the default value of two, this means that the Communication server will ask the two most active computers on each subnet to run the IP discovery feature. If you set it to 0, IP discovery will be disabled.
IPDISCOVER_LATENCY	Agent will pause for many seconds between each IP address scan during IP discovery.
IPDISCOVER_MAX_ALIVE	Maximum number of days between two inventories for an IP Discovery- enabled computer to hold its status of IP Discovery computer. An IP Discovery-enabled computer will lose its status if it has not been seen by the Communication server for more days than the number of days defined in this setting. Another computer in the same sub network will then be designated.
LOCAL_PORT	Port of the OCS-NG central server.
LOCAL_SERVER	IP address/DNS name of OCS-NG central server.
LOGLEVEL	Enable or disable detailed log for the Communication server. If enabled, the server will write logs to the file ocsinventory-NG log in directory /var/log/ocsinventory-NG for Linux and \xampp\apache\logs for Windows.
PROLOG_FREQ	Controls how often the windows service agent runs. Specified in number of hours 1-24. The agent will contact the OCS server every PROLOG_FREQ hours. The agent will not send an inventory if the inventory is not older than FREQUENCY days.
REGISTRY	Activates or disables the Registry query function (for Windows agent only).
TRACE_DELETED	Activates the tracking of deleted/renamed computers for integration with GLPI. Enable this feature only if you use integration with GLPI asset management software.
UPDATE	Not used, always set to OFF.

Maintaining a clean inventory: Solving common pitfalls and eliminating redundancies

One of the most common difficulties of inventories of all kinds is trying to keep them clean. Using the categorization mechanism, and automatically pulling out information can be more reliable than human-introduced data. However, algorithms cannot think rationally enough to comprehend some real world situations (unless they are programmed of course).

The eighth icon of the administrative toolbar on the right is called **Duplicates**. Let's go beyond that feature and understand how it works. Once loaded, it displays a summary.

The next screenshot shows the **Redundancy** function:

As we can see, there are some redundancy problems we need to address. The agents pull out relevant information that we can use to identify hosts uniquely, such as hostname, PC serial number, and MAC address. While the serial number of some hosts might be the same (manufacturers or OEMs don't fill in those appropriate fields correctly), we must accept that the likelihood of both the MAC address and hostname matching is quite low.

We have the following options for dealing with redundancies. First, we can organize these duplicates according to the aforementioned variables. It is generally recommended to pick a coupled summary, something like **Hostname + Mac address**, but that depends on infrastructure specific particularities.

The next screenshot shows the **Redundancy summary** option:

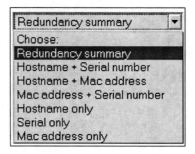

After choosing one of the options, the results are displayed. We can then examine each of them, and decide the right way to merge them (or not). In the preceding example, we will present two computers that are present as duplicates. This is because they both have a VMware virtual machine running, which is identified and inventoried once again. We can recognize this due to the **00:50:56:C0:00:08** ever-present MAC address.

☐	00:50:56:C0:00:08	PCNO_01	user_01	2048	1864	✕
☐	00:19:D1:08:95:2D	PCNO_01	user_01	2048	1864	✕
☐	00:1C:C0:59:8D:F4	PCNO_02	user_02	3072	2320	✕
☐	00:50:56:C0:00:08	PCNO_02	user_02	3072	2320	✕

From experience, we know that it stands for the **VMware Virtual Ethernet Adapter**. There are many other possibilities why redundancies might appear. For example, if a machine is migrated or given to another employee, and let's assume this process involves changing the hostname in your infrastructure, as a result, it is going to be inventoried again under a different hostname (new entry), but with an identical serial number and MAC address.

In order to identify the reality behind such a duplicate entry, it is advisable to check the PC's specifications. By clicking on the blue hyperlink (hostname), a new tab opens up with loads of information. Then we can navigate to the **Network** icon to find out more.

Continuing with the previous example, we look up one of the machines. We see the following screenshot:

Description	Type	Speed	MAC address
VMware Virtual Ethernet Adapter for VMnet8	Ethernet	100 Mb/s	00:50:56:C0:00:08 (Vmware, Inc.) ✕
VMware Virtual Ethernet Adapter for VMnet1	Ethernet	100 Mb/s	00:50:56:C0:00:01 (Vmware, Inc.) ✕
Intel(R) 82566DC Gigabit Network Connection - Packet Scheduler Miniport	Ethernet	100 Mb/s	00:1C:C0:59:8D:F4 (Intel Corporate) ◒

A while ago we mentioned the ability to include entries into the blacklist. In this case, we blacklisted those two VMware MAC addresses. The green mark next to the description **Vmware, Inc.** stands for removing those entries from the blacklist. The physical MAC address of the host is not blacklisted. Clicking on the red sign would blacklist it.

Implementing the Registry query function

The OCS-NG agent does an amazing job to pull out, and identify the installed software. In this way, we get to have an inventory filled with applications on every machine. It helps the process of software auditing and licensing, but that is not enough.

There are certain situations, when we may want to customize the way we track some registry keys. This is when the Registry query function pops into the picture. Thanks to this feature, we are able to manually specify the keys inside the registry hives that we plan to track. Sometimes, we may want to audit some fields due to malicious content. Other times we may want a second check for software that might not have been installed as they should have been.

The following screenshot shows the **Registry requests** function:

Registry requests	
Name (you choose) :	Blizzard Games
Registry hive :	HKEY_CURRENT_USER ▾
Path of the key (Ex: SOFTWAREMozilla) :	SOFTWARE\Blizzard Entertainment
Name of the key that will be read (* for all) :	*

Send   Cancel

The previous example is just for exemplification purpose. We can seamlessly identify games made by Blizzard Entertainment without registry querying too. The same goes for Valve's Steam, but it gives a sense of how to set up a new query.

We can set up queries for the **Run** fields in order to pull out the processes that are running on the hosts. This might help when troubleshooting malware and other malicious programs. Moreover, sometimes we are required to pull out ,and verify the product IDs or license information. Almost always, this type of information is stored within the registry. Otherwise, it is stored inside a file that we can get our hands on remotely anyway.

The summary of the **Registry** query function is shown in the following screenshot:

name	regtree	regkey	regvalue
Steam Games	1	SOFTWARE\VALVE	*
Blizzard Games	1	SOFTWARE\Blizzard Entertainment	*

The '*' is a wildcard that means 'for all'.

Uploading inventory data of hosts that are not networked

It might not seem that probable, but actually there are some hosts that might not be always connected to the network. There are various valid reasons for that. In the previous chapter, we covered how to set up and run an agent *locally* on hosts that are not networked.

The only drawback of this situation is that we need to import the inventory file manually. This file has the .ocs extension and has the following syntax: COMPNAME-2009-12-03-05-04-03.ocs. There are two methods which could be used to import this file. The first method is using the OCS web interface. The administrator logs in, selects the **Local import** function (11th of the 12 icons on the yellow toolbar), and browses for the path of the file. After clicking **Send**, it gets imported.

The **Local import** function is shown in the next screenshot:

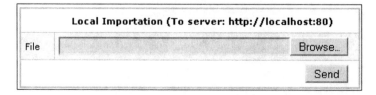

When dealing with routine administrative tasks manually, the thought of automating and scheduling the tasks comes to the mind of every system administrator. Fortunately, for us, the developers thought about implementing a Perl and batch script to aid the importing.

As expected, the Perl script can be used when the OCS-NG management server runs on Linux operating systems. The batch script works fine on Windows-based OCS-NG central servers. We can locate these scripts in the following directories, respectively:

- The Perl script on Linux distributions:

  `/usr/local/ocsinventory-NG/Ocsinventory_local.pl`

- The batch script on Windows systems:

  `C:\<INSTALLDIR>\binutils\local_import.bat`

The script can be launched in two ways. In either way, we specify the file to be imported, and by doing so, it uploads the file (along with its accurate path) we specified as an argument. Otherwise, we launch the script without any parameters, and this way it checks its own directory and imports as many `.ocs` inventory files it can find there (its own folder) into the database.

Therefore, on most setups we can think about automating the whole process. If the host computers are not networked, there still has to be some kind of access to the machine. Either the data gets copied weekly to a thumb drive or has limited mail access on schedules that are already defined and sends a mail to the administrator with the `.ocs` files. The real deal is that somehow the administrator gets all of the files stored at the same place.

Once this is done, perhaps on a specified schedule that occurs always at the same time, the script is executed to import all of the files from its directory. A log can be generated, and the administrator can be notified on how the importing process was carried out.

The script displays an output that counts the sum of the successful imports and errors, as shown below:

Successfully inventoried : 7

Errors : 0

Working with the inventory

As obvious as it seems, we have built and want to maintain a full-fledged inventory platform with the ability to gather and store data in a centralized solution. Ultimately, that is the goal of inventorying and asset management. The OCS-NG agents, are pulling out a huge amount of information that is stored in the central database. Through the OCS-NG web interface we have a user-friendly manner to access and work with this data.

Imagine how hard it would be to generate SQL queries inside some database interpreter. That would not really be a seamless inventory interface. The web interface does all of these behind the scenes. We just need to learn its functions and features.

Besides those five query functions that we talked about earlier, which are present on the blue toolbar on the left, the inventory is much more capable of performing other functions as well. As mentioned earlier, every time we click on a hyperlink, such as a hostname, a new browser tab is opened up. This tab loads up plenty of relevant information about the said host. Here's a quick screenshot:

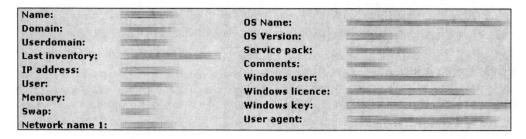

The previous screenshot is a brief summary. We have the following options in the next screenshot:

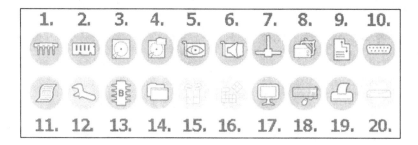

1. Processor(s)
2. Memory
3. Storage
4. Disk(s)
5. Video Card
6. Sound
7. Network(s)
8. Controller(s)
9. Slot(s)
10. Port(s)
11. Administrative Data
12. Customization
13. BIOS
14. Software
15. Deployment
16. Registry
17. Monitor(s)
18. Input Device(s)
19. Printer(s)
20. Modem(s)

We can surf through every component and find out every tidbit of information that the agent was able to pull out regarding that. On the bottom of every page, we find these two icons:

The first function pops up the print window. It's useful when we want to print the kind of information that is displayed. On the other hand, the second icon means "show everything". This is really useful. The query is really fast, and it barely takes a few milliseconds as long as you don't mind scrolling down through long pages. This way we can see all of the inventoried data regarding that host displayed on the screen, without being limited to specific areas.

Summary

The focus of this chapter was to achieve familiarity with the user interface of the OCS web console. First, we explained what each toolbar icon does, the kind of functionalities that are hidden beyond those tiny images, and so on. Practically, we can do almost anything inside the web console; even tune server-side variables that affect the behavior of the inventory. It's important to take some time to be comfortable surfing through toolbars.

We then elaborated on some configuration best practices and tips. We learned how to set up new users with privileged access rights. Then we introduced and explained the concept of TAG-based repartition. In case of medium-to-large organizations, this is a huge need, but if it's implemented appropriately it helps in case of small infrastructures as well. If the functionality is incorporated into OCS-NG, why not learn to use it the right way?

Practice has taught us that some preventive measures are to be taken in order to maintain a clean and ordered inventory. We not only discussed the techniques of eliminating redundancies, but we also understood why they happened, and how to solve other common pitfalls.

Furthermore, we got into overviewing the Registry query function. While the inventory agent does a great job on locating software on client machines, sometimes we want to be able to track specific registry keys and values. The examples we brought were mainly software based, but technically, we can track any field inside the registry.

Moving ahead, we also learned where to import the inventory data of hosts that are not networked. Once this is done and supposedly our inventory is clean, we got to spend some time understanding how to carry out common tasks. We elaborated tiny bits of how to search for software, generate reports, find out the hardware specs of inventoried hosts, and so on. After all, this is why we wanted to set up an inventory solution from the start!

In the next chapter, we will get into the depths of IpDiscover. We plan to go beyond the inventorying mechanism in order to fully comprehend how elevation happens. After these, we are able to make well-thought decisions on how to tune the retrieving process.

5
Investigating the Process of Gathering Inventory Data

At this point, our inventory is all set up and doing its job. Hosts appear in the database, and we have learned how to work with the results that we gathered, but what exactly happens behind the scenes? How can we identify the possible flaws of the system and recognize why some hosts remain uninventoried? Now we should go beyond this retrieving process.

In this chapter, we will explore the IpDiscover process. Elevation is the heart of the mechanism of this process. Based on some important criteria, the server is able to decide which client machine would be the best fit to delegate the discovery task. Each host, if activated as an IpDiscover computer, will scan its own subnet, and the results are sent back to server.

In this chapter, we will learn about the following:

- Understanding the IpDiscover process and demystifying the election mechanism
- Fine-tuning server-side variables to alter the discovery process
- Categorizing subnetworks by defining names and unique IDs
- Analyzing inventoried hosts and understanding the quality and fidelity columns
- Locating uninventoried hosts, determining their status, and finding and solving issues
- Managing and registering known hosts
- Using the IP Query function to find out details about the target host

Although our inventory might seem complete and functional, becoming proficient in using OCS Inventory NG does not stop there. By default, the server delegates discovery tasks to the clients, and these clients do their job quite well. However, in the case of complex network topologies that use diversified hosts, the chances are that the default configuration might omit some hosts and/or networks during the initial discovery process.

Our goal in this chapter is to present the meshing gears of the inventory. By the end of this chapter, we will know how to tweak the process of gathering data. The chances are we will also have a cleaner and more organized inventory without holes.

Going beyond the retrieval mechanism

OCS Inventory NG was designed to work seamlessly in infrastructures with tens of thousands of hosts. The central management server would be overwhelmed without any doubt if it had to scan, query, and gather the inventory data from all of the hosts at the same time. That is why the developers implemented a task delegation mechanism. We explained this mechanism in a nutshell in *Chapter 1, Introduction to IT Inventory and Resource Management*. Basically, in order to alleviate the network load, the central server delegates the task of discovering other hosts to other clients that are known to be faithful and also the most active.

What do we mean by this? The client agents are becoming slaves of the management server. The server rates these agents based on how frequently they contact the server. These variables are called as *Fidelity* and *Quality*. We will explain these in greater detail a bit later. Right now, what matters is that the server tracks all the activities of the agent.

This was rather obvious until now. Moving on, the server is able to delegate the task of discovering other hosts to a faithful agent that seems appropriate. These delegated agents are chosen using the **elevation mechanism**. The elevation mechanism evaluates the agents by checking the following parameters:

- **Fidelity**: The total number of connections from the host to the communication server
- **Quality**: The host to server connection (average calculated in days)
- **Netmask**: The subnet mask of the host, which can be at the most of class B (255.255.x.x)
- **Lastdate**: The last date of inventory data sent to the server (quality was computed)
- **Operating system**: Must be MS Windows-based or based on a Linux distribution

Based on the mentioned criteria, the server decides when to activate a specific host as an IpDiscover host. This entire process is called IpDiscover. Once a host behaves as an important delegated host, it scans its own subnet for uninventoried hosts. The computer will ignore the `frequency` server-side variable of inventorying and send in data more frequently.

After all, the quality of a host is the determining factor of its IpDiscover capability. It is always dynamically recalculated, and if another host turns out with a better quality rate, it will replace its predecessor. The Lastdate is crucial as an IpDiscover host might go down for a longer period of time, but with a great quality rating. By default, the server-side variable, on which this Lastdate is checked, is 7 days. If it's passed, another host is chosen.

These **IpDiscover** options can be configured from the **Configuration** menu of the administration (yellow) toolbar. From the drop-down menu, we pick the **Config** and then the **IpDiscover** tab. The variables are explained in green and are for exemplification purposes, as shown in the following screenshot:

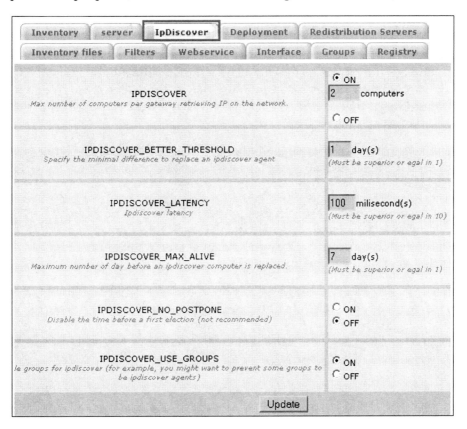

The **IPDISCOVER** option must be turned **ON** to enable this function. The number of computers to be delegated with scanning tasks must also be specified. This is on a per network basis. With the **IPDISCOVER_BETTER_THRESHOLD** variable, we can configure the minimal difference between an already elected host and another one that just sent in data. If this difference is exceeded, the IpDiscover activated agent is replaced with the new one.

The **IPDISCOVER_LATENCY** specifies how much time the agents will wait between scanning IP addresses. The default is 100 milliseconds. This suits most infrastructures. The **IPDISCOVER_MAX_ALIVE** variable sets that amount (in days). If that amount is exceeded, then the host loses its status, and another agent is picked to scan the said sub-network further on. The **IPDISCOVER_NO_POSTPONE** option disables time (**ON/OFF** option); thus, it enables or disables whether to postpone the first election.

Enabling the **IPDISCOVER_USE_GROUPS** option gives us the opportunity to customize group-based rules according to which agents are designed as IpDiscover hosts. We might have a group of computers that might not be suitable as hosts, but it is likely that their quality variable would be so high that the server might elevate them soon. With this option, we can eliminate this possibility.

Now that we know how computers are evaluated and designed as IpDiscover hosts, let's also find out how these agents can scan their own subnetwork. First off all, such a host determines the primary network interface through which it can communicate. Once that is done, it tries to contact every host through **Address Resolution Protocol (ARP)** in order to investigate their existence.

Each host will answer from its segment that it is available. In order to reduce the network load, a predefined amount of delay is specified as latency, which we have covered earlier.

Obviously, if a host can be resolved through ARP, but it does not have an inventory agent installed and/or for whatever reason it could not contact the OCS communication server, it means that host is an uninventoried host. The rest that are functional are inventoried.

We can query and analyze these hosts. Besides the server-side-based IpDiscover configuration parameters, the other functions can be found from the **Security** menu of the administration (yellow) toolbar. This is the second icon and it looks like a firewall. In some languages, it's translated as "IpDiscover" whereas mot-a-mot in English, it is known to be "Security".

This option loads up a new page inside the administration console with two or three options:

- **Network information**
- **IP Query** (only available when OCS-NG runs on top of Linux servers)
- **Config**

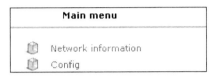

The **Network information** gives a general overview of the structure of the OCS-NG inventory infrastructure. We can see how many hosts are inventoried, uninventoried, how many hosts per gateway are designed and identified as IpDiscover-activated hosts. This count is in every case a hyperlink and clicking on it brings up a search query for those hosts. Clicking on **2** in the IpDiscover column narrows the search to display only those two.

Just after the heading, we can also see in parentheses the total count of uninventoried network interfaces. In a huge infrastructure, with complex topology, this count can be as high as thousands, but the inventory is complete and organized all the time.

			Network information			
		(6932 **uninventoried network interfaces**)				
			Uid:			
<= Back			Show everything ▾			
Click to edit	**Uid**	**IP address**	**Inventoried**	**Non-inventoried**	**IpDiscover**	**Identified**
-> Click to edit <-	-		1	0	0	0
-> Click to edit <-	-		33	37	2	0
-> Click to edit <-	-		32	43	2	0
-> Click to edit <-	-		86	37	2	0
-> Click to edit <-	-		69	29	2	0
-> Click to edit <-	-		1	0	0	0
-> Click to edit <-	-		1	1	0	0
-> Click to edit <-	-		4	40	2	0
-> Click to edit <-	-		2	2	1	0

Clicking on the **-> Click to edit <-** hyperlinks that are located in the first column is basically the same as going to the **Security | Config | Subnet names** from the administration toolbar.

The **Config** option also brings up two possibilities, as we can see from the following screenshot:

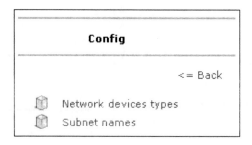

Both of these deal with configuration. Here we define, add, or remove, **Network devices types** and **Subnet names**. Organizing and linking these to the hosts is done on the previous pane (**Network information**). First let's add some devices here so that we end up with some device types to work with.

Defining network device types is beneficial to maintain an organized and neat inventory. In order to remove the benefit of doubt, when we examine the massive list of uninventoried hosts, we need to know for sure which hosts are legitimately non-inventoriable.

This varies from infrastructure to infrastructure. Sometimes we might not want to keep track and make an inventory of networking equipment such as routers, switches, access points, printers, and so on. Then again comes industrial automation devices such as motion control sensors, PLC Systems, SCADA systems, robots, and others. Even though these devices are connected to the network, we cannot make an inventory of them as no agents are supported. The following screenshot shows how we define network types:

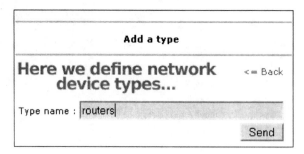

Adding new **device types** is trivial. Just type in the name and hit **Send**. A quick list will be populated right below showing the **device types** that we added.
If we want to delete one of them, we click on the red **X** icon at the end of a row.

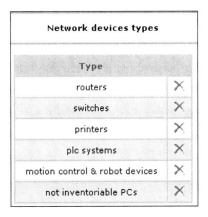

In the same fashion, we can also add a new **subnet name**. The real importance of these is due to the **Uid**. We can sort out and categorize them, later on, when we carry out the querying and analyzing of the overall structure of our inventory based on these Uids. It's useful if we have, say, N different subnets, and we name these appropriately, so we know which **Uid** stands for which.

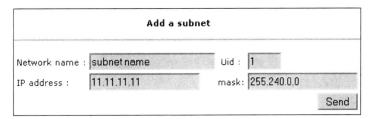

As we saw in the case of the network device types, the subnet list is populated right below. The more subnet names we define, the bigger the list becomes. In order to exemplify this, we created the following three subnet names. We can remove one of them with the red cross here too. This is shown in the next screenshot:

Subnet list				
Click to edit	Uid	IP address	mask	
Server Farm 1	1	1.1.1.1	2.2.2.2	X
Printer Room	3	4.4.4.4	4.4.4.4	X
Helpdesk Dept.	2	2.2.2.2	3.3.3.3	X

This sums it up for the **Config** pane of the **Security** menu option. Alright, but for what have we defined these? That's right, it's time to implement these changes. We go back to the **Network information** pane (first option) of the **Security** menu.

Surprisingly, we see that there is a drop-down box with Uids. The **Show everything** list is quite long, and it does not give an organized view of the structure. In the case of small companies, this is fine and the view is holistic, but at times, things can get disorganized. From this drop-down box, if we choose, say, **Uid 2**, then only hosts that are specified are displayed.

The following screenshot shows the **Network information** menu:

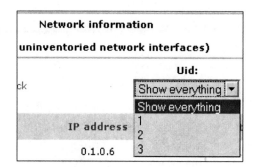

In the next example, only the **Uid** with the value **2** is displayed. **given_subnet_name** is the name we specified when defining the subnet with that **Uid**.

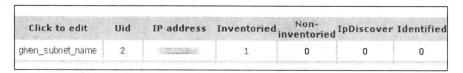

Click to edit	Uid	IP address	Inventoried	Non-inventoried	IpDiscover	Identified
given_subnet_name	2		1	0	0	0

We have seen where we use subnet names, but what about those network device types we defined? As we need to link these to individual hosts, we will initiate a query. This search query can be done from the **Network information** pane, if we click on any of those hyperlinked (blue color) numbers of the **Non-inventoried** column.

The result of such a query is presented in the next screenshot:

Registering un-inventoried but "known" hosts					
IP address	MAC address	DNS name	Manufacturer	Register	
			Canon Inc.	🧊	✕
			Cisco Systems, Inc.	🧊	✕
			Canon Inc.	🧊	✕
			Cisco Systems, Inc.	🧊	✕
			Vmware, Inc.	🧊	✕
			Vmware, Inc.	🧊	✕
			Vmware, Inc.	🧊	✕
			Vmware, Inc.	🧊	✕
			Vmware, Inc.	🧊	✕
			Vmware, Inc.	🧊	✕
			Vmware, Inc.	🧊	✕
			Vmware, Inc.	🧊	✕
			Vmware, Inc.	🧊	✕

As you can see, we have two **Canon Inc.** manufactured devices (Are they printers? What do you think?), two **Cisco Systems, Inc.** devices (network equipment), and the rest are **Vmware, Inc.** virtual machines. The **Register** column has those cubes on the left of the red crosses. That is where we can link a networking type that we specified with one of those devices.

The **IP address**, **MAC address**, and **DNS name** are crucial columns to determine whether that device really stands for what we want to name it. The chances are we have some company policy to implement the **DNS name** of the printers and network devices, so we can easily recognize their true identity. Now, we will click on the first Canon's cube.

A pane is displayed, as shown in the next screenshot:

Add a new network device	
MAC address:	
Description:	canon
Type:	printers
	Send

The **MAC address** field cannot be edited (obviously), the **Description** is taken from the DNS name (we can type anything in there), and at the **Type** field, we can pick any of those device types that we defined earlier. Of course, we pick **printers**. We send this information and that's all. Later on, we will know that this Canon is part of the **printers** group, and it won't create suspicions on why it's still not inventoried.

Let's analyze the **Quality** and **Fidelity** columns of the following inventoried hosts. This is shown in the next screenshot:

Quality and Fidelity Columns					
△ Last inventory ✕	Computer ✕	User ✕	IP address ✕	Quality	Fidelity
12/13/2009 18:03:27				1.2850	145
12/13/2009 17:03:41				1.3084	141
12/13/2009 14:08:20				1.4308	101
12/13/2009 12:39:04				0.1153	277
12/13/2009 10:33:28				1.2239	169
12/13/2009 06:32:57				1.2948	143
12/12/2009 22:09:25				0.9682	136
12/12/2009 15:04:26				1.9366	107
12/11/2009 16:42:35				3.1127	69

The higher the fidelity count, the lower will be the quality. The quality stands for the amount of days it requires (averaged) for the agent to contact the client. This is why the more frequently the agent succeeds in contacting the client, the quality value gets closer to zero.

Using the IP Query function

Assuming we have installed the OCS-NG server on a Linux distribution, we might also have the third option of the **Security** menu. This tool scans a manually specified host for a rather exhaustive list of details. It can also find out if the host was inventoried and/or just discovered. It determines the operating system (if available), DNS, and NetBIOS name.

The web interface of IP Query is basically a frontend to the `IPDISCOVER-UTIL` Perl script. That is why it is only available on Linux machines due to the Perl interpreter. Of course, there are workarounds for this too. It is based on the world-class security scanner and notorious penetration testing/security auditing tool, **nmap**. You can find more information about nmap from the following link:

`http://nmap.org/`

Alright, so we know that the heart of the IP Query function is `nmap`, but it has a few other requisite components as well, which are as follows:

- nmblookup (part of the samba suite, tested on 3.0.7/3.0.10)
- Perl module Net::IP
- Perl module DBI
- Perl module DBD::mysql
- Perl module XML::Simple

We need to specify the IP address and mask to carry out the scan. The output is shown in the next screenshot:

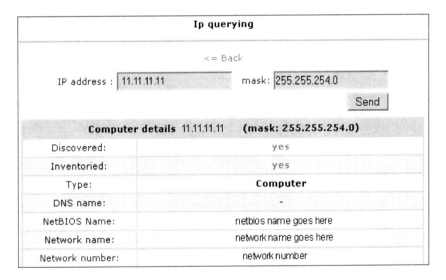

A final warning regarding `ipdiscover-util.pl` (Perl script); it requires write access (permissions) to the root directory. This warning message might appear in red. If we are running it on the Linux/Unix platform and we still cannot see the IP Query option from the **Security** pane, then write access permissions might be the cause for this warning message. Let's set the appropriate directory permissions by using the following commands:

```
#chown -R 775 /var/www/html/ocsreports
#chown -R 775 /var/www/html/ipd
```

Let's check out the results of running the previous commands:

```
#ls -l
drwxrwxr-x  2 root    apache 4096 Oct 30 16:51 ipd
drwxrwxr-x  9 root    apache 4096 Jan 26 14:07 ocsreports
```

Once the permissions are set, this warning message will disappear when looking at hosts that are not inventoried, and the IP Query option will also appear under the **Security** pane.

We can also verify the configured parameter under the **Config | Interface** tab. Look for the `IPDISCOVER_IPD_DIR` folder. This stands for the `IpDiscover` folder. As expected, it should point to the location where we actually have the IPD located.

The beauty of the IP Query function is that once it is working fine, it also adds a little *Analyze* function next to uninventoried hosts. This way, we can scan one of those hosts by clicking on it, instead of noting its network address and running a manual IP Query.

Summary

Throughout this chapter, we focused on the mechanism that fuels the OCS-NG inventory. We learned what separates the uninventoried hosts from inventoried ones, and how to track as well as analyze these. We elaborated on the IpDiscover process by explaining the elevation mechanism as well. Now, we know how some of the hosts become IpDiscover activated.

As there are no two identical infrastructures, we might be required to tweak those server-side variables that alter the behavior of IpDiscover. Thankfully, those parameters make sense and are clearly documented. In order to keep our inventory organized, we might want to define network types and name our subnets. These custom names and Uids can then be used to categorize the queries' results.

Finally, we have seen how the IP Query function works on Linux platforms that have the OCS-NG central management servers enabled. It's a useful Perl script based on `nmap` and other tools. The web interface makes a really straightforward interface.

The next chapter covers the nuts and bolts of package deployment and remote execution. In the next chapter, we will see how to get the most out of our OCS-NG inventory, how to create and deploy packages, customize this process, add another layer of security by involving certificates, and finally, how to monitor and troubleshoot the process (if required).

6
Package Deployment through OCS-NG

Having arrived at this point simply means that our inventory is together and we know how to use most of its built-in functions to get inventory-related tasks done. Each chapter, until this point, covered areas of our inventory solution that are required to fully comprehend and help us get our jobs done. Now we are going to continue our journey by presenting one distinctive functionality of OCS-NG: package deployment and remote execution.

It is not one of the most significant features of the inventory solution, but it is one of those functions which people expect to see support for. In the IT world, when there's a centralized server and many agents, we all want to see some kind of remote execution of commands. This is just an extension of the agents working for the server. Carrying out these sort of tasks remotely (deploying and launching packages) cannot be neglected.

The developers included support for this feature because the infrastructure of the OCS Inventory NG allows for remote execution of tasks. This built-in functionality is not frequently used as there are remote execution and deployment solutions already implemented within most environments. However, it's good to know about it, just in case it is needed.

In this chapter, we will see how to get the following tasks done:

- Learn to use the package deployment function
- How to build and activate packages
- Set up rules of affectation, and pick target computers for the packages
- Work with SSL certificates to enhance the security of deployment
- Monitor the progress and status of the deployments

Therefore, the goal of this chapter is to learn how to use this function. We must know that it is an in-built feature, and the mechanism of our inventory has this capability. When such a situation arises, we shouldn't struggle to find our way around. Each functionality of OCS-NG must be covered in sufficient detail in order to analyze when it is worthwhile to use a particular functionality in favor of other methods or solutions.

Getting to know the package deployment function

It should not surprise anyone that in this chapter, we are also going to spend most of our time using the web administration console of OCS-NG. For the first step, we need to fire up our browser and log in to the web interface. In *Chapter 4, Finding your Way through OCS-NG Features*, we read a rundown on each function of OCS-NG, and we presented glimpses of the package deployment menu.

It is located as the first icon of the yellow action bar. It is called **Deployment**, and we have three options under this drop-down menu. Their names are self-explanatory; the **Build** option deals with building a package, the **Activate** option manages the activation of those already existing packages (if there are any), and with the final option, we can set up, modify, and remove **Rules of affectation**.

Here's a screenshot of the **Deployment** menu:

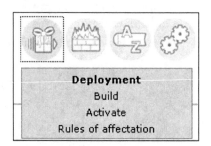

What happens behind the scenes when a package is about to be deployed? Firstly, when we create the package, it is stored on the deployment or central management server. Building a package assumes completing important factors of the process. Each package must have a *priority* and an *action* linked to it. The priorities are considered when more than one package needs to be deployed. These numbers range from zero (0) to ten (10).

Zero (0) is the highest priority, and respectively ten (10) is the lowest possible priority. As expected, the default priority is five (5). Let's assume that there are three packages which are about to be deployed at the same time, say with priorities: three, five, and eight. The corresponding order will be three (3), then five (5), and finally the one with priority eight (8).

There are three kinds of action that can be linked to a package:

- Store
- Launch
- Execute

While the store might seem obvious, the other two might be confusing at first.

Storing a package on a target computer means getting the package through to its destination, copying on the destination, and then extracting its content. Packages are either ZIP or TAR.GZ. The store action does not link with any other kind of action other than storing the package on the client machine. It does not execute, launch, or deal with the contents of the package. No command can be specified here. The only thing we need to set is the destination path.

Launching a package upon deployment refers to the action of launching an executable, which can be found inside the package (ZIP or TAR.GZ archive). Opting for this action requires specifying the name of the executable that must be included in the archive. This file can be executed with or without parameters. The content of the package is extracted into a temporary folder. The launch action allows retrieving the result code of the process.

Executing a package, once again, deals with execution of the specified command once the package is deployed on the client computer. However, the executable is not required to be inside the archive. This means that we can execute operating system-specific commands or any other third-party tool or application that is already on the target machine. Another major difference is the unavailability to retrieve result code of the executed command. The said command can be executed with or without parameters as it does not make a difference.

The obvious advantages of the store versus the other two actions are clear. We often want to get some files on the target computers. There are no other actions required to be taken other than getting those files through, that's all. The store action is simple.

The launch action is powerful when we deploy executables or self-extracting installers. Most third-party application installers support command-line parameters. As such, we can greatly benefit from their silent execution (for example, `/silent`) in the background. A little later, we will present two free installer systems that we can use to build our installers.

The most significant advantage of the execution action is the ability to run a command that is not just an executable inside the archived package. In essence, this is what we call remote command execution functionality of OCS-NG. The rest deals with package deployment. For this very reason, it gets the package through and works with its content. This execution action allows execution of commands without deploying anything.

For example, we might want to run a command that configures something on the remote machine in the background. Technically, we can do anything related to remote execution that other third-party tools support. It is up to us to decide when to use which, as other solutions (such as `PsExec` on Windows) have grown upon us over the years.

Every time we create a package, the OCS-NG system includes an `info` XML file that describes the package, including which action is linked to it. Besides this information file, a reference is made in the database. When we activate and/or affect a package or when the communication server asks to retrieve one of the packages, these tasks deal with that reference number. Moreover, each package can be split into N fragments. When we build the package, we can specify the fragment size.

Creating a package: Step-by-step approach

In this section, we will present a few steps through which we create a package. The **Package builder** can be found under the **Deployment** menu on the yellow action bar. The first option from the drop-down menu is called **Build**. It loads up the **Package builder**, as shown in the following screenshot:

Each package needs to have a **Name**. This is for identification purposes so that later on we can recognize the package we are referring to and working with. Let's not forget to enter something relevant to the package we are planning to deploy. The **Operating system** must also be specified: **WINDOWS** or **Unix/Linux**. Now, the only supported **Protocol** is the HTTP. Future development might expand the range of protocol support.

The **Priority** can be set from **0-10**, and it works as explained earlier. Next to the **File** field, we have the **Browse** button. Using this button, we need to point to the archive we want to deploy. In the **Action** field, we can choose from the three previously mentioned actions. If we choose **Store**, then we need to set the **Path**. If we choose **Launch** or **Execute**, then we need to specify the parameters and/or commands (or executable) to execute.

The **User notifications** are self-explanatory. In cases where we need a totally silent process, we can select **No** for both the **Warn user** and **Installation completion needs user action** options. The second option asks for user confirmation, and thus it requires user interaction.

Practically, the latter specifies whether the setup requires the user to go through some steps of the installation such as selecting an install path, picking some options, filling in information, and so on. This means user interaction. If this is the kind of application we are planning to deploy and launch, then it is critical to enable this by choosing **Yes**.

The **Warn user** functionality is more simplistic but nonetheless useful. Should we opt for that, we need to add text that will appear in a pop-up message box. Moreover, we can choose how long this window will be displayed and if the user needs to (or can) launch the deployment process right away, delay, or cancel it.

After clicking **Send**, we go on to the next step.

The **Package builder** creates a brief overview and generates the **Unique identifier** of the package. This is the reference number and finally digests an **MD5** sum in hexadecimal. In the **Fragments size** field, we have to specify the size of fragments. The package is split into numerous fragments that reduces the overall network load and adds another layer of practicality by downloading only those fragments which fail to get downloaded (if there are failed ones).

An example of this step can be seen in the following screenshot:

Package builder	
New package building [speedfan]	
File name:	installspeedfan435.exe
Unique identifier:	1261921999
Digest MD5 / Hexa:	6dac3513b411bfea229083b895fdfab4
Total size:	1739 KB
Fragments size (1 KB min):	512 KB
Fragments number:	4
	Submit Query

The **Fragments size** is **512 KB**. The file we are about to deploy is the **speedfan** setup kit, and it is approximately 1.7 MB, thus we got **4** fragments.

Once that is done, we can hit the **Submit Query** right away. This is when the package is created, and it is copied to the central management server/deployment server in the OCS-NG folder (for example, `/var/lib/ocs-inventory-reports/download/uniq_id_goes_here`).

The success notification is shown in the next screenshot:

Package builder
Your package was successfully created in the directory
/var/lib/ocsinventory-reports/download/1261921999

The **Unique identifier** is basically the timestamp, and this is the folder to which the package is copied on the Apache web server.

It should be mentioned here that in the case of command execution, when in the **Action** field **Execute** is chosen, the second window with the fragment size is not displayed. From now on, there is no package to be split into fragments. In these occasions, only the XML file called `info` is created and copied into the timestamp folder on the central server. The `info` file has all the necessary information to execute the said command remotely.

Let's see the contents of the package we previously created. As a memory refresher, we had chosen the **Launch** action, and we had split the package into **512 KB** fragments. The administration web console calculated the total count of fragments (four pieces), and decided to split it using the 445 KB size in order to make them almost equal fragments.

Name	Size	Packed	Type ⇧	Modified	CRC32
..			Folder		
1261921999-1	445,169	430,620	File	12/27/2009 4:10 PM	FF5E8F03
1261921999-2	445,169	445,309	File	12/27/2009 4:10 PM	6680FF96
1261921999-3	445,169	445,309	File	12/27/2009 4:10 PM	519FC75C
1261921999-4	445,170	445,310	File	12/27/2009 4:10 PM	7B5040CE
info	365	244	File	12/27/2009 4:10 PM	FCB68C82

selection.zip - SFX ZIP archive, unpacked size 1,781,042 bytes

The `info` file contains the package-specific information, which is useful for the agents on client computers. This file contains information such as which executable to launch? Are there any parameters? How to build the entire package (packet size, and so on.), the MD5 sum to verify integrity, and so on?

Server requirements for effortless deployment

There are a few important server requirement points that we need to address. These should be checked before we head further as they can create lots of headaches.

First, we need to check if the web administration console is running through the PHP engine. When we create a package and browse for the source file, this needs to be uploaded to the server. This uploading happens via `PHP POST`. For small files, this won't create problems, but in order to be sure, we need to check the file upload settings in the `PHP.ini config` file.

Please look into the official PHP documentation for more accurate and in-depth information as this depends on what version you are running. On PHP5, the configuration file is named `php5.ini`. The older PHP 4 versions are just defaulting on `php.ini`.

The `config` variables that we need to deal with (modify or add those lines) are given as follows:

```
memory_limit = 96M
post_max_size = 64M
upload_max_filesize = 64M
```

This kind of setup allows the maximum size of one POST instruction (post_max_ size) to be 64 MB. The upload_max_filesize will also be 64 MB. The memory limit (memory_limit) of PHP reaches up to 96 MB. In most circumstances, these options are alright during the modern computing era. If we are unsure of what we're doing, then we can open up security holes by making our PHP engine vulnerable to buffer overflowing, and/or open doors for miscellaneous activities.

Getting aggressive with server variables is acceptable, if the OCS-NG central management server is running inside the local network and it does not have access to the world outside, assuming, of course, that we have a robust monitoring solution and we know exactly what happens inside the environment. Some attacks do come from the inside. On the other hand, a bad script (or erroneous) upload can also lock up the PHP engine if those variables are not fine-tuned. That's why those limits are useful.

Those variables can be set via the settings.ini file as well using the following commands:

```
ini_set('memory_limit', '96M');
ini_set('post_max_size', '64M');
ini_set('upload_max_filesize', '64M')
```

Another warning regarding deployment is that the deployment server (in our case, the central OCS-NG server) is required to be SSL-enabled. The deployment info XML file is secured via SSL certificates. As with everything else that works based on certificates, on the server, we must generate the prerequisite certificate files, and then spread the private keys throughout the agents. The agents must have a copy of the certificate to be eligible for deployment. Soon, in this chapter, we will cover every tidbit regarding this.

Package activation and going beyond deployment

Now, let's see how we can activate packages. So far we have learned how to create packages; the next step is activating them. Activating a package means setting up server-specific information through which agents are able to pull out the packages. For exemplification purposes, we created a package called **speedfan**. It has **Priority 7** and is composed of **4** fragments.

When we navigate to the **Activate** option from the **Deployment** menu of the orange administrative toolbar, the following page loads up:

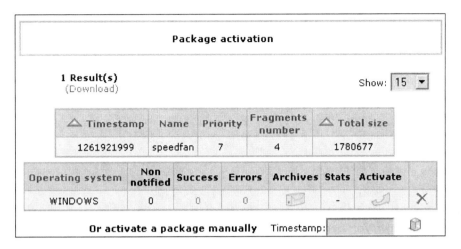

The table in the previous screenshot is split into two segments to enhance print readability.

A while ago, we described the process of deploying a package. As a first step, this info XML file is downloaded by agents through an **HTTP Transfer Protocol Secure** (HTTP over SSL, abbreviated as **HTTPS**). This file is really important because if someone tampers with this, the entire deployment can not only be broken, but also manipulated; thus, altering its behavior, injecting the execution of hazardous remote commands, and so on.

Once this info file is downloaded by agents, it proceeds further. The agent understands the syntax of this information file, and if it's a remote command execution, it does not ask for further fragments as there is no package to be downloaded. In other cases, it knows how many fragments to retrieve, what is their MD5 sum, their size, and so on. The agent will then grab these fragments and build up the package. This happens through normal HTTP.

The package activation window gives an overview of how many hosts are not notified, how many are successfully deployed, and how many have encountered some kind of error.

Activating a package can be done by clicking on that double-ended arrow mark under the **Activate** column. It loads up the page, as shown in the following screenshot:

Here we need to set up the URL of the server that sports the info XML file (HTTPS server, the one with SSL), and the URL of the server on which the fragments are stored (normal HTTP server). If we are using a non-distributed OCS-NG setup, then both URLs are the path of our OCS-NG central server.

The URL we type in the text field needs to be either hostname or IP based. This is the path through which the agents will contact the server(s) to pull out those files. As we can see, the unique identifier (timestamp) folder is already attached as a suffix at the end of the text-field. This is because we only need to type in the following:

    Httpsurl: ocs-server/download
    Fragments url: ocs-server/download

Otherwise, we need to type in the following:

    Httpsurl: 192.168.1.10:443/download
    Fragments url: 192.168.1.10:80/download

Let's not forget that we can use custom ports after the semicolon. The /download folder must also be specified as the package fragments and the info XML file is stored inside this folder on the Apache web server's root.

When we click on **Send**, the administration console verifies whether those URLs are valid and that the necessary files can be found under those paths.

There is a little **Stats** icon that deals with statistics. It brings up some percentage-based statistics regarding the number of hosts that are either not notified yet, have already been notified but encountered an error, or simply succeeded the deployment of the package.

The **deployment notification status** can be one of the following:

- **WAITING NOTIFICATION**: Server is waiting for agent communication in order to notify that there is something to download.
- **NOTIFIED**: Agent has been notified that there is something to download. Now, it is waiting for the result code.
- **SUCCESS [code]**: Agent has successfully downloaded the package and launched the command or stored extracted data.
- **ERR_ALREADY_SETUP**: Package was previously installed successfully on this computer.
- **ERR_BAD_ID**: Agent is unable to download the package because it cannot find the package ID on a deployment server.
- **ERR_BAD_DIGEST**: Downloaded data has bad digest, so agent does not execute associated command.
- **ERR_DOWNLOAD_PACK**: Agent was unable to uncompress the downloaded ZIP or TAR.GZ file.
- **ERR_BUILD**: Agent was unable to rebuild the package fragments.
- **ERR_EXECUTE**: Agent was unable to execute the associated package command.
- **ERR_CLEAN**: Agent was unable to clean downloaded package.
- **ERR_TIMEOUT**: Agent was unable to download package during DOWNLOAD_TIMEOUT days.
- **ERR_ABORTED**: User canceled package command execution (you've chosen to notify him/her, and allowed him to cancel command execution).

We also have a few possibilities to carry out some of the following tasks:

- **Validating success**: This will remove those hosts that have the success status as we don't need to deal with them anymore. They can be removed from statistics.
- **Unaffect not notified**: This will unaffect the package on those hosts that did not contact the OCS-NG central server since it was affected. The package is not inactivated, nor deleted from the server. The deployment order is just canceled on unaffected but notified client computers.
- **Validate all**: This will remove all of the hosts from the statistics; it's the same as clicking validating success and then unaffect not notified.

We can click on each status line to find out more information regarding that status. Moreover, we need to validate often to clear up the deployment database's log.

Affecting packages: Getting the packages through

When one or more packages have been activated, we can finally move to the final step and get them affected on one/more client computers. This can be done in various ways. One way is to affect some packages on these hosts one-by-one, but this process is time consuming, and it is only useful when we want to deploy on only one of the machines.

An alternative approach is affecting a package on multiple computers. In this case, we are going to use the query toolbar, and perform some sort of search based on various criteria. We can use the TAG-based search, if we want to affect packages on every machine that is located in a TAG specified location.

For example, we can also build up some custom search query. The choice is ours. What is most important is that we have the following **Deploy** option at the end of the query, right below the listed table. An example of this is shown in the next screenshot:

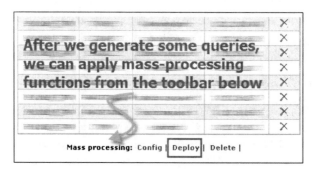

We already know that by using the query toolbar, we can generate table-based queries. At the bottom of these tables, we can locate the **Mass processing** mini toolbar with **Config**, **Deploy**, and **Delete** functions.

Clicking on the **Deploy** link loads up the **Affect a package** page. On this page, all the packages that are already activated are displayed. Remember, we first activate a package, and then we affect them based on which computers we are planning to deploy the said package.

In the previous example, we could see some part of a search query that returned **24** hosts. We clicked on **Deploy**, and it brought up the page on which we only have one package that was activated earlier. It's that **speedfan** package. We click on the **Deploy** icon, which is a tiny little cube under the **Deploy** column. If there are multiple activated packages, then we click on **Deploy** of the appropriate row for the package we want to affect.

An example where it calculates how many hosts were in the processed query is shown in the next screenshot:

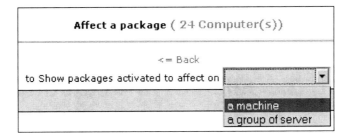

As mentioned earlier, we can also deploy a package on just one of the inventoried clients. We can do this by bringing up the full inventory screen of such a host. On this page, we have multiple actions to click, but we will click on the **Config** icon (the tool icon on the toolbar), as shown in the next screenshot:

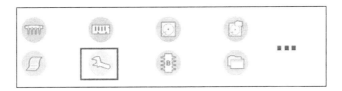

The web console then prints out the configuration information of the agent, but at the bottom of the table, we can find the **Add package** option. This loads up the same screenshot, as seen previously, but with **Affect a package on 1 Computer text**. The rest of the process is similar. The following screenshot shows the **Add package** option:

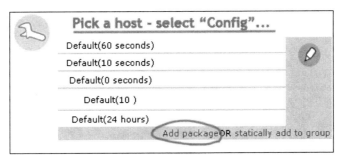

The mechanism of deployment is quite straightforward. Once a package has been affected on a host, the next time its agent contacts the OCS-NG communication server, it gets notified by the server that it has a pending package. The status changes from non-notified to a notified one. Before this, we can see under the **Config** page (where we added the package) the "status: WAITING NOTIFICATION."

This situation can be explained. If we affect a package on a host at hour 23, the client will start the download the next time PROLOG_FREQ is defined. If there are more packages, they will be downloaded the next time the PROLOG_FREQ occurs. The priorities are always taken into account (say, the first one has the priority 1, and the other, 5).

Managing the rules of affectations

The rules of affectations deal with automatic affectation of packages. These are useful in the case of redistribution servers when we opt for a distributed OCS-NG inventory setup, but there might be exceptions to this. This is the third option of the **Deployment** menu (first icon of the yellow admin toolbar). By default, there is no rule. It is shown in the following screenshot:

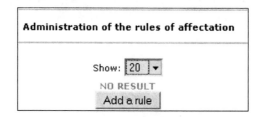

Should we want to add a rule, the interface is intuitive. Each rule needs to have a priority. This benefits scenarios in which multiple rules are meant to be implemented. Under most circumstances, the syntax of an affectation rule is: if **MACHINE VALUE** equals "=", does not equal "<>", or is **LIKE**, **SERVER VALUE**, both the **MACHINE VALUE** and **SERVER VALUE** can have one of the following options: **NAME**, **@IP**, **IPSUBNET**, **DOMAIN**, and **USER**.

The next screenshot shows how to define an affectation rule:

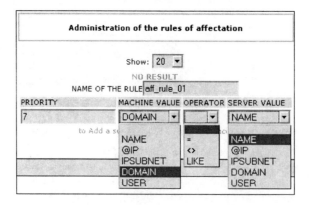

Setting up more than one redistribution server might require rules of affectations. Imagine the following situation. We have a redistribution server per IP subnet or DNS domain. The rule that deals with such a configuration is similar to the following lines:

```
Machine Value IPSUBNET =  Server Value IPSUBNET
```

The rule should make sense as it checks whether the machine's IPSUBNET equals to the server's IPSUBNET. In the case of DNS domain, we of course select the **DOMAIN** variable. On another note, if there is no distribution server within the same **DOMAIN/ IPSUBNET**, then the agent will use the central OCS-NG management server.

Finally, don't forget that if we want to use redistribution servers, it needs to be specified in the OCS Configuration Redistribution menu. At the beginning of this book, we kind of assumed a centralized suite, not a distributed one. This information should be more than enough to make our way around, if we feel the need to implement this.

Securing the process with SSL certificates

Now, we will cover the internal working of SSL certificates. As explained earlier, these are required as they enhance the security of deployment. Those info XML files are grabbed through HTTP over SSL protocol. We have two options to set up such a necessary SSL system.

Either we are going to work with self-signed certificates, or we opt for a more refined solution via the typical **Public Key Infrastructure** (**PKI**) scheme, having the certificate signed by a **certificate authority** (**CA**). In the very essence, the public key is linked with an identity. After that, anyone can verify whether that key really belongs to that identity. Therefore, it acts as a digital signature.

Describing in detail how the PKI scheme works is beyond the scope of our book. Chances are if you want to opt for the second methodology (that is having signed the certificates by a CA), then you either have an internal PKI or, you may have got yours issued by a commercial signer such as VeriSign or Thawte. We will see that even if you want to use this option, there is a free certificate authority at CAcert.org.

In the mean time, self-signed certificates should suffice for most environments. One of the key points to be careful about is the certificate validity period. As the generated certificates need to be spread around on the clients, we should set up an extended time. Otherwise, we need to repeat the process of deploying certificates quite often (each time they expire).

Apache web servers are shipped with sample scripts to generate SSL certificates. **OpenSSL** is a free, open source toolkit sporting SSL-related features that work well. Check out the following URL:

```
http://www.openssl.org/
```

Let's see an example of how to generate a certificate with OpenSSL using the following commands:

```
openssl genrsa -out server.key 1024

openssl req -new -key server.key -out server.csr
```

The first command generates an **RSA server private key** and a CSR certification request.

 CSR stands for **Certificate Signing Request**. **RSA** is a public-key cryptography algorithm, and its name comes from Rivest, Shamir, and Andleman.

We will see this in more detail in the next section, *Working with self-signed certificates*

Working with self-signed certificates

We can generate and self-sign our certificates. The OpenSSL toolkit allows us to carry out these tasks, and the certificates created by OpenSSL are robust and secure enough for testing or internal usage.

Generating and self-signing a certificate can be done using the following command:

```
openssl genrsa -des3 -out server.key 1024
```

This command generates the `server.key`, which is a 1024-bit RSA private key. The algorithm is Triple-DES encryption. The format will be in **Privacy Enhanced Mail** (**PEM**), which is in plain and simple readable ASCII but it is encrypted in Triple-DES.

 More information regarding PEM can be found by visiting the following link:
```
http://en.wikipedia.org/wiki/Privacy-enhanced_
Electronic_Mail
```

Now, we will run the following command:

```
Enter PEM pass phrase:

Verifying password - Enter PEM pass phrase:
```

The next step is generating the CSR certificate signing request. Once this is done, we can either self-sign it ourselves or issue it to a signing requestor service as mentioned earlier. The latter is the ideal situation. These services can verify the real identity of the requestor and if they match, then they sign the certificate. As such, the certificate becomes signed by the said CA authority. First, let's see how we can generate that CSR file by typing the following command:

```
openssl req -new -key server.key -out server.csr
```

Once this is executed, OpenSSL will ask you for the X.509 attributes. Those variables need to be filled in and attached to the certificate. The common name must be the server hostname that is going to be protected (for example, `ocs-server.mydomain.com`).

The list of X.509 attributes is as follows:

- Country name (two letter code)
- State or province name (full name)
- Locality name (for example, city)
- Organization name
- Organization unit name
- Common name
- E-mail address

After completing the previous steps, the CSR file is generated. As we opted for the Triple-DES encryption algorithm when generating the private RSA server key, we end up having to enter the passphrase each time the web server is started. Therefore, we need to remove the Triple-DES encryption. Alternatively, of course, we could have just neglected that option (-des3) when we generated the key in the first step.

Let's create a backup of our server key and then remove the Triple-DES encryption using the following command:

```
cp server.key server.key.bak
openssl rsa -in server.key.bak -out server.key
```

The `server.key` does not have the Triple-DES encryption anymore. The `server.key.bak` still has it. We need to specify the owners and permissions so that the unencrypted RSA private key does not get in the wrong hands (say, allow only root access). As always, in case of internal usage, these kinds of strategies might work as long as we are very careful.

Finally, let's self-sign the certificate. This is what we have been waiting for! We can do this by running the following command:

```
openssl -x509 -req -outform PEM -days 730 -new -key server.key -out
server.crt
```

A general prerequisite for Apache is `mod_ssl`, but we dealt with that in *Chapter 2, Setting up an OCS-NG Management Server*. Therefore, we just copy the certificates in the Apache `config` folder by typing the following commands:

```
cp server.crt /etc/httpd/conf/ssl.crt
cp server.key /etc/httpd/conf/ssl.key
```

Verify the path of these certificates inside the `mod_ssl` configuration (`httpd.conf`), and check whether the engine for this virtual host is enabled. If not, set these accordingly.

See the following examples of commands:

```
<VirtualHost _default_:443>
SSLEngine on
SSLCertificateFile /etc/httpd/conf/ssl.crt/server.crt
SSLCertificateKeyFile /etc/httpd/conf/ssl.key/server.key
</VirtualHost>
```

In our example, we have set the previously mentioned lines for our virtual host.

Now let's restart the Apache web server daemon using the following command:

```
/etc/init.d/apache2 restart or /etc/init.d/httpd restart
```

This can also be done on a Windows operating system. The XAMPP Apache Web server suite comes with a script that generates self-signed certificates. The script automates the process as we have the same OpenSSL toolkit in the `\bin\ folder of the \xampp`.

```
...\xampp\apache\makecert.bat
```

This means that, technically, we can follow the same steps as presented earlier under Windows as well, but if there is a script that does the entire job for us, we can use it. By default, it creates a key that is valid for 365 days (one year). You can edit this part of the `.bat` script. Keep in mind that the script also asks you for those X.509 directive attributes.

Once it is finished, the certificates are already installed as well. We just need to restart the Apache 2 service (that is all). As soon as you do that, our server is ready for deployment.

The `server.crt` needs to be renamed to `cacert.pem` and copied to each agent's folder.

Working with PKIs that have certificate authority

The only major difference between signing a certificate ourselves or sending it to a CA is that we don't self-sign the CSR file. The first step of generating the RSA private key is similar. Once that is done, we generate the CSR file, which means the second step is exactly same. Instead of creating the CRT (self-signed) file, we send the request to the appropriate certificate authority.

The validity test is usually receiving an activation link in your e-mail, then on clicking on the link, you pass the test. As a result, you end up with the CRT file signed by the certificate authority. The remaining steps can be carried out in the same fashion. Both of the keys (RSA private key and signed CRT) need to be copied to the appropriate places. The mod_ssl configuration part needs to be checked (see paths), and Apache 2 needs to be restarted.

Pay attention to the SSLCACertificateFile variable, and comment out (with '#') the previous line (remember, we previously used SSLCertificateFile when we self-signed).

```
SSLCACertificateFile /usr/share/ssl/certs/ca_root.crt
```

On a Windows operating system, we can generate both the RSA private key and the CSR request using the following command. Fire up a command-line window, and browse to the \xampp\bin\ path, then run the openssl command like this:

```
\xampp\bin\openssl req -newkey rsa:1024 -outform PEM -out server.csr
-keyout server.key -keyform PEM -days 730 -nodes
```

The ca_root.crt file needs to be renamed as cacert.pem and copied into the install folder of agents on every host. This can be done with a simple PsExec command or login script. The agents will match that certificate with the server certificate.

Getting the certificates deployed on agents

Regardless of the solution we have chosen, the signed certificates need to be deployed on the agent's installation folder on every host. If we self-sign our certificates, then we will end up renaming the server.crt file to cacert.pem. If the certificate is signed by a CA, then the file we receive, that is ca_root.crt, and this root key gets renamed to cacert.pem.

The name of the certificate must be exactly cacert.pem. This is the name of the file that the agent will look into for its installation folder. If it is not found, then no certificate can be used.

One of the easiest solutions to get the certificate file on every client's install folder is to ship the agents with this certificate included when we first set them up on the client machines. In these situations, we can use the OCS-NG packager to create a bundled agent installer with the certificate file as well, but this is not the only option.

We can use a login script or select our favorite remote execution tool. The script needs to be stored locally on one of the servers, then the login script would check for the existence of the `cacert.pem` file. If it is found, it does nothing; if it is not found, then it copies from that publicly available path into the agent's install folder. Once again, we are talking about internal usage. Let's run the following commands:

```
if exist "%ProgramFiles%\OCS Inventory Agent\cacert.pem" goto SCRIPT_END

cp \\public_serv\shared_folder\cacert.pem "%PROGRAMDIR%\OCS Inventory
Agent"

    :SCRIPT_END
```

The preceding script checks for the existence of the `cacert.pem` file. It is using `%ProgramDir%` environment variables to get the exact path of the program files. If it is found, then it jumps to the `Script_End` label. This label begins (and ends) at the end of the batch file. It literally does nothing. Otherwise, it copies from `shared_folder` of `public_serv` and shares the said `cacert.pem` file with the OCS inventory agent installation folder. Using a remote execution tool, such as `PsExec`, this can be done with a similar command line:

```
psexec \\targetmachine -u domain\administrator -p password -n 20 -c -f
get_cert.bat
```

We could also try to write a **Windows Script Host (WSH)** visual basic shell script. The previous command `PsExec` we just saw gets the said `get_cert.bat` file on `\\targetmachine\Admin$` and executes it.

Finally, the `xcopy` command could be used as well, if all we want is to just copy. This may not be one of the most robust solutions, but if the file is found, it won't overwrite, provided that we do not specify such an option when executing the command.

It would be better if we were to write a similar batch script as follows:

```
..@echo off
..set source=%1
..for /F ""tokens=1-3"" %%f in (targets.txt) do (
....net use \\%%f /u:%%g %%h
....xcopy /z %1 \\%%f\targetdir
....net use \\%%f /d
  ..)
```

This one works with `targets.txt` from which it gets the IP address (or hostname) of the computers and the username/password that it needs to log in. If we have a local administrator on these machines, chances are they are the same. This script can be used without any mods.

The `targets.txt` will look something like this:

```
192.168.1.24 localadmin localpass
192.168.1.28 localadmin localpass
192.168.1.37 localadmin localpass
```

These are just sample scripts, and we should do our best to modify them appropriately. The key behind this is that we open up the network share, and then we are able to copy the file to it. It's as simple as that! The script can be modified, so it only asks once for the administrator username and password. All in all, here we're given plenty of options to get the certificate on agents

Summary

In this chapter, we got into the nuts and bolts of package deployment and remote command execution functionalities of the OCS Inventory NG suite. It's a client-server (agent) model and remote execution is possible via those agents running on every inventoried client computer.

Over the course of this chapter, we learned how to create a package, the kind of steps we need to go through in order to build one. Once a package is done, it needs to be activated. To add a layer of security, the OCS-NG deployment mechanism is secured with HTTP over SSL. The metadata `info` XML file is retrieved via HTTPS protocol.

While a package is activated, it does not mean it has been deployed yet. As such, we learned how to select the target computers on which an already activated package will be deployed. This technique is called affecting the package on hosts.

Finally, we learned how to generate SSL certificates and get them either signed or self-sign them ourselves. We pondered on a few solutions to get the certificates on agents.

The next chapter will literally be the icing on the cake as it discusses GLPI. Our inventory solution is already powerful and feature laden. Yes, that's true, but there is always room for improvement. *Chapter 7, Integrating OCS-NG with GLPI* explains how to integrate OCS-NG with other tools. GLPI will be running on top of our inventory and adds even more features.

7
Integrating OCS-NG with GLPI

OCS Inventory NG is a powerful inventory platform that has plenty of capabilities right out of the box. As we progressed with the book, we learnt how to build the server foundation and spread the agents across the infrastructure. Each chapter discussed some aspects of OCS-NG, and we gradually got into the depths of it. The structure of the inventory that OCS-NG creates opens up possibilities for extensions.

Everything that the agents gather is stored in the OCS-NG database. This means that by taking one step further, there could be applications that run on top of our database, using the data that is already acquired and stored. In this chapter, we will present and overview the benefits of **GLPI**. This is an open source application that is an *IT Information Resource Manager*. It deals with the organization and management of all kinds of IT assets.

We will see how this extension can make our lives easier by supercharging our already robust and feature-laden OCS-NG inventory suite. It doesn't change anything. OCS-NG can be used individually. GLPI builds up its own database from ground up by importing the data of OCS-NG. Thereafter, it is able to synchronize to keep the content up-to-date.

In this chapter, we will cover the following topics:

- Introduce GLPI overviewing and what it brings to the table
- How to set up GLPI and configure it to import OCS-NG database
- Learn to use the features of GLPI to track and manage IT assets
- Understand the report generation mechanism and see how to view statistics

- Carry out administrative tasks inside GLPI, fine-tune its configs, and set up users

- Get the most out of software license and issue tracking/helpdesk functions

- Go one step further and see how GLPI can also be extended with plugins

By now, we already have a sense of the tasks we can do with the help of GLPI. Tedious tasks such as administering an inventory can become easier with this combo of OCS-NG and GLPI. Throughout this chapter, we will try to cover most of its aspects. However, the suite is extensive enough that we cannot possibly cover each tidbit within a chapter.

Introducing GLPI: IT asset management on steroids

It goes without saying that inside any IT-centric environments, the hardware components need to be organized and administered. These assets, such as computers, monitors, phones, and so on need to be tracked, inventoried, monitored, and maintained. Some kind of application is required to track everything and update their status while servicing. GLPI comes to serve this scope, aside from many others as well.

The name of this application is a four-letter acronym of **Gestion Libre de Parc Informatique**. It is an open source project of French origin. The project's website can be accessed at `http://www.glpi-project.org/`.

GLPI is a robust and well-rounded product. It is used all over the world, and at the time of writing, over 1,650 entities reported publicly that they are using GLPI in their IT department. According to the reported numbers, almost one million computers are administered.

Therefore, these should make us sufficiently confident to rely on this application. If in doubt, you can give it a try. If you don't like it, feel free to uninstall it without harming your existing OCS-NG data. It's as simple as that! It does not cost anything—just a few minutes.

In essence, GLPI has an administration interface that provides easy access to tasks that deal with its database. As it is an IT Information Resource Management software suite, we need to build its database. This database is going to be the inventory. Once this database reflects the reality, we can do anything within the admin console.

The somewhat tougher job is creating the database, right? We can manually add entries, set up templates according to which we pre-specify some form field values, and so on. But these are still exhaustive. The good news is that we already have an inventory database. GLPI can mass import the OCS-NG inventory into its own database format. This way, the actual OCS-NG database remains intact but allows you to use GLPI.

This can be done seamlessly with an OCS mass importer plugin. We will cover this as we arrive to that part. Right now, let's focus on the benefits of using yet another asset manager suite as well. For some of you, this dilemma might pop up. As we have seen, OCS-NG already fulfils our needs, so why should we bother with another resource manager? To keep them updated, synchronized, and all that? Good question.

Well, it is up to us to decide by weighing the benefits. The overall setup of GLPI should not take more than five minutes as the AMP (memory refresher: Apache, MySQL, PHP) solution stack is ready. It's not heavy on resources, so we can install it on the central OCS-NG server. If we opted for a distributed OCS-NG configuration, decide on which server you set up to balance out the load. By itself, GLPI needs an Apache2 web server with PHP support and MySQL.

Drifting back to its set of features, aside from an extensive list of *inventoried assets*, we can also associate the items with extra information such as location, costs, technicians who are responsible, and so on. We can include vendors and manufacturers and then link them together. All these help the IT department's staff to organize a rather diversified environment.

Tracking the status of an asset is valuable. We can flag these as faulty, sent to servicing, or asked for an RMA. By having associated to the appropriate vendor, we can query its contact information (such as name, phone number, address, and so on) right away. If we have more than one supplier (say, one dozen), then taking note of everything is a huge deal.

Consumables are yet another sticky area that is quickly delegated from IT departments. Tracking the different types of consumables is often handled by assistants or suppliers. However, if we have a centralized solution, we can get notifications such as when our stock is running out, from which vendor to order, and so on. Everything can get easier. The location fields are especially useful in the case of large companies (multiple floors or dozens of offices).

Should we have the same type of multifunctional printers on every floor, we can easily label these accordingly in the location field. Such as the printer003 inventory number is situated "on the back of fourth floor, in front of the PR department."

The incorporated *helpdesk* and *issue tracking* functionalities are somewhat expected. If we have an application with which we track and manage IT assets, then implementing the helpdesk isn't far away. GLPI is multi-user by its nature. We can set up user levels such as administrator, technician, and user. The users can post issues and/or request service. The GLPI platform handles the notification of administrators and technicians automatically.

At first, if no rules are set up, the administrator receives the ticket and needs to deploy the task to one of the technicians. Once the ticket is associated with a technician, its status can be further tracked by both the technicians and the administrators — obviously, the issuer user as well. The follow-ups are received only by the technician if set up that way.

The *notification system* is not only used in the case of helpdesk tickets, but also in running out consumables as mentioned earlier. The GLPI suite sports enhanced *license tracking* features. One way is automatically detecting the software running on a machine (this is imported via OCS-NG), but the advanced way is monitoring the usage of licenses. We often have N kinds of software licenses; tracking their count seamlessly is necessary.

Some licenses are volume license, others are OEMs. Some licenses are life-long, while others are timeline based. GLPI can deal with all of them, and if we set up the count of licenses within our portfolio accordingly, then we can receive notifications when their count is running low or they are soon to expire.

Generating *reports* and *statistics* is something that a system administrator needs to know from where to pull out. We're required to generate reports on maintenance histories, user logons, status of assets, financial contracts, and basically anything else. GLPI supports various export formats for these reports such as PDF, CSV, SLK, or XML.

Its *search function* is advanced as well. We can search based on any column information, including status, vendor, history, and all of these "new" variables when compared to OCS-NG. When displaying results, we can widely configure the fields to fit our needs.

Getting familiar with the web interface of GLPI

The user interface of GLPI is straightforward. It comes in 22 languages.

The main menu bar is long and sports seven drop-down menu items. In the next screenshot, we can see four of these menu options. In order to maintain visibility, we have split everything into two segments. In a printed book layout, we cannot really go further than 800 pixels in width. In real life, you will see everything merged together.

The following screenshot shows the left part of the toolbar with the first four menu items:

The **Inventory** is where we can deal with the inventory per se. This is where we add, remove, edit, or search for inventoried assets. The place where we track and manage the assets is also here. The **Assistance** option is also self-explanatory. Under this drop-down menu, the **Helpdesk**, **Tracking**, as well as **Planning** and **Statistics** functions are situated. **Planning** is nothing more or less than a basic scheduler.

The **Management** part is where the "paperwork" would go. Under this option, we can find the **Contacts**, **Suppliers**, **Contracts**, and **Documents** functions. We set up and modify valuable information related to these items. On the **Tools** option, we find **Notes**, our **Knowledge base** repo, **Reservations**, **Reports** (where we generate them), and **OCSNG**-related direct tools.

The second part of the toolbar, as shown in the next screenshot, is situated right next to the part of the screen shown in the previous screenshot.

Here we find the other three menu options: **Plugins**, **Administration**, and **Setup**.

Plugins	Administration	Setup	
Cacti	Users	Dropdowns	
Objects	Groups	Components	
management	Entities	General	
	Rules	Notifications	
	Dictionaries	Authentication	
ems	Profiles	Receivers	Landscape
	Transference	OCSNG Mode	
	Data	Document Type	
Inventory number	Logs	External Links	Warranty duration
Statu		Plugins	
			36 month
			36 month
			36 month

Under the **Plugins** menu, we find the name of the plugins we have installed and activated. Not every plugin will have its own menu option under that drop-down menu. In our case, we have a few plugins, but only those two have their own menus: **Cacti** and **Objects management**. Under basic setups, there is nothing under **Plugins**. This is to be expected.

The **Administration** menu is where administrative tasks are rolled into. This is where we set up users, or import them via LDAP, add and/or modify groups, entities, rules, dictionaries, profiles, transference; reach data (backup and restore) and logs-related tasks.

The final **Setup** is where we configure the display of GLPI, document types, how OCS-NG mode is set, and lots of configuration regarding notifications, authentication, and so on.

Setting up GLPI on top of our OCS-NG server

There are a few prerequisite server components as mentioned earlier. This section will assume that our intention is to install GLPI on a server that has the full AMP solution stack installed, configured, and running. The standard solution that is supported by most distribution communities is installing software via their official repositories.

On various Linux distributions, this is possible in the case of GLPI too. There are some repos that contain the OCS-NG + GLPI combo as one package. If you prefer to use the package manager to keep things consistent, then just check out your list of supported applications. If GLPI is present and its version is at least recent, then we say go for it. Choose the method that you find the most comfortable.

The latest version of GLPI can be found at `http://www.glpi-project.org/spip.php?article41`. If the site changes its structure, we can still rely on the main page, and then click on the **Downloads** section. Don't be scared if the site loads up in French at first. On the top-right corner, we can select either French or English.

The latest version at the time of writing is 0.72.3. It's archived in TGZ (`tar.gz`).

We can download it via the basic `wget` command or with our favorite browser. We can find all of the project archives in the following folder available online:

`http://www.glpi-project.org/IMG/gz/`

As such, we can download the currently latest version with the following command:

#wget http://www.glpi-project.org/IMG/gz/glpi-0.72.3.tar.gz

And we extract the contents into the `/var/www` folder or to your web server's root folder, by using the following command:

#tar xzvf glpi-0.72.3.tar.gz

The setup has an automated installation script that is web based. The installation process begins when we visit the URL `http://our-server/glpi` for the first time. Once it finishes, and assuming the setup finishes successfully, it won't reappear again.

But before we type in that URL and start the setup, a few points need to be mentioned. The setup needs to create and work within the MySQL server. It needs to create its own database. We need a user with sufficient privileges to do so. The script also needs to write to setting files, document files, session files, and even cron files.

In order to meet these requirements, we are going to give '777' permissions to two folders as follows:

#chmod 777 config/ files/

By now, we should have everything ready to launch the setup.

Nevertheless, the installation script asks for the root administrator of MySQL to create its own database. We allow this by launching the setup at this time and then supplying it with the required username and password (root and its password) or we do this before. Alternatively, we could supply the required username and password before launching the setup.

The more secure approach is by creating the database ourselves. This way, we can be sure of what we are doing. We also set up two new users, one with more permissions to be able to write inside the GLPI database and another one to use for OCS synchronization. The latter user will have only minimum "read" rights on the `ocsweb` database.

The installation instruction from the Remi's blog gives us an example of this:

`http://blog.famillecollet.com/pages/OCS-GLPI-en`

The following MySQL command snippet performs the the tasks just mentioned:

```
# mysql -u root -p rootsecret
mysql> CREATE USER 'glpi'@'%' IDENTIFIED BY 'glpisecret';
mysql> GRANT USAGE ON *.* TO 'glpi'@'%' IDENTIFIED BY 'glpisecret';
mysql> CREATE DATABASE IF NOT EXISTS `glpi` ;
mysql> GRANT ALL PRIVILEGES ON `glpi`.* TO 'glpi'@'%';
mysql> CREATE USER 'synchro'@'%' IDENTIFIED BY 'syncsecret';
mysql> GRANT USAGE ON *.* TO 'synchro'@'%' IDENTIFIED BY 'syncsecret';
mysql> GRANT SELECT ON `ocsweb`.* TO 'synchro'@'%';
mysql> GRANT DELETE ON `ocsweb`.`deleted_equiv` TO 'synchro'@'%';
mysql> GRANT UPDATE (`CHECKSUM`) ON `ocsweb`.`hardware` TO 'synchro'@'%';
mysql> FLUSH PRIVILEGES;
mysql> exit
```

A few notes regarding the previous sample: The name of the database we create for GLPI is called `glpi`. The first user is going to be called `glpi` and it has `glpisecret` as the password. This user will have all privileges on the `glpi` database. The other user we create, that is, the `synchro` user, will have limited privileges (usage, select, delete, and update) on `ocsweb` database. The password of the `synchro` user is `syncsecret`. At the beginning of the script, the `root` and `rootsecret` are the root user and password to launch the MySQL shell.

Please don't forget to replace these passwords with the actual ones! Do not attempt to create these two users with those sample passwords.

Moving on, we can now finally execute the web-based installation script. We can do this by navigating to the following URL:

`http://our-server/glpi`

The installation page loads up. The first page asks us to select our language. The default language is English. We click on **OK** and the next step follows. The license agreement is displayed, and once we go through it, we should accept it. The setup then continues.

We are asked whether we want to install or update GLPI. Unless we are updating from a previous version of GLPI, we need to pick installation. This way, the data imported by GLPI will be the default one (for example, users). Moving on, the setup script will check the compatibility with your server environment. This is when it checks those permissions, the existence of PHP parser, MySQL extension, sufficient memory, and so on.

Everything should be alright. If this is not the case, then the notes are clear enough for us to recognize what's the trouble, where and how to fix it. Assuming this succeeded, we click on **Continue**, and the setup follows along.

This is the page where we need to supply the database connection parameters. If the MySQL server is located on the same server where we are installing GLPI, then we write "hostname" to the MySQL server field. The MySQL user and password fields need to be filled appropriately. If we followed a safer approach, like the one from Remi's guide, then we need to enter the glpi user and its password.

The next step asks for the database connection details. We can create a new one or use an existing one. Once again, if we have already created the glpi database, then we select this. Otherwise, we let it create a new database called glpi or anything else.

Next, the setup tests the connection and it finishes the configuration files. The setup is verbosely logged, so we know what has happened in the background. The final step just displays the default logins. The admin account is glpi/glpi.

Alright, the setup is finished. Now, by visiting the URL of http://our-serv/glpi, the setup is not going to be displayed anymore. The following login screen greets us:

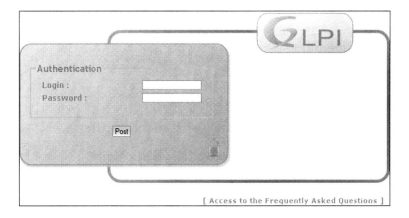

Configuring GLPI to integrate with the OCS-NG mode

At the beginning of this chapter, we presented GLPI as an individual resource manager of IT assets. By default, the OCS-NG mode integration is not enabled. This means that we need to activate this OCS-NG mode and then configure the database connection parameters.

First, let's navigate to the **Setup** from the top menu bar and then pick **General**.

The following window loads up. Right now our purpose is to activate the **OCSNG Mode**. We can find this under the **Restrictions** tab. There are lots of other configuration variables, and depending on your preferences, you can take a glance at them.

The following screenshot explains what we are talking about:

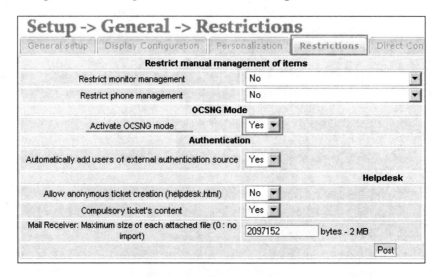

Moving on, we need to configure the database connection parameters.

We navigate within the toolbar to the **Setup | OCSNG Mode**. Now we select **Yes** in the **Acivate OCSNG mode** field after which we have to click on the **Hostname**.

A new page is displayed that asks for the name of the OCS server (we can type anything), the hostname of the OCS database (`ocsweb`, if default), and the username/password credentials.

Once we type in these details and select **Post**, the connection to the OCS-NG database will be tested. It also checks whether the configuration and version of OCS-NG is valid.

We can see how to configure these on our sample setup, shown as follows:

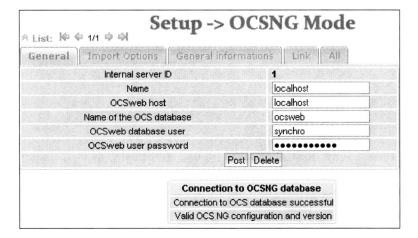

We should also go through the other tabs of this menu. The **Import Options** specifies the way GLPI imports data from OCS. Items can be managed globally or unit-wise as is. Managing items globally is known as "global import" while the latter is known as "unit import". This is the place where we can limit the import of specific OCS-NG TAG items. Say, we have different locations, the central OCS server is the same, but we want to import only one location.

In the **General informations**, we can select the type of data we want to import, including computer and components specifications and even OCS administrative data.

Under the **Link** tab, we can configure how automatic connections are created. We can set up the existence parameter of a computer. A link means associating a computer from GLPI with the same computer of OCS-NG. This way, the changes are reflected in GLPI.

Now we can go to the **Tools** menu and select OCS-NG. We can set the OCS-NG server address to *localhost* in our case because both GLPI and OCS-NG run from the same physical server machine.

Extending GLPI with plugins

GLPI is a modular application and it allows the usage of plugins. The tricky part is that the plugins are officially supported, meaning you cannot really get your hands on plugins that are not supported. However, with this comes the guarantee that they will work without any problems. We can find an updated list of plugins at the following URL:

```
http://plugins.glpi-project.org/spip.php?lang=en
```

Right now there are a total of 87 plugins ranging on various areas such as **Inventory, Network, Management, Reports, Data, Export, Helpdesk, Import, Calendar, Appliances, Buying, Entities, Graphs, Logs, Meta-plugin, Snort, Syslog-ng, Web, Accounts, and Ocs-ng.**

When we select a plugin, we can find its description, state, languages, and lots of other vital information. The details of the OCS Import plugin are attached below it, which is by far the most frequently used plugin. It deals with automation import of OCS-NG.

Of course, we can use the manual import or rely on the *pseudo-cron* job that the GLPI does by default, but there are dedicated OCS-NG import plugins as well. The pseudo-cron job is launched (to synchronize) each time there is activity on the remote end.

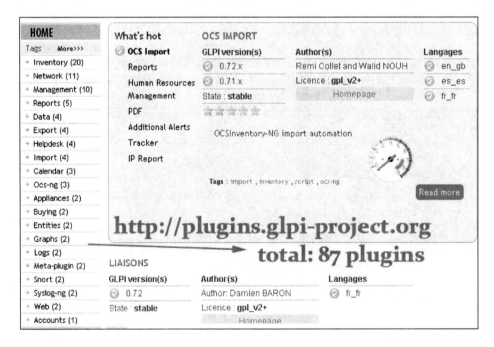

When we download a plugin, it comes inside a `.tar.gz` archive. Uncompressing this archive leads to a subfolder that is the name of the plugin. The contents of the plugin are inside that directory. Thereafter, every plugin will have its own directory. There is a `plugins` folder inside the `/glpi/` folder. On default, this is on the following path:

`/var/www/glpi/plugins/`

We are required to extract and copy each plugin within its own folder inside the `plugins` folder. This process should make sense, as it's quite straightforward. Once we placed the plugin inside, we need to log in again to GLPI—this means log out and log in. Every time we log in to GLPI, it re-checks the contents of the `plugins` folder and refreshes its list.

By navigating to the **Setup | Plugins** from the top menu bar, the following list is displayed on the screen:

Plugins list						
Name	**Version**	**Status**	**Author**	**Website**		
barscode	1.4	Not installed			Install	Uninstall
Cacti	1.6.1	Enabled		🐾	Deactivate	Uninstall
Inventory number generation	1.3.0	Installed		🐾	Activate	Uninstall
Objects management	1.1.1	Enabled		🐾	Deactivate	Uninstall
OCS import	1.3.0	Not installed		🐾	Install	Uninstall
Reports	1.3.0	Enabled		🐾	Deactivate	Uninstall

This list changes from setup-to-setup. Our example here has six plugins inside the folder. It is important that the newly extracted/copied plugin appears within the list. Then we can work with it. We have a few actions available: install; then activate or deactivate, or uninstall. Obviously, when to use which action is self-explanatory. When you install a plugin, it means that its setup is launched, its requirements are checked, and so on—but it isn't functional.

At first launch, after a new plugin is installed, when we navigate to the **Setup | Plugins**, we might be greeted with a message that notifies us that our newly installed plugin needs to be configured. Then, clicking on its hyperlink leads us to the initial configuration. The **Select a plugin to configure** message appears and your plugin appears as the choice.

The advanced plugin configuration page can be reached from **Administration Setup | Plugins**, and then click on the name of the plugin. It should be noted that not every plugin has an entry here. Only those plugins that have configuration options have an entry.

Always check out the official plugin repository as it happens that some of the plugins get depreciated after the release of a new version. Their functionality might be implemented into GLPI by standard or simply the plugins structure doesn't fit the changes introduced into GLPI. If this is the case, then the plugin may or may not be developed again in order to release a new version.

Using GLPI to track and manage inventory assets

The way we use GLPI depends on our needs. The framework is flexible enough, and it ends up just as useful as we make it. Should we decide to use only 10 to 20 percent of its capabilities and features, then we might claim that GLPI isn't worth the time. It all depends on our requirements. This chapter focuses on describing the possibilities and features that GLPI sports. We then know where to find them and how to use them, if we want to.

Logging into the central web console gives us a welcome screen. This is customizable as well. We can select the kind of things we want to see inside personal views. Either way, the global view usually gives a sufficient idea of what has happened since our last login.

Check out the following screenshot for such an example:

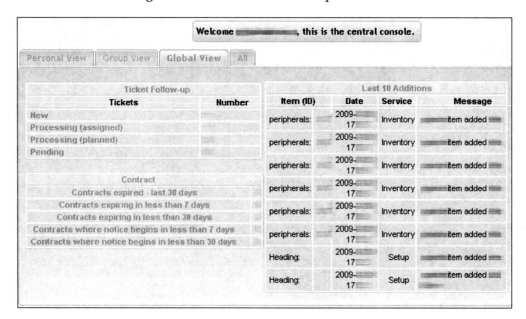

We can find an up-to-date status of contracts, tickets, additions (new entries into the database), planning (remember—this is the scheduler), personal notes, and latest events.

In order to configure what and how many items to display at pretty much anywhere in GLPI, we can set these parameters at **Administration | Setup | Display Configuration**.

There are two kinds of notes that we can work with, namely, personal and public ones. Super admins can set up public notes and every user can see them, while the personal ones are private and hence are visible only to you. These notes can be added into the planner.

In our day-to-day lives, we are only going to view the inventory. Yeah, that's right. Why would we want to create an inventory if not to view and administer it? There are multiple ways we can visualize the inventory, based on our (searched) parameters. We can also configure the behavior of displayed tables.

We can modify and alter the inventoried variables of each item, one-by-one, or perform some massive actions on a selected list. The entire user interface is intuitive.

A descriptive user guide on the central console can be found at the GLPI wiki:

```
http://www.glpi-project.org/wiki/doku.php?id=en:manual:admin:centralh
elp_en_gb
```

The following is a screenshot of an inventory page. This is just the left side of the entries.

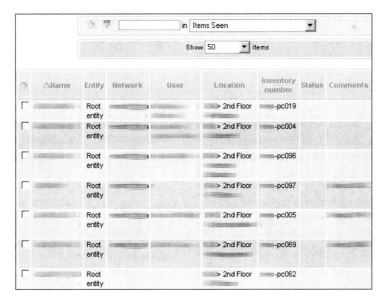

And here is the right side of the inventory page. Due to resolution restrictions, we have split the screenshot into two segments. We can add/remove columns in order to fine-tune to our needs the kind of variables we're always looking for. Our setup is quite common and suffices for most environments.

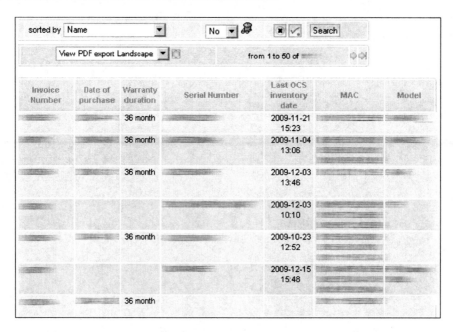

We are not trying to explain how to use GLPI, but rather briefly, we are giving an idea of the useful tasks that can be done with it, which may or may not be done that easily with OCS-NG alone. So we skip many "how to use" elements. Please refer to the official GLPI documentation (known as Doku/Wiki) and make sure you go through it:

```
http://www.glpi-project.org/wiki/doku.php?id=en:welcome
```

Another interesting concept that GLPI does amazingly is the detection of **connections**. We call these direct connections, and they mean a connection of a peripheral component or device to a computer. It detects the connection of monitors, printers, cameras, phones, and so on. We can manage these connections as well as track the history of a device.

The **network connections** are handled in the same way. GLPI calls these as network ports and it assigns to them an IP and MAC address. When they are interconnected, we can see which port is connected to which—usually this is the case of a computer and a switch, for example. It supports the addition of VLANs as well.

The beauty of **software management** is thanks to the enhanced license tracking functions. We can do basic software auditing with OCS-NG, but the automatic count of licenses and their management and other such things is only possible if we use GLPI. This is going to be covered in a later section.

Apart from figuring out what kind of equipment is connected to a computer (by following the connections) or auditing the software that someone installs (software management) we can also track the lifecycle of a machine. This is vital from an inventorying perspective.

At first, the device (for example, a computer) is collected and placed into the inventory. GLPI grabs all of its characteristics, and we can link more information to the item as well. Generally, we have the choice to monitor the following parameters apart from technical specifications:

- **Management information**: User, group, responsible technician, location, inventory number, and so on
- **Network information**: Network, port, MAC address, IP address, VLAN, and so on
- **Financial information**: Acquisition date, warranty time, amortisation, supplier, vendor, vendor's contact information, contract info, licenses data, and so on

The management of duplicates eliminates the possibility of redundancy. If a computer gets replaced, GLPI auto-detects this by constantly checking the parameters of the computer name, serial number, and MAC address. Should a duplicate be detected, we are asked for a merge action. Computers do not disappear from the inventory.

If a computer is removed from activity, meaning it 'dies', then its status won't get updated any more, but it does not get deleted. Nothing will happen to it. We can find out historical data regarding it at any time. If we want to delete a machine, then we can do so by sending the item into the trash. Fortunately, this does not delete either, it marks the item as 'deleted' but we can still bring these back to life and query for these.

The **tracking of consumables** and **cartridges** is beneficial. It is important that when we define a cartridge type, we also specify and take into account with which printer it is compatible. First, we define the type of consumables, and then we can add different models of that element under that category. The financial information can be associated per element.

The default threshold for consumables and cartridges count can be set at **Setup | General.** However, this value can be modified for each type of consumable individually.

Carrying out administrative tasks with GLPI

The most important administrative tasks deal with users. GLPI is a multi-user environment. Therefore, we need to set up the users. The default users are recommended to be removed as well, except the helpdesk one. There are four kinds of user levels:

- **Super Admin**: No holds barred full access
- **Admin**: All permissions to everything except "Setup"
- **Normal**: Read-only access to every part of GLPI
- **Post-only**: Helpdesk section + Reservation + Viewing the FAQ

As expected, we have the possibility to add users manually. However, if we want to implement and use GLPI on the organization scale, then we have to set up each user. If we don't plan to use the helpdesk and tracking feature, then perhaps this might not be necessary. Carefully evaluate the needs. If only the IT department members and financial department/management staff wants access, then those few people can be set up manually.

Let's navigate to the **Administration | Users** drop-down menu. Here, we can set up new users, list the existing ones, and modify their attributes.

The following screenshot gives a sense of what to expect. As a cherry on the top of the cake, we can monitor and audit the history of a user—what did he/she do, when, and how. This is great—it gives another layer of security by allowing us to take a glance at technicians.

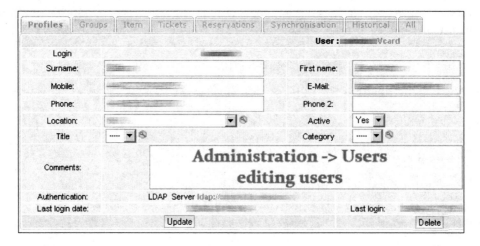

Alright, moving on with the multiple user import scenario, thankfully there are solutions. GLPI supports *LDAP authentication*. This also makes it possible for Microsoft Active Directory. Once enabled, the users are created (imported) inside the GLPI database too. The beauty of this is that we can log in via the GLPI users or via the LDAP authentication mechanism. This entire bravado needs the PHP's LDAP module on server.

In order to implement this, let's jump to the following on the menu bar: **Setup | Authentication | External Authentication**. The entire process of how to do this, the different kinds of connection modes that are highly depending on your LDAP/AD structure are all documented in the GLPI Wiki. For more details, please refer to the following URL:

```
http://www.glpi-project.org/wiki/doku.php?id=en:ldap
```

Another administrative task apart from the management of users is taking care of *backup*. It is plain and simple common sense that inventories need to be backed up. This applies to the physical world as well—building gets on fire, documents get compromised, and you name it. It's better to be safe than sorry. GLPI incorporates an inbuilt SQL dump function.

We can find this at **Administration | Data**. It can create two kinds of dumps, SQL and XML. The SQL dump is pretty simple—it's the same one, and we could do with a one-liner MySQL command to dump the GLPI database from a console terminal on the server. The second one is in an XML format. The advantage of using the inbuilt backup is that we can perform these tasks, assuming we're privileged to do so, inside a web browser.

Most administrators like to be in charge of updates. In the *Extending GLPI with plugins* section, we explained how the "pseudo-cron" job synchronizes GLPI with OCS-NG. It detects when there is some activity and then launches the task. We can set a task for this in crontab instead of needing to rely on that ambiguous activity-detection rate. GLPI comes with a PHP script that does this synchronization—it's called cron. php. It is scheduled to run every five minutes.

```
*/5 * * * * /usr/bin/php5 /var/www/monsite.com/glpi/front/cron.php &>/
dev/null
```

Generating reports and statistics with GLPI

A centralized inventory solution must have the ability to generate reports. Statistics are also useful in certain situations, if we need to bring up some points and back up our assumptions. Statistics are largely focused on helpdesk and issue tracking.

The report generation can be found under the **Tools | Reports** menu.

Statistics can be displayed from **Assistance | Statistics**.

We have a few predefined default report styles. For example, we can create reports for financial information, history of hardware information, or installed software. Depending on the amount of parameters we fill into our inventory, the parameters based on which we can create reports is also higher.

Unless asked for specific kinds of reports, we frequently use the following ones: reports based on duplicate computers, detailed license reports, and by license expiration dates. The financial reports, including contracts, location trees, and so on might be asked by higher management. And as such, it's quick for the system administrator to create them.

The following screenshot exemplifies the report generation page:

Tools -> Reports

Select the report you want to generate:

Default report
By contract
By year
Hardware Financial Information
Other Financial Information (licences, cartridges, consumables)
Network report
Loan
Reports - Detailed license report
Reports - Duplicate computers
Reports - Financial Information
Reports - History of last hardware's installations
Reports - History of last software's installations
Reports - Licenses by expiration date
Reports - List all devices of a group, ordered by users
Reports - List of groups and members
Reports - Location tree
Reports - Number of equipments by location
Reports - Number of items by entity
Reports - Rule's catalog

The statistics are dealing with tickets. Basically, we have lots of criteria upon which we can pull out statistics. The main categories are—global statistics, by user, by technician, by company, title, category, priority, and so on. These are the determining elements according to which the statistic is queried.

From the list of possible statistics, we have the following choices:

- Total number of tickets
- Number of unsolved tickets
- Average problem solving delay
- Maximum problem solving delay
- Real average ticket solving duration
- Real maximum problem solving delay
- Minimum delay of ticket handling time
- Average delay of ticket handling time

Statistics are composed by a summary table and/or an additional graph.

Check out a quick screenshot on a test scenario where we added five new tickets in March.

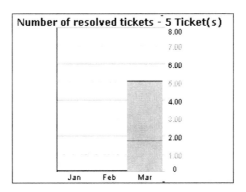

In the next screenshot, we can see a summary table. The **Average resolution delay** is 0 seconds as we added already solved tickets for this example.

		Number of tickets	Number of resolved tickets	Average resolution delay
		4	3	0 Sec(s)
		1	0	0 Sec(s)
		1	0	0 Sec(s)
		4	2	0 Sec(s)

License tracking and software auditing with GLPI

GLPI has enhanced license tracking functionalities. In essence, it grabs the software list, which is installed per computer from the OCS-NG database, and then administers this list of software applications (along with licenses, if it's the case) itself.

Tracking licenses are possible as it auto-detects and categorizes the applications. It is able to decide and associate a said license with its application. The applications are recognized by their names and manufacturers. GLPI uses dictionaries to do this.

The dictionary can use either the OCS's incorporated one or the one that comes with GLPI. We can opt for either of these. These dictionaries contain rules based on which applications are recognized and associated with their manufacturer.

The more complete a dictionary is, the higher is the likelihood of recognizing every application correctly. We can add our entries as well. It's based on criteria, such as if the name of the program begins with, say, "Microsoft", then it's a Microsoft Corporation product. Fortunately, both dictionaries are vast, so regardless of which dictionary we decide to use, it will likely recognize most applications.

OCS-NG has three main categories of software: *New*, *Unchanged*, and *Ignored*. GLPI imports the software that appear within the Unchanged category. By default, OCS adds every application into the New category. We can manually set up the ignored pieces of software into the Ignored group. All that we need to care about is maintaining the software we want to manage within the Unchanged group. In this way, they get imported into GLPI.

Furthermore, we also have the option to create custom groups. Either way, the way we organize this is up to us. What matters is once the software are pulled out from OCS into GLPI, they can be administered from GLPI.

The next step is adding some license count in order to see summaries. But first we need to understand how licenses are managed. There are a few kinds of licenses:

- global (these are valid for the entire site — unlimited installs allowed)
- standard (has a serial number and an expiration date)
- free (the keyword 'free' is specified at the serial field — unlimited installs)
- "to buy" (no license available; new software, license needs to be bought)

Additionally, we can categorize software if they are part of OEM, bought, or upgrade (such as extending the expiration date) licenses as well. Licenses can be moved back and forth.

For example, some workstations inside a specific department might get a new license. This step requires unglobalizing the previous license group, then we can pick the licenses we want to move to the newly created license. The same can be applied when an application changes from a paid (license) version to the free one (perhaps light edition). We don't want to track its license anymore, so we move them to a new "free" license.

The interface of GLPI calculates and displays the number of installations and matches these with the specified number of licenses. We can see the following in action in the next screenshot:

	Name	Entity	Manufacturer	Name - Versions	Number Installations	▽Number Licenses
☐	Microsoft Window	Root entity	Microsoft Corporat			
☐	Microsoft Visual	Root entity	Microsoft Corporat			
☐	Microsoft Office	Root entity	Microsoft Corporat			
☐	Microsoft Visual	Root entity	Microsoft Corporat			
☐	Microsoft Office	Root entity	Microsoft Corporat			
☐	Kaspersky Anti	Root entity	Kaspersky Lab			
☐	Microsoft Office	Root entity	Microsoft Corporat			
☐	Microsoft Visual	Root entity	Microsoft Corporat			
☐	Microsoft Office	Root entity	Microsoft Corporat			
☐	Microsoft Visual	Root entity	Microsoft Corporat			
☐	Microsoft Office	Root entity	Microsoft Corporat			
☐	Total Commander	Root entity	N/A			
☐	Microsoft Window	Root entity	Microsoft Corporat			
☐	Nero OEM	Root entity	N/A			

There are situations when we use a wide range of versions of an application but from a licensing point of view, they are the same. An example of this is version 1.7 and 1.8 of some piece of software. The license we acquired is valid for both versions. On some workstations, we might still have the older version and on the new rigs the latest. The dictionary of OCS-NG comes to the rescue. This is when we can benefit of categories.

In OCS-NG, we create a new category where those applications would be placed (regardless of version number). This category would appear along with the default ones: New, Unchanged, and Ignored. However, let's not forget that GLPI imports the full data of the software listed in the Unchanged section. The new section we created is just good for those two applications that don't need version number differentiation.

To sum it up, the greatest benefit of this software management capability is the automated license tracking mechanism. We can specify our dozens of licenses, their number, including their types, then the software take count of installations. We can specify our status on licenses at any time (how many to buy, still available, and so on).

Conducting software audits is also possible with GLPI in a similar fashion. This does not mean we won't use OCS-NG any more. That couldn't be farther from the truth.

Helpdesk and issue tracking functions of GLPI

The issue tracking and helpdesk features can be found under the **Assistance** section of the top menu. The first one is simply called "tracking" functions, but it deals with tickets. The interface allows two kinds of searching mechanisms: basic and advanced. There are lots of criteria and parameters based on which the results are queried. Tickets are used to report issues, ask for servicing/help, and helpdesk-related tasks.

At the **Helpdesk** section, we can add tickets. This form can be loaded up by any user. The previous **Tracking** is only possible for technicians and administrators. Tickets can be added both retroactively (meaning historical, just for archiving purposes) or as new ones.

Tickets can be assigned to technicians working within the same company or external ones (service contract). This step assumes that we added more than the required companies to that category. The planner is used to schedule intervention of tickets, if this option is enabled.

Users with the least privileges are post-only users. These can only post "follow-ups" to an already existing ticket. Basically, their area of eligibility is reduced only to the helpdesk. At the **Setup | General Setup**, this option can be modified. Notification options are at **Setup | Notifications | Notification Options**.

There is a status linked to each ticket. This can be one of the following: new, assigned, planned, on hold/standby, unsolved but closed, and closed ticket (and solved).

The following screenshot shows the system in action—posting a new ticket:

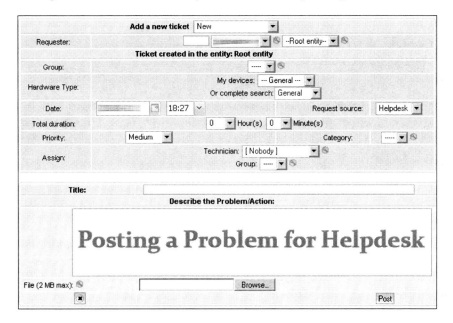

The status of a ticket can be modified by a user with sufficient privileges at any time. This includes reopening a closed ticket. Tickets can only be deleted if their status is closed. Should we intentionally want to delete a ticket, we first need to close it and then delete it.

The advanced search mechanism lets us specify each of the parameters.

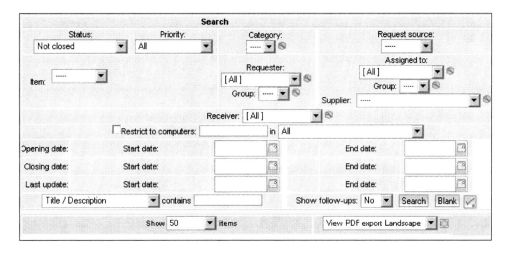

As expected, each ticket is identified by its ID. Apart from that, tickets have a status, as previously mentioned (there cannot be a ticket without a status), requester, and priority level. Additional parameters assigned are technician, opening and closing date, last update, description, and tracking information. You could also have supplier, material, and category.

Please refer to the GLPI wiki documentation in order to understand how costs work within the helpdesk system. There are multiple types of costs and all of these combined have an effect on the **total cost of ownership** (**TCO**). Therefore, it's vital to understand the concepts and use them accordingly. See the **Assistance Section** at the following URL:

```
http://www.glpi-project.org/wiki/doku.php?id=en:manual:admin:centralh
elp_en_gb
```

The page which shows a general overview of current tickets can be seen in the following screenshot. Due to width-space restrictions, the image was split into two segments at the middle (between requester and assigned columns) and merged on top of each other. The basic information, which is reported of a ticket, is sufficient. This column setup can also be altered.

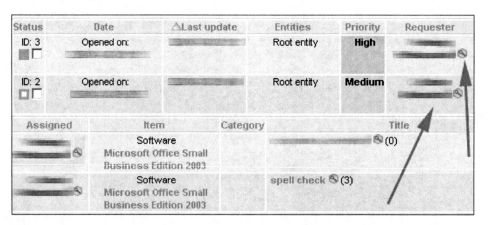

By combining the planner into the helpdesk and tracking mechanism, make this into a feature-laden ticketing system. It should suffice for most environments. Of course, by now, every corporation and organization has its own ticketing solution, one that was implemented within their infrastructure for years and has been present ever since, but this is still worth considering an option. The obvious advantage is directly working with inventory.

Summary

The course of this chapter was flexible. Our purpose was to present the capabilities of GLPI and give a sense of what it is able to do. It is a valuable extension and it fully integrates into our OCS-NG platform. And if it does not mess up anything, why not give it a go and play around with it? Thus, we have seen how to set it up and configure briefly.

We presented most of its features, while always bringing up associations from the real-world. This way, we can see when and how and if we need to use some of those functions within our environment. GLPI can also be extended by the use of plugins. Sometimes we are asked to create reports, and if such a situation happens, we need to get those papers printed as fast as possible. GLPI has an inbuilt mechanism to generate all kinds of reports.

Once we get the hang of GLPI, we endeavored into carrying out administrative tasks with it and how to manage the database to get the most out of it. It incorporates an advanced helpdesk and issue-tracking feature. We have seen how to use these. The same goes for the enhanced license tracking function. There were little reminders that we need to consider in order to eliminate possible problems. Tracking licenses automatically is great.

The purpose of this chapter was to give a taste of GLPI. It is beyond the scope of this book to have an extensive GLPI manual-style chapter that covers every tidbit of this application. By all means, you are advised to use the documentation of GLPI as reference material: http://www.glpi-project.org/wiki/doku.php.

The next chapter deals with all-around repetitive tasks related to IT inventories and management needs and how to get them solved with our setup. It presents useful scripts and the "know-how" of working with this combo for years in a production environment. We will see some best practices and other backing up tips of the database. In short, we will witness a collection of probable scenarios that can happen and need to be resolved seamlessly.

8
Best Practices on Inventorying with OCS-NG

One of the most significant challenges of inventorying in the real world is keeping the inventory up-to-date and clean. We want inventories of all kinds—whether it is an IT assets inventory or the stock of a hypermarket retailer to be easy to work with. We do not want to keep an inventory just for the sake of having one. We would rather be able to pull out reports and carry out administrative tasks on the imported data. That is the key.

OCS Inventory NG marks most of the requirement checkboxes of our inventorying needs but, as with anything else in the world, there are best practices to follow. Sometimes the obvious tasks can be misleading, while the rather complex issues can be narrowed down to simple steps that make sense. In this chapter, we will shed a bit of light on these topics.

Furthermore, we need to look into the updating mechanism of OCS-NG inventory suite. The development team releases updates frequently (not that often, but updates are carried out progressively, whenever necessary). Right now, the latest agent update adds official support for Windows 7. By the end of this chapter, we'll tackle a bit on how to update both the central management server of OCS-NG as well as the agents on clients.

During this chapter, our focus will lie specifically on the following:

- Learning how to back up and restore the OCS-NG database
- Writing trivial backup scripts for scheduling, which deal with backup archiving
- Looking into OCS-NG management server tuning to tweak for better performance

- Understanding why we cannot retrieve some model-specific data of hardware components; trying to find a working solution (this depends on the environment)
- Carrying out administrative tasks via scripts, thus speeding up our everyday tasks
- Getting around to update the OCS-NG management server, if needed
- Mastering the art of updating the agents on client computers—even remotely!

This chapter is a distillation of the experience gained through daily usage of OCS-NG.

Backing up and restoring the OCS-NG database

Each time we deal with data, experience has taught us that we can't underestimate the slight chances of hardware failover or any other sort of "all hell breaks loose" events. In database administration, our data is organized into tables. Everyone knows that the content of these tables can be dumped. Dumping is a technical term and in plain and simple English it means "exporting" the data into a file.

This exported file can be saved and stored at some safe place. It is generally advisable to store these important backups at a remote location. Many companies exchange backups between locations (if they have more than one) or pay for an expert service that does this for them. The key is to have the backed up drives (or tapes) stored at a different location, that is, by common sense, somewhat safe from natural catastrophes.

Of course, these are general backup guidelines as the OCS-NG database is not that crucial compared to the other services a company uses, but if we're dealing with backups, we shouldn't neglect these either. An entire dump of a database with details of a few thousand computers is less than two megabytes.

Dumping the database with mysqldump

MySQL is the database management software on top of which OCS-NG runs. This means that we can use the popular utilities such as *phpMyAdmin* to manage and carry out administrative tasks with our databases. But there's no need to go that far for our needs. The MySQL server comes with a standard command-line utility—mysqldump that allows us to dump the content of a database into a .sql file.

Here is a quick command-line example that backs up our OCS-NG database:

```
mysqldump --add-drop-table --complete-insert --extended-insert --quote-
names --host=localhost --user="ocs-user" --password="pass" ocsweb > /
backup/mysql/mysqldump_ocsweb.sql
```

Keep in mind that in the preceding sample, `ocs-user` is the MySQL user that has administrative privileges to work with the database. Generally, we can assume that this user is root, and the `pass` string needs to be replaced with the password of the previously mentioned user. This command dumps the `ocsweb` database into `mysqldump_ocsweb.sql` file.

As we all know from the earlier chapters, `ocsweb` is our default OCS-NG database.

If our setup deals with another database, then let's not forget to backup accordingly. To make things even neater, we can compress the backup file on-the-fly. We are going to add the following command at the end of our last two-liner code sample. We will be using the pipe operator '|'. It looks like this:

```
mysqldump --add-drop-table --complete-insert --extended-insert --quote-
names --host=localhost --user="ocs-user" --password="pass" ocsweb | bzip2
-c > mysqldump_ocsweb.sql.bz2
```

Dumping the database with phpMyAdmin

Over the years **phpMyAdmin** has become one of the most widely used MySQL third-party tools. It provides a seamless user-friendly web interface to databases. Backing up the database is done with a few clicks. The same process when importing and so on.

However, phpMyAdmin has some limitations. By its very nature of being web based and working with PHP posts, it depends on your PHP configuration variables. As such, sometimes (by default), it is not able to work with really large databases. In those cases, we need to split up the queries into segments, or, of course, tune our PHP configuration to allow us to work with large sizes.

In order to dump a database, we click on **Export** of the menu, and the following screen appears:

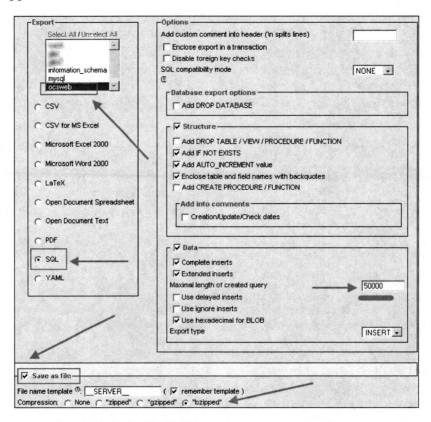

In the last screenshot, we can see the fields we should deal with. First, we need to select the database(s) we are planning to export. In our case, that is **ocsweb**. We pick **SQL**. The next step is to **Save as file**, as that is what we want. And eventually set up a template for naming the file and pick a compression. The **__SERVER__** template yields the result of `localhost.sql.bzip2` if bzipped compression is chosen as well, and the **ocsweb** is on the same server from which phpMyAdmin runs. This is the reason why `localhost` appears in the filename.

 We can use the **__DB__** template to name the file similarly to the database (**ocsweb**).

If our database gets large enough to cause troubles, then we can either fine-tune the variables from PHP.ini to allow us to work with larger files, or set a "maximum length of created queries" on the backup page of phpMyAdmin. In the first case, we need to check for the post_max_size and upload_max_filesize. If we pick the second variable to split the dump files, then we should reduce the number of queries until it suits the limitations.

Importing the dumped SQL file can be done via the **Import** from the menu. We browse for the location of the file and let phpMyAdmin do its work.

Restoring SQL dump files via MySQL's CLI

The structure of a .sql dump file is standard, and we can import it via any other tool or the basic **command-line interface** (CLI) of MySQL. The dump file is a compilation of SQL commands that build up the database scheme in an exactly identical way to the backed up database. They also fill it up with the data contained within the tables (obviously).

In order to import such a dump file, we just need to execute the .sql file that we saved. It has all of the necessary commands to bring the database to that state. We first bring the MySQL command-line interpreter by typing the following in a terminal console:

```
$mysql -u root -p ocsweb
```

As a next step, the utility asks for the root password, and the interpreter loads up.

```
mysql>source <location_of_the_SQL_file>
```

We need to give the source of the SQL dump file. It executes and sets up the scheme and tables. As a final step, once everything is finished, we can quit by typing exit.

Regardless of what tool we opt for to import, the results of those dump backup files, such as MySQL administrator or phpMyAdmin, are the same either way.

In the case of Windows operating systems, we can find the command-line tools of MySQL in the folder of \xampp\mysql\bin\ — depending on where XAMPP is located, and if we picked XAMPP as our Apache-MySQL-PHP combo suite.

Automating and scheduling dumping backups via scripts

In the earlier pages, we saw how we can manually export and import SQL dump files. Nevertheless, the final question is how we could somehow automate the backup task. In the case of Linux operating systems, we write a tiny script and put it into crontab. Likewise, on Windows systems, we write a .bat/.vbs script to execute the command we want (mysqldump with our arguments) and place that script into Windows Scheduler.

Adding the scheduled job into crontab on Linux OS

As a matter of fact, we don't even need a script in case of Linux. We can write the entire dumping command in one line and set that as a cron job. Check it out below:

```
30 10 * * * mysqldump --user=ocs-user --password=pass --host=127.0.0.1
ocsweb > /var/backups/ocsweb-`/bin/date +\%Y\%m\%d`
```

As a memory refresher, in the next screenshot, we can see a quick sketch on crontab's scheduling syntax. Those asterisks mean "any" value, while we can also delimit more values by a comma. For example, every second day, we'd write something like this: 55 22 * * 1,3,5 task_goes_here. This translates into Monday, Wednesday, and Friday, every month, and on 22:55 (10 pm and 55 minutes).

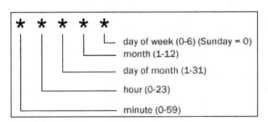

The previous cron job is launched every day at 10:30, and it backs up the ocsweb database from the 127.0.0.1 server (localhost) under the ocs-user with its pass passkey. Please be aware of the escape character delimiting the /bin/date file naming template.

This script cron job generates the following kind of output dump files:

/var/backups/ocsweb-20100201 — in this case it is 2010, February, 1.

Writing the batch script and adding into Windows Scheduler

There are numerous ways in which we could write a script that does this trivial task. In a nutshell, we want to first retrieve the date in order to delimit into segments. Once this step is done, we can call the `mysqldump` with the required arguments. It dumps depending on the file template we created, which includes the actual date in its name. It's as simple as this! Let's do it!

Open a text editor, copy the following, edit wherever necessary, and save it as `.bat`.

```
@echo off
SET Dmp="%ProgramFiles%\OCS Inventory NG\xampp\mysql\bin\mysqldump.
exe"
FOR /f "tokens=2 delims= " %%D in ('echo %DATE:/=%') do SET
Dateprefix=%%D
%Dmp% --add-drop-table --complete-insert --extended-insert --quote-
names --host=localhost --user=root -password=password-goes-here ocsweb
> d:\backup\ocsweb_%Dateprefix%.sql
```

This script begins with turning off echo—this way, nothing is written on the output message console, unless it's intentionally echoed. The second line sets up a `Dmp` variable that points to the `mysqldump.exe`—it can be found within the `\xampp\mysql\bin` folder. It retrieves the current date and sets up the `Dateprefix` variable according to the required format of date. And finally, it calls the dumping command with the necessary arguments.

As a final step, we can add this into Windows Scheduler. Add a new task as follows:

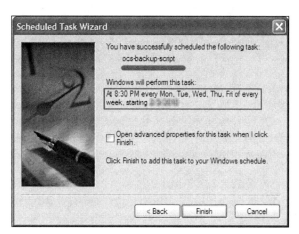

Before we finish, we'd like to also mention a few other GUI tools for MySQL that might be useful when importing the dumped SQL files. However, we always recommend using the command-line interpreter of MySQL. Once you get the hang of it, it's really easy to work with. Anyway, check out the following freeware third-party MySQL frontends:

- MySQL Workbench (`http://www.mysql.com/products/workbench/`)
- Toad® for MySQL (`http://www.quest.com/toad-for-mysql/`)
- Aqua Data Studio (`http://www.aquafold.com/`)
- HeidiSQL (`http://www.heidisql.com/`)
- Sequel Pro (`http://code.google.com/p/sequel-pro/`)

The latter runs on Mac OS X platforms. There are many others, just Google for more...

Tweaking the OCS-NG server for performance

One of the most significant advantages of OCS Inventory NG comes mainly from its performance. The inventory for every machine is really lightweight thanks to its XML syntax. It requires little-to-no CPU processing power. This way, it does not put any load on most of today's processors. However, in the case of large environments, it needs a relatively beefy server with a big RAM size.

Keep in mind that the software was designed in 2005. Back then, most mid-sized enterprise servers had around or less than 3GB of RAM. We should not forget about the 32-bit limitations as well. The official documentation states that when working with inventories with as many as 70,000 clients, they needed 3GB of memory. They also picked a distributed setup that spread across 3x 2.8GHz Xeon servers.

Nowadays, one new generation server can cope with such a similar load, assuming it has more or at least 4GB of RAM—preferably 8GB. But if we dedicate such a workhorse power for OCS inventory, then our hardware platform will be ready to support up to 100,000 clients, and even more with the right tweaks. In the case of the small-to-mid size environments, even a half-ancient machine is more than enough.

OCS-NG can make an inventory of hundreds and even thousands of machines powered by a rather old generation Pentium 4 processor dating back to 2002-2004 with 1-2GB of RAM. After all, if your inventory target is not over 2,000-3,000 clients, then probably any kind of computer that you get is good enough—here we include remaining computers from the basement.

Nevertheless, this is not a reason to waste resources. Tweaking MySQL databases always leads to increased performance no matter which new backend technology our server shows off. It is also relatively understandable that we might want to virtualize OCS-NG.

Tweaking the OCS-NG server is basically tuning MySQL and Apache. Some correlation needs to be set between maximum simultaneous connections. This makes sense because, if we increase the HTTP requests of the communication server without increasing the MySQL connection amount (maximum allowed), then it won't be able to answer each of those requests.

We must point out that, by default, MySQL is limited to 100 connections. This variable is called `max_connections`. This needs to be tuned in correlation with Apache's `Maxclients` directive. This parameter defines how many simultaneous connections can be served. As soon as this value is surpassed, the rest of the queries are queued.

It is important to know how much load our server can handle. Increasing these variables without proper testing can lead to server instabilities. We can play around with values as high as 128-200 on a 2-4GB system. Dynamic web applications can load the server more than static content (images, texts, and so on.). The improper tuning of these values can lead to a symptom called **thrashing**. That's when traffic spike or bottlenecks can occur.

Thrashing is basically the excessive amount of virtual memory swapping that can take place without doing any real work. This can happen when too many new connections are requested and the older requested connections (thus, forked new processes per each connection) cannot be served.

As such, the server runs out of its physical memory and starts to allocate those new connections while swapping. The process goes on and on as the values are misconfigured. In the case of OCS-NG, we might not see this happening, but it is one of those issues we should always be careful about. **Content management systems (CMSs)** are notoriously popular for these thrashing symptoms.

If we are sure our platform can handle the load, then we can go as high as 512 for those upper limits. As long as we monitor the logs of our server daemons and know what's happening behind the scenes—and we feel comfortable troubleshooting, benchmarking, and tuning our server backend for performance—then these should not yield problems.

The official MySQL documentation gives general guidelines when tuning our MySQL daemons for performance, depending on how much memory our server has. Check out the following table:

Parameter	800 MB	1.7 GB	2.4 GB
Table_cache	64M	64M	64M
Key_buffer	128M	256M	256M
Sort_buffer_size	2M	2M	2M
Read_buffer_size	2M	2M	2M
Read_rnd_buffer_size	4M	4M	4M
Myisam_sort_buffer_size	64M	64M	64M
Query_cache_size	128M	128M	128M
InnoDB_buffer_pool_size	384M	1024M	1700M
InnoDB_additional_mem_pool_size	20M	20M	20M
InnoDB_log_buffer_size	8M	8M	8M

The entire list of tuning parameters of MySQL can be found at the following URL:

`http://dev.mysql.com/doc/refman/5.0/en/server-parameters.html`

The following few articles are also worth checking out:

`http://www.devshed.com/c/a/MySQL/MySQL-Server-Tuning-Tips-and-Tricks/`

`http://www.devshed.com/c/a/MySQL/MySQL-Benchmarking-Tools-and-Utilities/`

`http://ebergen.net/wordpress/2006/03/06/3-minute-mysql-tuning/`

Useful scripts that make our everyday life easier

OCS Inventory NG by itself gives a huge portfolio of functions that help us during our daily routine tasks. One of the most frequent similar scenarios is generating reports of all kinds, depending on such criteria. The OCS-NG web interface does this natively, we just pick the elements (columns) and add the operators (and operands, if needed). The reports are generated right away. We can export the results of the inventory in **comma-separated values** (CSV).

This is all great when we want to manually create reports based on the requested criteria. For example, find all computers with less than 2GB of disk space or the ones with less than 1GB of RAM. We build up the query and we're done with it.

However, there are situations when we would like to be notified when a situation like this happens. In a real world implementation of this, let's imagine that we want to monitor the hardware specification changes/differences. The chances are quite slim that someone might change the processor, but replacing (or removing) one of the memory modules is entirely viable (though highly unlikely within a remotely moral community).

The same goes with hard drives in case of multiple HDD setups (or replacing them).

The integration of OCS-NG with GLPI was covered in *Chapter 7, Integrating OCS-NG with GLPI*. GLPI brings these features, but what if we don't want to implement GLPI. If, until this point, OCS-NG satisfied all of our inventory requirements, and we did not want to specifically use GLPI's ticketing/helpdesk and software license/tracking functionalities, then sticking with an OCS-NG setup is fine.

Implementing PHP notification-sender scripts

Thereafter, a practical solution is writing a PHP script that solves our problem. We want to take a snapshot of the current hardware configuration (hardware table from `ocsweb` database) and then compare it with the previous snapshot that we have taken yesterday (a day before). If changes are found, then we report these to some predetermined e-mail addresses. We export the results (that is, differences) into a CSV file so that we can attach them to our notifications.

As soon as the identification is done, the old snapshot is overwritten with the current one (the one we did today) and the execution of the script is complete. This gets scheduled to be run every day.

The notification messages are similar to the following:

Computer name $computername last logged into by user $userid RAM has changed from $snapram to $currentram

Computer name $computername last logged into by user $userid used to have $snapdskcnt hard drives and now has $curdskcnt

This idea was thoroughly implemented and developed by *Mike Seigafuse*. We can find and download the PHP script called `ocsdiff.php` directly from his website:

`http://seigafuse.com/2008/12/19/ocs-diff-script/`

It also needs an `ocsdiff_conf.php` script that can be found under this link too:

`http://seigafuse.com/2007/07/26/daily-diskspace-alerts-using-ocs-inventory-ng/`

At the last link, we can also find a threshold notifier for disk space below a threshold. This is useful in case of servers, but we can, technically, monitor any kind of computer. Both, the `diskreport.php` and the `ocsdiff.php` scripts(the aforementioned differentiator) are based on the `ocsdiff_conf.php` script. The latter PHP file serves the purpose of the configuration PHP header. Inside this file, we specify the variables of OCS-NG for our setup and e-mails.

`diskreport.php` is the daily disk report checker and notification sender. We implement either or both of them in the same way. We set up a new folder at `/var/www/html/ocsreports`, which we might name anything, but it's advisable to name it something self-explanatory (like `reports`).

Final reminder:
Do not forget to set the same permissions and ownership for that folder.

Extending OCS-NG inventory via .vbs scripts

The OCS-NG development team added this feature starting from agent version 4061. The OCS agent supports the addition of various `.vbs` scripts, which we write into the final XML file that it sends to the OCS-NG central server. Basically, the standard STDOUT output (that is, `Wscript.Echo`) is added into the XML that the agent will send to the OCS-NG server.

This VBS scripting function is explained in the official wiki documentation of OCS-NG at:

`http://wiki.ocsinventory-ng.org/index.php/Admin_center:Windows_Scripting`

We need to use the same XML-specific syntax that OCS agents use to deliver the inventory to the central server. For example, the last logged user is delimited inside the `<HARDWARE>` and `</HARDWARE>` tags. Of course, the `<LASTLOGGEDUSER>` and `</LASTLOGGEDUSER>` is where the actual name of the user name goes.

Before trying to make such a script from scratch, we should check out the XML file our agent creates and use its syntax to format the output via our VBS/WSH script. Finally, the output is passed on to the server accordingly and it gets imported into the inventory.

A script can be found on the aforementioned wiki page. It's about the last logged on user.

Uninstalling the OCS agent via batch script

The title of this section might seem counterintuitive at first. Why would we want to uninstall the OCS agent from one or more of our client computers? Regardless of the reason, we need to know how to do it remotely. Remote execution comes to mind. In addition, we want a silent uninstall. We can create a batch script that does this.

On Windows machines, the following script silently uninstalls the OCS agent:

```
#File uninstall_agent.bat
cd %programfiles%
cd OCS Inventory Agent
if exist uninst.exe call uninst.exe /S
del *.* /s /q
cd ..
rmdir "OCS Inventory Agent" /s /q

#File schedule_uninst.bat
copy uninstall_agent.bat C:\
for /f (tokens=1) %%a in ('time /T') do set /A heure=%%a + 1
at %heure%:10 "C:\uninstall_agent.bat"
```

We can publish this script via the *Package Deployment* functionality of OCS-NG. The next step is creating an archive of the two files, that is, `uninstall_agent.bat` and `schedule_uninst.bat` files. Then, we set up a new package of the launch type (explained in *Chapter 6, Package Deployment through OCS-NG*). The command we're going to launch is the `schedule_uninst.bat`. The final step is activating the package. We need to select the client machines on which we want this script to be deployed.

The algorithm, in the simplest terms, is the following: the script is deployed and the remote client machine launches the scheduling batch. Accordingly, the other uninstall batch script is copied to the root `C:\` volume. It then launches the uninstaller script after at least 11 minutes, but less than 1 hour 10 minutes. This way, the deployment of the agent is ensured.

For more information regarding this solution, please refer to the following OCS-NG wiki link:

`http://wiki.ocsinventory-ng.org/index.php/Tools:Uninstall_agent`

Another option is just remotely executing the first `uninstall_agent.bat` script via `psexec` as follows:

```
psexec @comps.txt -u mydomain\domainadmin -c -n 10 uninstall_agent.bat
```

Once again, we supply the name of the computers in a `comps.txt` file. The timeout of each remote execution is 10 seconds. If it times out, the host is surely unreachable.

On Linux operating systems, we can execute the following command:

```
#rm -Rf /etc/ocsinventory-client /usr/sbin/ipdiscover /bin/ocsinv /usr/
sbin/ocsinventory-client.pl /bin/ocsinv /etc/logrotate.d/ocsinventory-
client
```

Best practices on retrieving model-specific data of various computer hardware components

In the real world, inventories needs be as complete as possible. In the case of IT assets, it is especially important to retrieve and archive all sorts of model-specific data of hardware components. Specifically, we want the manufacturer, model number, serial number, and if possible, firmware and other hardware specifications. These are useful when dealing with automated administration of warranties.

Typically, the warranties of hardware components are given out according to their serial number. In other cases, it's per manufacturer and model number. This depends on our infrastructure and the retailer suppliers for those IT assets. If we have hundreds of similar pre-made builds, then we might not necessarily care about the individual warranty period of each component. But should we have built the computers ourselves, then we do.

In the case of hard drives, sometimes we also need to know the exact firmware. Not that long ago, it had happened that one of the popular hard drive manufacturers released their latest HDD models with a rather buggy firmware. The issue was widely documented, and they released a new fix right away. But in case of large environments, who would have known for sure which computers had those problematic HDD firmwares?

It is clear that we need some sort of script that retrieves the firmware of each HDD. The rest is child's play for a system administrator. We can then deploy and remotely execute the script or application across the entire domain. It is our choice whether to opt for PsExec and other tools or the inbuilt package/command deployment of OCS-NG. Alright, the idea was formed, and now we need to actually get down to the implementation.

Retrieving model-specific data of HDDs

Our instincts said that we could throw together an easy WSH VB script, based on the appropriate WMIs; we could retrieve and echo the model-specific data we were looking for. However, the results were not so promising. Therefore, we looked further.

 WMI stands for **Windows Management Instrumentation**. It is a set of extensions to the **Windows Driver Model** (**WDM**), and provides an interface to the operating system through which instrumented components provide information and notification. In our case, WMI allows us to work with scripting languages and query hardware-specific information directly.

Fortunately, we found the CodeProject article *Get Physical HDD Serial Number without WMI* at `http://www.codeproject.com/KB/mcpp/DriveInfoEx.aspx`.

The author of the source code and article, *Decebal Mihailescu*, explains quite thoroughly how to use the code. We can use any .NET language (at least 2.0 Framework). The code he posted returns all of the model-specific data within a collection. The way we organize and deal with the rest is up to us. We can format the output and pick the ones we want.

Therefore, we do not have to deal with the inner-workings of the application. We just implement the collection it returns when we retrieve the data. Even though the level of the project is quite advanced, the implementation part does not require higher than an intermediate level of programming. We opted for **C Sharp** (**C#**) programming language.

Once the project is compiled, we will get our `.exe` and the `.dll` files. The dynamic link library contains the unmanaged code with which we are going to work. It is not necessary for us to understand how it works on the algorithmic level. It does low-level calls to the hard drive via `DeviceIoControl` API. The code is *object oriented* and that's why building on top of the foundation is rather easy, as one function fills up the collection.

Now that we are throwing together an application like this, we need to look ahead and think out of the box. As we're going to remotely execute this tiny program across every machine of the domain, the output will be logged in a text file. In order to ease the logging and searching, it would be awesome to retrieve the name of the computer and IP address. Print these out along with the model-specific information. Then put some delimiters.

Check out the next screenshot. This is a snippet of the output log of the application that we have put together in less than 30 minutes based on that CodeProject publication.

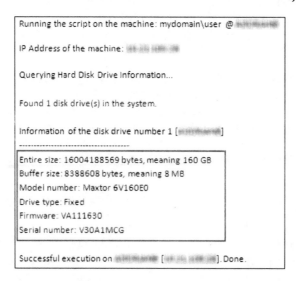

Here is a quick implementation of the things we mentioned. Things might seem a bit complex at first. The source code is rather simple, but if you don't have C# experience, then this part of the chapter might have caught you off-guard. Either way, we will supply the source code of this project along with a ready-to-run executable.

```
DriveListEx m_list;

m_list = new DriveListEx();
m_list.Load();

string currUser = System.Security.Principal.WindowsIdentity.
GetCurrent().Name.ToString();
string currComp = Environment.MachineName;
IPHostEntry ipEntry = Dns.GetHostEntry(currComp);
IPAddress[] addr = ipEntry.AddressList;

Console.WriteLine("Running the script on the following machine: {0} @
{1}", currUser, currComp);
Console.WriteLine("IP Address of the machine: {0}", addr[0].
ToString());
Console.WriteLine(" ");
Console.WriteLine("Querying Hard Disk Drive Information...");
Console.WriteLine(" ");
Thread.Sleep(500);        // sleep to ensure querying finishes
```

```
if (m_list.Count < 1)
{   // nothing to do if there are no disk drives detected
Console.WriteLine("Could not find any disk drive attached to the
system.");
Console.WriteLine("Nothing left to do. Done.");   }
Console.WriteLine("Found {0} disk drive(s) in the system.", m_list.
Count);
Console.WriteLine(" ");

for (int i = 0; i < m_list.Count; i++)
{
Console.WriteLine("Information of the disk drive number {0} [{1}]",
i+1, currComp);
Console.WriteLine("-------------------------------------");

Console.WriteLine("Entire size: {0} bytes, meaning {1} GB",m_list[i].
DriveSize/10,m_list[i].DriveSize/1000000000);
Console.WriteLine("Buffer size: {0} bytes, meaning {1} MB",m_list[i].
BufferSize,m_list[i].BufferSize/1000000);
Console.WriteLine("Model no:{0}",m_list[i].ModelNumber);
Console.WriteLine("Drive type: {0}",m_list[i].DriveType);
Console.WriteLine("Firmware:{0}",m_list[i].RevisionNumber);
Console.WriteLine("Serial number: {0}\n",m_list[i].SerialNumber);
}


Console.WriteLine("Successful execution on {0} [{1}]. Done.",
currComp, addr[0].ToString());
```

You can find the implementation of this project at the following URL:

`http://www.primeranks.net/storage/queryhdd`

Our implementation is compiled into `QueryHDD.exe`. You can grab the executable.

Please keep in mind that this would not have been possible without the contribution of the author to the CodeProject. Respect the **Code Project Open License (CPOL)**.

The original link is `http://www.codeproject.com/KB/mcpp/DriveInfoEx.aspx`, and you should always use this as a starting point. I do not claim any ownership of the code sample. My goal is to share this as a viable option to get our job done.

If we want to remotely execute this application, let's call it QueryHDD, then we first need to deploy its `DriveInfoEx.dll` file too on every machine. We copy that file on a public share within our intranet, and run the following script remotely across the domain:

```
copy /Y "\\serv_name\path_here\QueryHDD\DriveInfoEx.dll" %WINDIR%\
system32
```

Running this script via PsExec on every machine of the domain simply copies the dynamic link library files from that public share to the `%WINDIR%\System32` folder of local machines. The computers are ready for our mass execution of QueryHDD.

```
psexec @allcomps.txt -u mydomain\domainadmin -c -n 10 QueryHDD.exe >
logging.txt
```

The last command launches the `QueryHDD.exe` on every machine name within the `allcomps.txt` file. If we want to execute it on every machine of the domain, then we can use the wildcard of PsExec, namely, two back slashes and one asterisk *

The output is logged into `logging.txt` and the `-n 10` gives a 10 seconds timeout per computer. Hosts that are unavailable (shutdown or unreachable) are timed out after 10 seconds.

I have published an article on ASP Free based on our QueryHDD implementation and how it solves our real world inventorying needs. For further information, check it out!

The article is titled **Inventorying HDDs Remotely on Windows**. If you want to look into this implementation, then that article should provide you with a more thorough overview.

```
http://www.aspfree.com/c/a/Windows-Security/Inventorying-HDDs-
Remotely-on-Windows/
```

Retrieving model-specific data of RAM memory modules

The same situation happens in the case of memory modules. Retrieving the model number, manufacturer, and serial number of RAM modules can be a tricky process. In theory, it is quite seamless. We have a dedicated WMI abstraction that queries the SMBIOS and returns all of model-specific data. However, in the real world, unfortunately, it isn't like this.

A quick Google search leads to dozens of WSH scripts that retrieve information about the memory modules. Sometimes, these work fine, but on other occasions, they retrieve "null" on lots of fields. Within our company, around 75 percent of the machines failed to retrieve the manufacturer, let alone the model number and/or serial number.

There are those exceptions when the memory module manufacturer does a poor job at filling in the **Serial presence detect (SPD)** information into the EEPROM of the chips. This is when we physically retrieve the SPD data via low-level calls and get 0x0000000 as the serial number.

Either way, if we want to mess around with these scripts, here is one WMI-based script.

```
Set objWMIService = GetObject( _
"winmgmts:{impersonationLevel=impersonate}" _
& "!root\cimv2")
Set colItems = objWMIService.ExecQuery("Select * from Win32_
PhysicalMemory",,48)
For Each objItem in colItems
myVar = ""
If Not IsNull(objItem.Capacity) Then
myVar = myVar + "Capacity: " & formatnumber(objItem.Capacity) & VBCr
End if
If Not IsNull(objItem.Manufacturer) Then
myVar = myVar + "Manufacturer: " &objItem.Manufacturer&VBCr
End if
If Not IsNull(objItem.DeviceLocator) Then
myVar = myVar + "DeviceLocator:"&objItem.DeviceLocator&VBCr
End if
If Not IsNull(objItem.BankLabel) Then
myVar = myVar + "Bank Label: " & objItem.BankLabel & VBCr
End if
If Not IsNull(objItem.PartNumber) Then
myVar = myVar + "Part Number: " & objItem.PartNumber & VBCr
End if
If Not IsNull(objItem.Speed) Then
myVar = myVar + "Speed: " & objItem.Speed & VBCr
End if
Wscript.Echo myVar
Next
```

As we can see, the script does not print out if one of the returned fields is `Null`. On my workstation machine, the results were not so great. We got the capacity, device locator, memory type (0?), and their speed (667 MHz). It failed to retrieve the manufacturer and the part number. It displays the message boxes one-by-one but we merged them in the following screenshot:

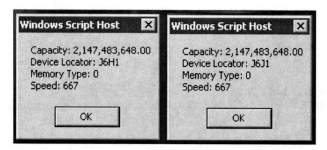

On some machines, the preceding script works fine. Nonetheless, sometimes it just does not suffice. Thankfully, we have found a CodeProject that targets this issue once again.

```
http://www.codeproject.com/KB/system/SMBIOS_Peek.aspx
```

The author, *wjfrancis*, realized that the WMI approach does not return many of the missing SPD data of memory modules. He explains why this limitation occurs and presents his workaround. In the CodeProject article, he shows us the C++ project that dumps the entire (literally!) content of the SMBIOS. This means tons of information.

It is amazing if we want to go so in depth. Nevertheless, if our sole purpose is just retrieving memory-specific SPD information via the SMBIOS, then it is quite overkill for us. If we run the script remotely on hundreds of computers, then the output log would be huge. The entire SMBIOS dump for one machine is already many pages long.

Therefore, we can fine-tune the source code of the posted CodeProject application. If we open up the source file, we find the following functions being called:

```
show_bios_information();
show_system_information();
show_system_enclosure();
show_processor_information();
show_cache_information();
show_system_slots();
show_physical_memory_array();
show_memory_device();  // this is _only_ line we need
show_memory_array_mapped_address();
show_system_boot_information();
```

Unless we want some other information, we can comment out all of the other function calls and leave the `show_memory_device()` alone. Another option is to implement a parameter choice based on which we can select, namely, mode 1 or mode 2. Mode 1 would be our memory-related SMBIOS dump, while mode 2 would be the original complete dump.

Commenting out a line of code can be done by adding `//` at the beginning of the line (one line at a time) or delimiting the segment of code between the tags `/*` and `*/`. The former tag will be at the beginning and end with the latter tag. This way, the delimited part is simply ignored. This is what is meant by "comment out" in the context of software development.

This is up to us, and the results are either way promising.

```
Executing script on computer name: SUSANPC
total width: 64; data width: 64
size: 2048 megabytes
form factor: DIMM; memory type: DDR2
device locator: J1MY
bank locator: CHAN A DIMM 0
additional memory details: synchronous
speed: 800 mhz
manufacturer: 0x7F7F7F7FCB000000
serial number: 0x8D2A19DB
Finished. Successful execution on computer name: SUSANPC
```

Please keep in mind that this would not have been possible without the contribution of the author to the CodeProject. Respect the CPOL (CodeProject Open License).

The original link is `http://www.codeproject.com/KB/system/SMBIOS_Peek.aspx`, and you should always use that as a starting point. I do not claim any ownership of the code sample. My goal is to share this as a viable option to get our job done.

From the previous output, we can see that the serial numbers and manufacturer fields were reported accordingly. We recommend using an identification utility like CPU-Z or some other third-party utilities to test each module manufacturer independently, at least once. This way, we can figure out which kind of HEX value matches the manufacturers.

Within our organization, the most dominant memory manufacturers are the following:

0x7F9800000 — Kingston

0x7F7F7F7FCB — A-Data

I have published an article based on this PeekSMB implementation and how it gives a solution to memory auditing needs. For further information, check it out at `http://www.aspfree.com/c/a/Windows-Security/Inventorying-RAMs-Remotely-on-Windows/`. The article is titled **Inventorying RAMs Remotely on Windows** and it's on ASP Free (DevShed).

Updating OCS-NG agents on clients (when needed)

Just like with anything else, we need to check the official website of OCS-NG often. New versions and updates are released from time to time. Generally, these updates are not frequent at all, but when they do happen, we need to know how to approach the process.

The latest Windows agent at the time of writing is 4061.1. The UNIX unified agent is 1.1.2. The method for installing newer agents is similar to the way we could update from earlier versions to the current version. We have two (or more) reasonable options for updates.

There is a widely documented bug with Win32 agent versions lower than 4030. There was no silent uninstall available in those versions. As soon as an update was attempted, the uninstall dialog box would pop up. There is no way to eliminate this, except for automating the user click through the uninstall process (with AutoIt, for example). The agent client versions lower than 4030 date back to early 2007's. Reading this book in 2010 (or later), the chances are slim that you will have to deal with those versions anymore. It has been fixed.

Updating the Windows agent

First, let's cover the typical agent updating process on Windows operating systems.

As mentioned earlier, we have at least the following two methods of updating the agents. Which one we choose depends on our OCS-NG setup. If we use the agent set up as a Windows service, then we can use the package deployment mechanism of OCS-NG. The other option is using the OcsLogon launcher to force an update. Either way works fine.

The package deployment method requires us to create an archive (`.zip`) with the update file titled `OcsAgentSetup.exe`. This setup is the latest agent client that we download from the official OCS-NG website's **Downloads** section. We pick the `execute` kind of package when we create the package (remember, deployment package types from *Chapter 6, Package Deployment through OCS-NG*). Moving on, we execute the executable with the necessary arguments as follows:

`OcsAgentSetup.exe /S /UPGRADE /NOSPLASH /SERVER:ocs_serv_address /DEBUG`

Feel free to include additional arguments, if need be such as `/NP` (no proxy), `/PNUM:` xxx (port no), and so on.

Refer to *Chapter 2, Setting up an OCS Inventory NG Management Server* for the complete list of switches supported by agents.

Another option is specifying the `/DEPLOY:version` via OcsLauncher. The version number stands for those 4-digit version numbers, for example, 4061 (latest). This way, the client will download and install the appropriate version number agent from the server.

Let's not forget that we can use the web-based administration console of OCS-NG to upload agent version archives (`.zip`) to the communication server. These are called update_xxxx.zip. As in the previous example, xxxx represents the version number.

As another extra modality, we can use PsExec to update the clients. The same agent setup can be launched via PsExec remotely as long as the switches are similar to the one we created earlier when we opted for the package deployment function.

Updating the UNIX agent

On Linux operating systems, the process might be a little more time consuming as there are no practical remote "reinstall" or "upgrade" solutions. Almost all of the possibilities focus on deploying the package onto the machine and then running the `setup.sh` agent installer script manually.

As of the latest agent version (1.0+), we have package deployment functionality under Linux as well. This means that we can generate the same package as we did under Windows. However, there is one difference. We will execute the `setup.sh` install script via those command-line switches that we require. This way, the updating can become unattended.

If this option fails, we can force a remote uninstall of the agent. Once that is done, we can use our methods to get the installer script deployed onto the machine and then run it via our command-line switches. In a nutshell, all that we want is just getting the installer script to be executed via our arguments on the Linux machine. The rest are just details.

Updating OCS-NG central server (when needed)

OCS Inventory NG is a healthy project that is still supported and has a dedicated small team of developers behind it. While updates are not that frequent, this doesn't mean that there are no updates. There are rarely major updates concerning the OCS management server or communication server. However, when that happens, we need to know how to install the update.

First of all, let's consider a safety tip. We need to back up our database. Yes, back it up! NOW! Read that sentence again. This is crucial as newer updates always bring a little bit of schema update and change the structure of our OCS database (`ocsweb`, in our case). The steps for backing up the database were explained at the beginning of this chapter.

Moving on, we download the latest OCS-NG central server archive and extract it into the `/var/www/ocsreports/` folder depending on our configuration (or `\xampp\ocsreports\`). We overwrite our files and move on. From this step, there are two little distinctions comparing a Linux OS versus Windows Server (with XAMPP).

In the case of Linux based operating systems, we need to follow the instructions of the install script. As expected, we will skip the Perl modules and all of these preliminary steps, unless they are specifically required to be updated as well. Either way, the install script will know what to do. Once it is done, we navigate to `http://ocs-server/ocsreports`. The same old page loads up when we started our OCS-NG installation for the first time.

It will automatically update the database schema and other table-specific information if required and finally verifies if everything is fine and ready to go. Then it asks the user to input the MySQL database information. As a final step, the updating is already finished!

Under Windows operating systems, we launch the OCS setup wizard. By default, it should auto-detect that there is an already existing OCS installation on the computer. Therefore, it will not select the XAMPP components and also completes the path of the OCS installation directory. Verify these and only if they're fine, move on. Keep in mind, it is pointless to update and mess with XAMPP components if we update only OCS-NG.

The rest of the procedure is the same. It updates the database schema and everything else. The process is verbosely logged within your web browser via dynamically-generated PHP pages. Should there be errors, their reason is clearly pointed out. But if you are updating, you should not encounter any of them. The final step asks for MySQL information.

Updating the OCS-NG central server is following the same fashion of installing a fresh new OCS-NG server, except it updates the database schema and does other tiny fixes so that the new server components match with the database (tables, data, and so on) that was created with the older version.

Summary

Over the course of this chapter, we presented a distillation of best practices. These are either useful when implemented in the real world and save us lot of time or are well-learned lessons, which we recommend not going through anymore.

At first, we went through the various backing up modalities. System administrators have a saying and it goes like this—*Backups that are not automated are not done. (Source:* `http://www.fief.org/sysadmin/`). This law could not be truer. Knowing this, we designed automated backup scripts. This way we can sleep well knowing that our job is done.

Moreover, we discussed MySQL database tuning and how to squeeze every drop of performance out of our OCS-NG inventory platform. We have dealt with common setups, hardware specifications, and software-based variables that can be tweaked. We have also overviewed a few scripts that can make the daily life of a system administrator easier: notification sender, `.vbs` scripting extension to OCS, and remote agent uninstaller.

Before ending the chapter, we decided to show one of the everlasting frustrations when inventorying and auditing hardware components. Sometimes grabbing important data is hardly seamless. We identified some problematic situations and tried to find solutions. We did succeed. Finally, we have seen how to update agents and eventually, if need be, the OCS-NG central server management as well.

Moving on, the next chapter continues the string of practical tips and tricks and good-to-know strategies. It helps in identifying issues, diagnosing common pitfalls, how to troubleshoot them, and finding solutions. Technically, we will focus on finding out when some agents aren't doing their job and how to get them back on track. We're going to deal with all sorts of other problems, from the admin console up to the server backend.

9

Troubleshoot Confidently—Find Solutions and Workarounds

Over the course of this book, we have touched every area of our complete inventorying solution. We all know the adage "if it works, don't fix it", but the truth is we still need to be familiar with the troubleshooting methods beforehand. This gives us confidence while presenting the solution to the superiors, getting the idea accepted, and ultimately—which matters the most—the on-field experience and the "know-how".

There are several problematic situations that need to be addressed. What happens if some agents are not sending in their inventory? Where should we begin troubleshooting? What if the admin console throws MySQL errors? And what if we're facing issues, and the error logs are filling up? We should not lose hope. Verbose logging is great. It can help us big time!

As an incentive, here's a quick glance at what we are going to cover in this chapter:

- Learn how to keep an eye on the behavior of agents
- Diagnose and troubleshoot agent-related problems
- Look into several ways to solve the admin console-based issues
- Identify and fix issues of the server backend, if need be
- Understand how to ask for help the "right way" (for example, providing logs)
- Read about practical workarounds to not so common situations

This chapter deals with headache alleviations. We cover techniques and methods that help us to diagnose situations and detect problems. Once these issues are identified, we will look into ways to solve them. Most of the time, these errors are common and they are fairly well documented. This chapter strives to be a reference for these kinds of struggles.

Nevertheless, we know that when it comes to administration, sometimes we are just meant to be striving with the most bogus and unknown situations. We have all been there: those errors that throw seemingly pointless messages, or things that simply refuse to work appropriately. Thus, we are presenting a feasible solution for these kinds of situations too. Our purpose is to gather all appropriate and relevant information and then ask for help via the forums.

Keeping an eye on the behavior of agents

There are situations when everything seems to work alright, agents are uploading their inventory, the server backend accepts the connections and handles the queries appropriately, but then we recognize some client agent is not reporting status. There are more than a handful of reasons why an agent does not upload its inventory to the OCS-NG server and logging is the key to keep an eye on their behavior.

A closer look at the agent's logfile

Thankfully, OCS-NG has inbuilt logging mechanisms. Using the /debug parameter when launching the agent forces it to automatically create the logfile. This can be found in the directory of the agent under the following naming scheme: hostname.log, where the hostname stands for the name of the computer on which the agent runs.

In the case of Linux agents, the parameter is -debug and the logfile can be located in the /var/log/ocsinventory-client folder. The filename is called the same as hostname.log.

The logfile is quite verbose. Here is the beginning of a sample agent logfile:

```
HTTP SERVER: Connection WITHOUT proxy
TAG FORCE: Tag forced by /tag, value is <TAG-NAME>
WMI Connect: Trying to connect to WMI namespace root\cimv2 on device
<Localhost>...OK.
Registry Connect: Trying to connect to HKEY_LOCAL_MACHINE on device
<Localhost>...OK.
CHECKINGS: read <COMP_NAME-2009-12-17-08-22-47> and <00:14:54:9F:DA:27
00:42:BC:35:C7:5D> in ocsinventory.dat
IpHlpAPI GetNetworkAdapters...
```

```
IpHlpAPI GetNetworkAdapters: Calling GetIfTable to determine network
adapter properties...OK
IpHlpAPI GetNetworkAdapters: Calling GetAdapterInfo to determine IP
Infos...OK
IpHlpAPI GetNetworkAdapters: OK (2 objects).
CHECKINGS: write <COMP_NAME-2009-12-17-08-22-47> and <00:14:54:9F:DA:2
700:42:BC:35:C7:5D> in ocsinventory.dat
HTTP SERVER: Creating CInternetSession to get inventory parameters...
OK.
HTTP SERVER: Getting HTTP Connection to server ocsng-serv.mydomain.org
port 80 using no authentication...OK.
HTTP SERVER: Sending prolog query...HTTP status 200 OK
OK.
HTTP SERVER: Receiving prolog response...OK.
```

These are the preliminary steps at the beginning of an agent's first launch. It connects to the OCS-NG server, but to do that first, it needs to grab the network adapter information. Once this is done, it grabs the `prolog` variable from the server, and after a successful query retrieval, it sets this value to the agent config file and moves ahead with the inventory.

This is when the agent begins to build up the inventory XML. It first queries the logged in username, last logged in user, its operating system, and later on via WMI, all of the hardware components, software, and so on. The inventory is then built ground up.

A sample of this part can be seen as follows. This section is in the middle of the logfile.

```
Retrieving Device informations...
getUserName: Trying to get logged on User ID...
getUserName: Will using Process32...OK
User found (explorer): john.doe.
Registry NT GetLastLoggerUser: Trying to get the last user who'd been
logged in...OK (john.doe).
WMI GetOS: Trying to find Win32_OperatingSystem WMI objects...OK
(Microsoft Windows XP Professional 5.1.2600 Service Pack 3 2 1).
WMI GetDomainOrWorkgroup: Trying to find Win32_ComputerSystem WMI
objects...OK (mydomain.org)
Registry NT GetDomainOrWorkgroup...OK (MYDOMAIN).
WMI GetBiosInfo: Trying to find Win32_ComputerSystem WMI objects...OK
(INTEL_ D946GZIS)
WMI GetBiosInfo: Trying to find Win32_Bios WMI objects...OK (Intel
Corp.)
WMI GetProcessors: Trying to find Win32_Processor WMI objects...
Intel(R) Core(TM)2 CPU        6600  @ 2.40GHz 2401 (x86 Family 6
Model 15 Stepping 6). OK
WMI GetProcessors: 2 processor(s) found.
```

```
getMemory...Physical: 3478777856 bytes, Swap: 4905226240 bytes. OK
[ --part cut out-- ]
WMI GetSystemPorts: OK
WMI GetSystemSlots: Trying to find Win32_SystemSlot WMI objects...OK
(7 objects)
WMI GetSystemControllers: Trying to find Win32_FloppyController WMI
objects...Failed because no Win32_FloppyController object!
WMI GetSystemControllers: Trying to find Win32_IDEController WMI
objects...OK (5 objects)
WMI GetSystemControllers: Trying to find Win32_SCSIController WMI
objects...OK (1 objects)
```

As expected, the inventorying process is not finished yet. There is still plenty of other information to retrieve, just that we have purposefully selected the last snippet as a sample to demonstrate a few key elements of the logfile. It is indeed verbose. Every WMI object query is logged on a step-by-step basis (each line). Their results are on the right of the key, for example, OK, and in parentheses, the retrieved values or their count. In the case of failed queries, for example, no floppy controllers found in the previous situation, they are specified as well.

Next the agent retrieves the leftover information such as software, network information, product keys, and licensing information (via registry queries—HKLM hive); and finishes the inventory. It opens up the previous inventory state (if there is any) and compares it with the current state. In the case of changes, it updates the inventory XML file.

Let's exemplify this part from the agent logfile:

```
Trying to open database on folder <C:\Program Files\OCS Inventory
Agent\> with XML...OK.
Reading last inventory state file...
XML Read last inventory state from file <C:\Program Files\OCS
Inventory Agent\last_state>...OK
Checking last inventory state...
   Logical drives inventory state changed.
   Video adapters inventory state changed.
   Inventory changed since last run.
XML Update Device properties...
   XML Update Logical Drives...
   XML Update Logical Drives: OK (4 objects).
   XML Update Softwares...
   XML Update Softwares: OK (304 objects).
[ --part cut out-- ]
   XML Update Video Adapters...
   XML Update Video Adapters: OK (1 objects).
XML Update Device properties: OK.
WMI Disconnect: Disconnected from WMI namespace.
```

In a nutshell, this is how the inventory is built up. Now, the next step is sending it in. The agent will open up an HTTP connection towards the server, send it in, wait for feedback, and finally check whether there is something new to download (for example, a new agent version).

```
HTTP SERVER: Creating CInternetSession to send inventory results...OK.
HTTP SERVER: Getting HTTP Connection to server ocsng-serv.mydomain.org
port 80 using no authentication...OK
HTTP SERVER: INV : SEND received, sending inventory...HTTP status 200
OK
OK.
HTTP SERVER: INV : no account info update
HTTP SERVER: Closing HTTP connection....OK.
DOWNLOAD: Download is off
Writing last inventory state file...
  XML Write new inventory state to file <C:\Program Files\OCS
Inventory Agent\last_state>...OK
Execution duration: 01:25:34.
```

Under a successful execution, this is the fashion through which the inventorying is logged. Generally, there are two kinds of problems that might occur. At first, the agent cannot contact the OCS-NG communication server for whatever reason. This is specified at the beginning when it tries to initialize the connection the first time. HTTP status/errors are printed in the log. Thus, we can see the notorious errors such as HTTP 500, 404, 301, and so on.

The second situation can happen at the end when it tries to send the inventory. If there are some missing modules from the OCS-NG server, for example, XML interpreter, then it cannot retrieve and understand the inventory the agent is trying to send in. If this is the case, then the same error should happen on every agent, obviously.

Regardless of what errors we are getting, especially in the case of internal errors such as HTTP 500, we need to look into the Apache logfile (`error.log`) that is located, by default, on the following path: `/var/log/httpd`. Under Windows, this is located at the directory: `C:\xampp\apache\logs\`. The filename is the same `error.log`.

If all goes well, by now, we should be familiar with the agent logging. This means that we are ready to move on to troubleshooting. We are going to cover some of the most frequent agent-related problems—how they appear in the logs, along with solutions to fix them.

As a final note, in case of Linux agents, the parameter that forces logging is `--debug` instead of the `/debug` one on Windows agents. Please refer to *Chapter 3, The Zen of Agent Deployment* for a complete list of agent switch parameters. There are many of them!

Troubleshooting problems related to agents

As mentioned earlier, quite often, there are connection-related issues, for example, the agent cannot establish a connection with the OCS-NG server. This can happen because of various reasons. First, there is a proxy required, and the agent is launched with the /NP parameter; thus, it sets "no proxy" mode and fails the connection. Linux agents have the -NP parameter.

By default, the agent retrieves the proxy address set in Internet Explorer (IE) under Windows. This means that if there is a required proxy to go outside and surf the Net, but that proxy is not required to reach the internal OCS-NG communication server, which is within the intranet, then the agent will fail again. In this situation, we need to specify the /NP switch to disable proxy detection. It ignores the one set in IE and things will work.

In the situations we just discussed, the connection times out as the destination is unreachable. Based on our network topologies, we must know whether or not we need a proxy (if we have any) to reach the OCS-NG communication server from workstation computers.

Another possible error occurs when the OCS-NG server is not configured accordingly. We can see this from the following log sample:

```
HTTP SERVER: Connection WITHOUT proxy
HTTP SERVER: Creating CInternetSession to get inventory parameters...
OK.
HTTP SERVER: Connecting to server ocsng-serv.mydomain.org 80...OK.
HTTP SERVER: Sending prolog query...
HTTP SERVER: The server ocsng-serv.mydomain.org is not a well
configured OCS server
HTTP ERROR:
<!DOCTYPE HTML PUBLIC "-//W3C//DTD HTML 3.2 Final//EN">
<html>
 <head>
  [ --part cut out-- ]
 </head>
 <body>
```

The cut out part is where the Apache web server automatically responds with an *HTTP Error 500* as there is an internal server error. Under most circumstances, this is the "generic" error, as the OCS-NG server cannot be found, and hence the server will not answer in an understandable language for the agent. This means it can detect whether or not the address you specified runs an OCS-NG server.

The communication between agents and the OCS-NG central communication server happens via a pre-determined protocol (syntax, semantics, and so on), and if those are not kept, the communication fails and is reported as an "internal server error", as the responses do not match the required kind of answers. The easiest way to determine their real cause is by looking at the Apache HTTP logfile (`errors.log`).

While the HTTP Error 500 is the most common one, it's not the only one. We can face any of the possible HTTP status codes. Not all of them are errors either. When initiating the connection, the status OK, HTTP code 200 means everything is fine. But there are situations when we face the *404* or the *301* error.

For a detailed list of HTTP status codes, check out the following URL:

```
http://en.wikipedia.org/wiki/List_of_HTTP_status_codes
```

Whenever struggling with an error message, we need to try debugging the config file of the Apache web server, that is, `apache_config`. This is where lots of directives are set, and if there are duplicates or mistaken variables, it can easily become a source of many issues. For example, error 301 appears when there are multiple redirections and the `/ocsinventory` directory already exists. We need to set where the directive points and determine why the conflict happens. We can either rename that folder or sort out the Apache directive.

Nevertheless, the error 404 might hit us in the face when we least expect it—especially when we rush through the Apache installation and initial configuration. This error means that it cannot find the `/ocsinventory` directory. Often, the directory might be there physically but the Apache configuration file remains the default and does not match our specific configuration. Of course, then it cannot locate the required folder.

Forcing an agent to report inventory

When we are troubleshooting a specific computer's agent, we want to see the results of our modifications right away. No one wants to wait for the agent to try again by itself (`prolog_freq/tto_wait variables`), and then who knows when we might see some results. The solution here is to force the agent to contact the OCS-NG communication server and report its inventory data. This can be done by creating a batch script.

Here's an example on Microsoft Windows:

```
@ECHO off
NET Stop "OCS INVENTORY"
COPY /Y "\\path-here\service.ini" "C:\Program Files\OCS Inventory
Agent"
NET Start "OCS INVENTORY"
PAUSE
```

This script is launched on the remote client and then it retrieves a pre-configured `service.ini` file from a shared/network host. It stops the OCS Inventory service, copies that file, and restarts the service. The service will then read its newly copied configuration file and act accordingly. Let's call this batch script as `force-ocs.bat`.

The most important component of the newly configured `service.ini` file is the `TTO_WAIT` variable. It equals zero. This value traces the countdown to the next run in seconds. This means that the service is going to launch the `OCSInventory.exe` right away. For further information, refer to *Chapter 3, The Zen of Agent Deployment* where we discussed agent switches.

By default, the `PROLOG_FREQ` is set to `10`. This means 10 (ten) hours until it contacts the OCS-NG server for the first time. On first installations (the first time the agent reaches the OCS server), this value is always the same unless we replace the config file. A common misconception is that administrators set a low `PROLOG_FREQ` value in the web-based admin console, and they expect the agents to send in their data right away.

However, it does not work like that. The agents will wait patiently for those 10 hours (value set by default), contact the OCS server, retrieve the configurations we set via the admin console, and then update the newly configured `PROLOG_FREQ`. They will send in their inventory data, and from that point onwards, the current actual configuration variables are set.

Drifting back on topic, here's our modified `service.ini` file for the batch script just mentioned:

```
[OCS_SERVICE]
NoProxy=1
Server=ocsng-serv.mydomain.org
Pnum=80
Miscellaneous= /tag:"tag-name" /SERVER:ocsng-serv.mydomain.org /
PNUM:80 /NP /DEBUG
PROLOG_FREQ=24
OLD_PROLOG_FREQ=24
TTO_WAIT=0
auth_user=none
auth_pwd=none
```

This script launches the OCS service with the new configuration file. However, there are some situations when there is a problem with the service. It does not fail because of the configuration but rather because there are not enough privileges to run that service. The question whether the user has local admin rights or not varies from situation to situation. Therefore, we need to debug this with **Event Viewer**.

The **Event Viewer** is a useful MMC snap-in. We can launch this by either navigating through the **Control Panel | System and Maintenance | Administrative Tools**. It resides inside that folder or we launch the `eventvwr` command from **Start | Run**.

Once it's up and running, we want to check the application-related logs. The events are categorized such as Application, Security, System, and so on. We want the first one. The next step is sorting the queried results within the table based on **Source**. This way, we can check all of the logs related to OCS inventory service at the same place. The source field contains the name of the application, that's why we are sorting it that way.

Here's a quick glance at a segment of the **Event Viewer** focused on what we need. Double-clicking on an event brings up the details regarding the event for that said issue.

Information	2/23/2010	9:16:48 PM	OCS INVENTORY SERVICE
Information	2/22/2010	7:24:45 PM	OCS INVENTORY SERVICE
Information	2/21/2010	5:34:21 PM	OCS INVENTORY SERVICE
Information	2/20/2010	3:43:01 PM	OCS INVENTORY SERVICE

We need to check what happens when the OCS Inventory Service is about to start. This is logged in the **Event Viewer**. So, we should not forget about reminding ourselves to look into the **Event Viewer** in the case of Windows machines. In the case of Linux, there are logs everywhere, and if the service refuses to start, we will know that right away. Apart from that, the Apache HTTP logs are totally the same and this also applies to the OCS agent logs.

Here's a screenshot from when we double-clicked on the event from **2/21/2010**:

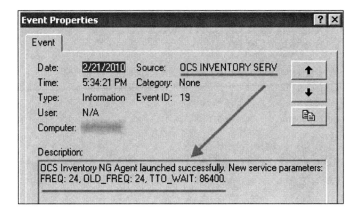

Solving administration console-based issues

The backend of the administration console is based — as we very well know — on PHP and MySQL. The web server platform is Apache. In most situations, when we do have some problems, they are almost always related to either Apache not working accordingly or PHP not being able to execute the scripts. The MySQL part can also be troublesome if the OCS-NG server was not set up correctly.

Generally, once the web-based administration console is set up, things will always go fine. The chances are slim that it will refuse to work from one day to another. Therefore, on the scale of likelihood of issues, these stand on quite a low level. The agents can act strangely more frequently than the administration console.

By default, every server component has some built-in limitations. These are alright for most situations, but if our queries end up larger than normal or if we try to upload a slightly larger sized package for remote deployment, then we might hit another limitation. These limitations are not pointless, but in most cases they conserve bandwidth, reduce server load, and alleviate the possibility of hang-ups due to bad commands.

Solving MySQL limitations the right way

Let's discuss some common MySQL limitations at first. The way these upper caps or limitations are implemented are quite simple. They are specified as server-side variables in the MySQL configuration file. As such, let's fire up our favorite text editor and load up the MySQL config file. This file can be found as `my.cfg` (or `my.ini` under certain circumstances).

Under Windows operating systems, this configuration file resides under the `\xampp\mysql\bin\` folder. On Linux, we can `grep` for their correct location.

Here is a complete list of server-side variables from the official MySQL documentation:

`http://dev.mysql.com/doc/refman/5.0/en/server-system-variables.html`

The logging mechanism is intelligent enough, so when we face a server-side problem caused by such a limitation, the error log tells us which variable causes the issue. For example, the following error message can be thrown at us: *Got a packet bigger than 'max_allowed_packet' bytes*. Without any doubt, it really tells us the problematic value.

This was just an example, but it can happen. By default, the size for the `max_allowed_packet` variable is set to 1MB. The official OCS-NG documentation recommends 4MB. In this day and age, we can easily increase this tenfold if not on the hundreds scale. Nevertheless, well written SQL code should not meet this limitation if it is not working with the importation of large databases (over few gigabytes+).

The `max_allowed_packet` variable applies both ways. The default for the client side is 16MB and it suffices for almost every situation. In the case of OCS-NG, that's a 100 percent. The server-side variable is the only one that should be upped a bit from the default 1MB. It is pointless to increase it that much if the client side is not tuned accordingly. MySQL 5.1 has the limitation of 1GB when it comes to setting the highest value for that variable.

In the configuration file, find the following part and set the variable accordingly:

```
[mysqld]
max_allowed_packet=16M
```

This is one of the many errors that MySQL might report while working alongside the administration console. We described the process of troubleshooting, understanding and interpreting the error message, and pinpointing the exact location (source) of the error. We should always refer to the official MySQL documentation first, and then, for further clarification, we can check other sources. The process is the same for any other error like this.

Solving PHP limitations the right way

Similar to MySQL data packet limitations, PHP also suffers from similar limitations. These problems are the ones most people encounter at first when struggling to manage their own blogs, photo albums, CMS, or other PHP-driven web-based applications. PHP has well thought "max" limitations in order to minimize the chances of a server getting overloaded due to poorly written script or malicious ones.

The issues we will cover in this part are related to the package deployment functionality of OCS-NG, but they are reported via the administration console or we can grab notice of them after an action that we did from within the administration console. When we upload packages, these limitations come into play if our packet sizes are larger than the predefined limits.

The PHP configuration file is called `php.ini` and there are at least two modalities to find where this file resides. The first is to `grep` for it (or using `find`) or use the simple Windows-based file search in case of Microsoft operating systems. The `.ini` file can be at `/usr/bin/php5/bin` and also at `/etc/php5`. This is under Linux. Try running the following command:

```
find / -name php.ini
```

The other solution is much neater and actually gives us the entire dump of PHP configuration options and variables. This is a sure-fire method. The command is called phpinfo(), but we need to call it from within an HTML page with PHP code — like this:

```
<?php phpinfo(); ?>
```

Create any .php file with the previous line of code, save it, and copy it anywhere on the web server's folder. Now navigate with the browser to that file — say we named it phpreport.html. Then we open up that link. The following table appears on the screen:

PHP Version 5.2.8		php
System	Windows NT WINDOWS7-B1-EN 6.1 build 7000	
Build Date	Dec 8 2008 19:46:19	
Configure Command	cscript /nologo configure.js "--enable-snapshot-build" "--enable-debug-pack" "--with-	
Server API	CGI/FastCGI	
Virtual Directory Support	disabled	
Configuration File (php.ini) Path	C:\Windows	
Loaded Configuration File	C:\php5\php.ini	
Scan this dir for additional .ini files	(none)	

The sample screenshot is from a PHPini() execution on a PHP 5.2.8 on Windows 7.

The table is much longer, but we have cut out the variables section. They are listed in a two-column fashion, the left side showing the variable name and on the right its value. The default values need to be tuned to enhance the file uploading capabilities (>2 MB).

The official documentation for the PHP.ini core variables can be found at the following URL:

```
http://php.net/manual/en/ini.core.php
```

We need to fine-tune (read as: increase from the default values) the following variables:

- `upload_max_filesize`: The maximum file size we want to upload, it is self-explanatory.

- `max_input_time`: Recommended value is `-1` to disable this input time.

- `memory_limit`: OCS-NG recommends `16M`, we can go for `32M` or even `64M`. The error message this throws is: `Allowed memory size of ___ bytes exhausted`.

- `max_execution_time`: Recommended value is `-1` to disable this input time. The error message this throws is: `Maximum execution time of __ secs exceeded`.

- `post_max_size`: Maximum packet size we want to deploy plus 1MB for headers.

Due to additional overhead involved (for example, encoding MIME headers) when uploading packages, OCS-NG recommends that you set the `post_max_size` variable to 1MB larger than your `upload_max_filesize` variable. For example, if you set `upload_max_filesize = 200M`, you would need to set `post_max_size = 201M`.

There is one final pointer regarding larger file uploads. Apache has a configuration directive that is called `LimitRequestBody`. By default, this value is set to `512KB`. This value is really low and due to that, some Linux distributions are pre-shipping configured variables of this directive, but we cannot take this for granted. It is much better to override this limitation or disable it entirely. Please find the following directive within the Apache configuration:

`#LimitRequestBody`

In the previous example, we placed the hash (#) in front of the line. This way, that line is ignored as a hash sign indicates a comment in the Apache configuration file. Alright, now we explained how to fix it, but what's the purpose of this value? It specifies the maximum length of a POST data. This is a global rule, and applies to any sort of data transfer, regardless of scripting language, protocol, or target server.

Keep in mind that if we want to specify a limitation, then this value can go from 0 (unlimited) to 2147483647 (which is exactly 2GB). For more information, check the following URL:

`http://httpd.apache.org/docs/1.3/mod/core.html#limitrequestbody`

Identifying and fixing issues on the server backend

This section is going to be a distillation of server-related issues and recommended solutions, which occur frequently on standard OCS-NG installations. Keep in mind that over the years these were the common troubles that most users struggled with. As such, it's more likely to face these issues once again than some undocumented weird scenario. Just remember that logging is everything and immerse yourself within logfiles.

First and foremost, we might struggle with connection problems via the OCS-NG server.

At the moment, the OCS-NG communication server does not support *SSL connections*. This means that if your Apache is configured to use SSL with the communication server, you will experience problems. The deployment server is using SSL. This was a feature proposed a while back but was then placed on hold. As of the latest rumors, the development team might have started implementing this functionality, but it is not a priority.

The second chapter of this book covered the installation of the necessary modules for Apache in great detail. We might still run into situations where an Apache error is thrown regarding a mod requirement. Here we are listing a few of these error messages:

`Unknown directive PerlRequire /path-goes-here/.../some-startup.pl`

The `PerlRequire` directive executes the `startup` Perl script. This preloads the module `mod_perl`. This is where it fails and this means that `mod_perl` is not installed or loaded. We can query the version of mod_perl by typing `rpm -q mod_perl`. Now, this depends on the package manager we are using. Either way, we can also GREP for `mod_perl`.

Having the `mod_perl` module installed is not enough. We need to enable the automatic loading of this module within the Apache configuration file (`httpd.conf`). Please find the following line and uncomment if it's commented out (# hash sign is the comment):

`LoadModule perl_module modules/mod_perl.so`

If, for whatever reason this, line cannot be found, then write it. This enables the `mod_perl`.

After this step, Apache needs to be restarted — follow the logs closely for further information.

Other possible causes of problems are due to rushing into and/or not knowing exactly the exact version of mod_perl module we are using. Consequently, we end up misconfiguring the OCS-NG server during installation. If we select the older type of mod_perl version, then it's going to throw lots of Apache errors regarding not being able to find some perl modules such as the compat.pm.

To be honest, this error is highly unlikely because nowadays it's quite hard to grab, install, and use such an old mod_perl version that is lower than 1.999_21. This is why, by default, the installation script of OCS-NG already picks the mod_perl version 2.

If you checked the version of your mod_perl, you can query the environment variable's value by typing in OCS_MOD_PERL_VERSION, and if it's 2, then this isn't a problem. If it's 1 and you have the VERSION_MP 2, then this is the root of your problem. Find the following in the ocsinventory.conf file:

```
# Which version of mod_perl we are using
# For mod_perl <= 1.999_21, replace VERSION_MP by 1
# For mod_perl > 1.999_21, replace VERSION_MP by 2
PerlSetEnv OCS_MODPERL_VERSION 2
```

In order to help us troubleshoot problems with OCS-NG server, we need to enable detailed logging. This can be done in the web-based Administration Console. Navigate to the **Config** drop-down menu option from the yellow action bar, and then select **Config**.

You will be directed to a page similar to the one that appears in the next screenshot. The variable we need is located under the second tab called **server**. What we're looking for is called **LOGLEVEL**, and we need to enable that for detailed logging.

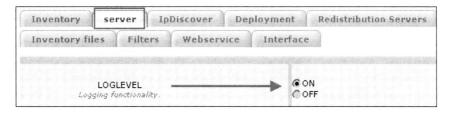

Another cause for problems is permissions. Here is the table from the official OCS-NG documentation:

Directory	File	Owner	Group	Permissions
/var/www/html/download		root	apache	-rwxrwxr-x
	All directories	apache	apache	-rwxrwxr-x
	All files	apache	apache	-rw-rw-r--
/var/www/html/ocsreports		root	apache	-rwxrwxr-x
	dbconfig.inc.php	apache	apache	-rw-rw-r--
	All others	root	root	-rw-r--r--
/var/www/html/ocsreports/ipd		root	apache	-rwxrwxr-x
	All files	apache	apache	-rw-rw-r--
/var/www/html/ocsreports/css		root	root	-rwxr-xr-x
	All files	root	root	-rw-r--r--
/var/www/html/ocsreports/files		root	root	-rw-r--r--
	All files	root	root	-rw-r--r--
/var/www/html/ocsreports/image		root	root	-rwxr-xr-x
	All files	root	root	-rw-r--r--
/var/www/html/ocsreports/js		root	root	-rwxr-xr-x
	All files	root	root	-rw-r--r--
/var/www/html/ocsreports/languages		root	root	-rwxr-xr-x
	All files	root	root	-rw-r--r--
/var/log/ocsinventory-NG		root	apache	-rwxrwx-r-x
	All files	apache	apache	-rw-rw-r--

You can find this at the following URL.

```
http://wiki.ocsinventory-ng.org/index.php/Documentation:Errors#Commun
ication_server_errors
```

The official documentation has plenty of frequent problems addressed, and you can read about these in the link just mentioned. Pay special attention to the FAQ section. It deals with common situations like what's the cause of an issue if you see such errors.

Communication server fails to write a logfile on Linux

Alright, we have been talking about logfiles here and there, but sometimes this is the actual problem. The Communication server might yell at us asking for help in panic that it cannot open the logfile. The reason for this is either because the path is invalid or because it doesn't have sufficient privileges. The exact error message is shown as follows and it appears within the Apache logs. Obviously, the communication server fails to create the logfile.

```
Cannot open log file: __path-goes-here__
```

This error can be easily debugged. There is an environment variable that we have set during the OCS-NG Server installation procedure. Please refer to *Chapter 2, Setting up an OCS Inventory NG Management Server*. This value can be found within the `ocsinventory.conf` configuration file. Locate the config file and open it. Then, search for the `OCS_LOGPATH` variable.

```
PerlSetEnv OCS_LOGPATH "/var/log/ocsinventory-NG"
```

As expected, we need to verify what is wrong with that path—or if there isn't anything specified, then please do write one! Logging is not just necessary, it's an absolute must! If the path seems alright, we need to check the directory permissions. The Apache web server is the communication server, so it must have sufficient privileges (logging means writing access!—that is akin to `-rwxrwx-r-x` at least).

We can check the permissions by listing the content of that directory with the notoriously popular `ls -l` command. A full reference on Linux file permissions can be found at the following URL:

```
http://www.zzee.com/solutions/linux-permissions.shtml
```

Setting permissions can be done with `chmod`. Definitely we won't struggle with that!

Diagnosing uncommon pitfalls—asking for help

We have all been there. Sometimes we might face such a weird situation that despite all of our efforts, we cannot solve it by ourselves. That's the beauty of communities and helping each other as more eyes can be more attentive to details and the know-how and experience is merged together. The OCS-NG site offers support forums that are active.

As the members of the community are not able to troubleshoot and debug on your setup and infrastructure, it is extremely important to provide the maximum amount of information you can. This means gathering all of the logfile outputs, including agents (those that are struggling), communication server logs, Apache logs, and even the configuration files. The specification details of your platform and version numbers are required.

Keep in mind that the vast majority of the community is from France. English for most people is their second if not third (or even more) language. This means their answers might not always sound so clear and understandable. Don't be afraid to ask for clarifications. They are always doing their best to provide meaningful replies if they can help.

On another note, the forums are split into three major categories:

- **Divers**: This category is about general discussions, newspaper articles, and so on
- **Help in English**: This is the support forums in the English language categorized
- **Aide en Français**: These are in French and categorized just like the English ones

It might seem a bit hilarious at first, but Google Translate or any other alternative works surprisingly well with French-to-English translations. The French support forums can be translated on the fly and then browsing, surfing, knowing what happens inside those forums is possible as well. This means we can use this extra option and find solutions even faster. Thus, we may think it feels weird – but let's not neglect this opportunity.

The threads are organized into those different sub-forums based on categorization of issues such as the following ones:

- OCS Inventory NG Server for Unix
- OCS Inventory NG Server for Windows
- OCS Inventory NG Agent for Unix
- OCS Inventory NG Agent for Windows
- Mobile devices management
- Administration Console
- Package Deployment
- IPdiscover
- Active Contributions
- OCS Inventory NG and GLPI
- Developers

As soon as we join the community, we should always search for some key terms regarding our problem. It is likely that someone has already faced your issue, and after similar struggles, somehow found a solution. We can learn from each other's mistakes, especially in the world of IT where things seem so straightforward and normal but can behave differently when we least expect.

The forums have a dedicated topic for the OCS-NG with GLPI integration. Same goes for the GLPI forums which were already covered in sufficient depth in *Chapter 7, Integrating OCS-NG with GLPI*. For more information, we can always refer to either of the forums when striving with issues.

Never lose hope! Do try some global search engine queries as well, maybe you are lucky and someone blogged about your issue. On another note, apart from the support forums, you can always ask for help from the OCS Inventory NG partner companies. They provide consultancy and expertise related to the OCS-NG platform. Find the entire list of service partners at the following URL:

```
http://www.ocsinventory-ng.org/index.php?page=service-partners
```

Contrary to popular belief or what anyone might think at first, these service partners were elected based only on their competence—nothing to do with financial support. In order to become a partner, these companies completed a questionnaire and the OCS-NG development team granted them their partnership title.

As a conclusion, this means we can ask for a reference or their services at any time when we require them. The service partners are building, deploying, and managing OCS-NG solutions.

Summary

This chapter delimited the kind of problems we can encounter. Soon enough, we get to know the ropes of possible issues of each component of the OCS-NG inventory solution and how to begin with troubleshooting in the respective situations. Logging is without any doubt the most important practice that any application can do. During this chapter, we presented where the logs are stored and how to take the magnifying glass on them.

We started out with probably the most common problem. We understood how to identify those computer clients that do not send in their inventory. When managing a significant number of machines—more than a dozen—we need to recognize when some of the devices are skipped. When we administer just a handful of clients, leakages are obvious.

The likelihood of running into issues with agents is evidently higher than with the main server backend. The reason for this is mostly because we have to deal with hundreds, if not tens of thousands, of agents on different machines running various operating systems on numerous platforms. All can be a source of trouble.

Once we knew how to analyze the behavior of agents, then finding solutions was just a few steps away. The inbuilt debugging functionality helps a great deal. Usually, the problems can be narrowed down to the agents not being able to contact the central OCS-NG server. Understanding the HTTP errors returned by Apache was necessary.

Moving on, the server backend is not immune to problems. We carried out some possible roots of problems, such as permissions, missing modules, or bad configuration tags. The administration console is a PHP-based web interface that queries the MySQL server. As such, there are many factors in the game that can go wrong. Queries can go wrong (PHP can refuse to work accordingly). We explained these packet and protocol-related issues.

Summing these up, this chapter was a definite problem-oriented one with a sense of practicality. Our target was to give modalities that develop into a habit when diagnosing and fixing issues with the OCS-NG inventory platform. This is the universal essence of troubleshooting everywhere: finding solutions or workarounds in limited time.

Keeping Pace with Version Updates—Glancing over the changelog of the Latest Release

The version number of OCS Inventory NG that appears on the cover of this book, and which is discussed in great detail during the book, is 1.02. This version was one of the longest standing stable versions. Exactly when I had finished the book, and the chapters were pretty much wrapped up, the development team released a newer version, which is 1.3.

The development team finally increased the version number by a seemingly large increment. In this appendix, we are going to analyze and go beyond the *changelog* of this release. As we will see, there are no major changes when it comes to installation, implementation, and usability. Nothing really changes except for a bunch of bug fixes and a set of additions that provide better compatibility with the latest hardware and software.

Definition of changelog:

This is a file that contains a log of every change that is made during the lifetime of a project. It includes all of the bug fixes, additions, and new functions brought to the project accompanied with their date/time and version number. Sometimes, we might come across these files named as changes or news on the Wikipedia reference link at:

http://en.wikipedia.org/wiki/Changelog

What we want to point out is that this version number change should not make us tremble in fear. Everything that we read about and learnt in this book applies to the good old 1.02.x and the latest 1.3 as well. Nevertheless, it should make us happy to see that the team behind OCS-NG is still heavily involved and active in the development of this project. These are clear signs that the heart of the project is still beating.

At the time of writing this appendix (April 20, 2010), the latest version of OCS Inventory NG is 1.3.1 (released on February 17, 2010). Visit the official website of OCS Inventory NG, and check the latest version at:

```
http://www.ocsinventory-ng.org/
```

Analyzing the changelog

Once we download the archive of the latest release, we extract the files. We can locate the following two files that contain the detailed logging of individual project files:

- **ChangeLog-ocsreports**
- **ChangeLog-server**

Please check out the screenshot below to see what we are talking about.

Name ⬆	Size	Packed	Type	Modified
..			Folder	
Apache			Folder	2/17/2010 5:32 PM
binutils			Folder	2/17/2010 5:32 PM
dtd			Folder	2/17/2010 5:32 PM
etc			Folder	2/17/2010 5:32 PM
ocsreports			Folder	2/17/2010 5:37 PM
ChangeLog-ocsreports	6,312	6,312	File	2/17/2010 5:49 PM
ChangeLog-server	67,463	67,463	File	2/17/2010 5:49 PM
LICENSE.txt	17,987	17,987	Text Document	2/17/2010 5:32 PM
README	3,946	3,946	File	2/17/2010 5:32 PM
setup.sh	55,139	55,139	File sh	2/17/2010 5:32 PM

The `ocsrepcorts` file deals with the web-based user interface of OCS-NG. Basically, it contains the changes that are made to the administration interface. As their names suggest, the server file is the log file of the changes suffered by the server backend of OCS-NG. By this, we mean the MySQL related queries, fixing security vulnerabilities, adding support for new functions, and so on. As expected, the server changelog is ten times larger.

Let's see what the changelog looks like from the inside by taking a look at an example of the following excerpt of the **ChangeLog-ocsreports** file:

```
2010-01-27  Paul Simons  <simonsp@calumet.purdue.edu>

        Changed an sql statement in doublons.php so that if a computer does
not have a mac address, it does not dissapear from hostname or serial
listings.  Currently if a comptuer does not have a mac address, and it had the
same serial or hostname as a computer that had a mac address, only that
computer would show up in the doublons report.  It was then impossible to
merge a computer that did not have a network adapter before, and has one
now.
```

The syntax of the log is quite simple. It starts with the date when the change occurred. It then continues with the name of the developer that introduced the change along with their contact information. Next, the change is described. The previously mentioned example is quite self-explanatory. Sometimes, the descriptions of these changes are understandable for the public as well, but that is not always the case.

Here's another important change that is relevant to the public, and it's documented as shown in the following screenshot:

```
2010-01-20  Paul Simons  <simonsp@calumet.purdue.edu>

    The changes that have been made address the following issue.

    When a computer is inventoried using a local standalone audit
    on one subnet, it stays on that subnet in the ipdiscover page.
    If the computer is moved to a different subnet, it still does
    not show up on the new subnet at all, even though it exists in
    the netmap table on the new subnet. The changes in the
    ipdiscover file modify it so that the inventoried subnet and
    the scanned subnet are compared for each mac address. If the
    subnets are not equal, the computer is now listed as
    non-inventoried. This is done through only modifying sql
    statements.

    The statements that have been modified are as follows:
    The two statements that give the total have been modified
    to compare subnets.
    The statement that selects non-inventoried for each subnet
    has been modified to not exclude all inventoried mac
    address, but only inventoried mac address on that subnet.
    The statement that lists the non-inventoried computers has
    been modified the same way.
```

Especially in case of bug fixes or issues, only the developers know what that specific part applies to, why they phrased that description like that, and what exactly that change deals with. In those cases, we should leave them alone. They are not meant for the general public, unless we are planning to get involved in development as volunteers. Thus, do not worry if you are reading the changelogs and find something you do not understand!

Alright, but then why are we explaining how to analyze changelogs, and why are we bothered about them? Answering that question is simple. Major changes that either directly or indirectly affect the public and the community of users are detailed and explained — always! This means that when new features are introduced, they are documented. In case of fixes or additions that alter the behavior of the software, we can find these to be mentioned.

The previously mentioned description of changelogs is pretty general to every open source project. The developers of OCS-NG are doing a great job of explaining each modification, even if it's just in a few words. The descriptions make sense and when there's a major one, it can get few sentences long.

It is important to understand how to read changelogs as their use is quite preponderant, especially as more and more open source projects are gaining popularity.

As a conclusion to this appendix, this new version did not bring anything new to the table that would alter the behavior of OCS-NG. Everything we learned about OCS-NG up to now during the entire course of this book still applies to this new version, and we could pretty much say that it's going to be valid for the entire course of the project.

Good luck with your OCS Inventory NG setup. This book should be used as a reference material along with the official documentation, even after the inventory is up and running.

I'm sure that you won't regret going on the path of OCS-NG. It sports one of the most flexible and modular platforms for inventorying and a simple agent-querying mechanism that works for all kinds of IT-related assets. Eventually, when integrated with GLPI, it becomes a powerful all-in-one suite that brings to the table out of the box solutions for most inventory necessities.

Let me hand out a few final goodbye points:

- Visit the forums, and don't hesitate to ask for help
- Check at least once a month whether there's a new release on the official site
- Do not skimp on the scheduling of automated backups stored somewhere else
- Whenever you face errors, check the logs and locate the cause of the trouble
- Once found — try search engines for the exact phrase

Index

networking equipment and office
  peripherals information, gathering 11
requisites 8
solution 8, 9
ticketing system, integrating with 10

J

J9 JDK 91
Java virtual machine (JVM) 91

L

Label file configuration function 111
LAMP 29
LAN 13
Lastdate 124
latest release
  changelog 233
launching action 139
LICENSE.txt file 69
license, types
  free 180
  global 180
  standard 180
  to buy 180
Linux agents
  --debug, parameter 217
  -debug, parameter 214
  log file 214
Linux operating systems
  agents, deploying 85
  AMP stack installing, with APT 35
  AMP stack installing, with emerge on
    Gentoo 35, 36
  AMP stack installing, with XAMPP
    precompiled package 36
  AMP stack installing, with yum 33-35
  modules, setting up 37
  OCS-NG management server, setting up
    38, 39
  software prerequisites 27, 28
Linux OS
  scheduled job, adding into crontab 192
local area network. *See* LAN
local import function 118
LOCAL_PORT 114
LOCAL_SERVER 114

LocalService 66
LocalSystem account, Windows OS
  demystifying 66, 67
LOGLEVEL 114

M

MAC address field 132
Mac OS X operating systems
  agents, deploying 89
management server, OCS Inventory NG 16
Maxclients directive 195
mobile devices
  agents, deploying 91, 92
mod_perl module 226, 227
model-specific data
  of computer hardware components,
    retrieving 200
  of HDDs, retrieving 201-204
  of RAM Memory Modules, retrieving
    204-207
MySQL
  GUI tools 194
  limitations, solving 222, 223
  tuning parameters, list 196
mysqldump
  database, dumping with 188, 189
MySQL's CLI
  used, for restoring SQL dump files 191

N

Netmask 124
network agent, OCS Inventory NG 16
NetworkService 66
nmap tool 19

O

ocsagent.exe file 69
OCS agents
  uninstalling, via batch script 199, 200
OcsAgentSetup.exe file 69, 72
ocsinventory 39
OCS Inventory Mobile 91
ocsinventory-ng 76
OCS Inventory NG
  about 7, 15

Thank you for buying

IT Inventory and Resource Management with OCS Inventory NG 1.02

About Packt Publishing

Packt, pronounced 'packed', published its first book *"Mastering phpMyAdmin for Effective MySQL Management"* in April 2004 and subsequently continued to specialize in publishing highly focused books on specific technologies and solutions.

Our books and publications share the experiences of your fellow IT professionals in adapting and customizing today's systems, applications, and frameworks. Our solution based books give you the knowledge and power to customize the software and technologies you're using to get the job done. Packt books are more specific and less general than the IT books you have seen in the past. Our unique business model allows us to bring you more focused information, giving you more of what you need to know, and less of what you don't.

Packt is a modern, yet unique publishing company, which focuses on producing quality, cutting-edge books for communities of developers, administrators, and newbies alike. For more information, please visit our website: www.packtpub.com.

About Packt Open Source

In 2010, Packt launched two new brands, Packt Open Source and Packt Enterprise, in order to continue its focus on specialization. This book is part of the Packt Open Source brand, home to books published on software built around Open Source licences, and offering information to anybody from advanced developers to budding web designers. The Open Source brand also runs Packt's Open Source Royalty Scheme, by which Packt gives a royalty to each Open Source project about whose software a book is sold.

Writing for Packt

We welcome all inquiries from people who are interested in authoring. Book proposals should be sent to author@packtpub.com. If your book idea is still at an early stage and you would like to discuss it first before writing a formal book proposal, contact us; one of our commissioning editors will get in touch with you.

We're not just looking for published authors; if you have strong technical skills but no writing experience, our experienced editors can help you develop a writing career, or simply get some additional reward for your expertise.

SAP Business ONE Implementation

ISBN: 978-1-847196-38-5   Paperback: 320 pages

Bring the power of SAP Enterprise Resource Planning to your small-midsize business

1. Get SAP B1 up and running quickly, optimize your business, inventory, and manage your warehouse

2. Understand how to run reports and take advantage of real-time information

3. Complete an express implementation from start to finish

4. Real-world examples with step-by-step explanations

iReport 3.7

ISBN: 978-1-847198-80-8   Paperback: 236 pages

Learn how to use iReport to create, design, format, and export reports!

1. A step-by-step, example-oriented tutorial with lots of screenshots to guide the reader seamlessly through the book

2. Generate enterprise-level reports using iReport 3.7

3. Give your reports a professional look with built in templates

4. Create master/detail reports easily with the sub-report feature

Please check **www.PacktPub.com** for information on our titles

CPSIA information can be obtained at www.ICGtesting.com

230199LV00003B/58/P